LAYER 3 SWITCHING

A Guide for IT Professionals

Prentice Hall Series in
Computer Networking and Distributed Systems
Radia Perlman, editor

LAYER 3 SWITCHING
A Guide for IT Professionals

Jim Metzler
Lynn DeNoia

To join a Prentice Hall PTR Internet mailing list, point to
http://www.prehnhall.com/register

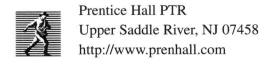

Prentice Hall PTR
Upper Saddle River, NJ 07458
http://www.prenhall.com

Editorial/production supervision: *Mary Sudul*
Cover design: *Design Source*
Cover illustrator: *Tom Post*
Cover design director: *Jerry Votta*
Page formatting: *FASTpages*
Manufacturing manager: *Alexis R. Heydt*
Marketing manager: *Miles Williams*
Acquisitions editor: *Mary Franz*
Editorial assistant: *Noreen Regina*

©1999 Prentice Hall PTR
Prentice-Hall, Inc.
A Simon & Schuster Company
Upper Saddle River, New Jersey 07458

The publisher offers discounts on this book when ordered
in bulk quantities. For more information, contact:

Corporate Sales Department
PTR Prentice Hall
One Lake Street
Upper Saddle River, NJ 07458

Phone: 800-382-3419
Fax: 201-236-7141
E-mail (Internet): corpsales@prenhall.com

ISBN 0-13-919838-5

Printed in the United States of America

10 9 8 7 6 5 4 3 2

Prentice-Hall International (UK) Limited, *London*
Prentice-Hall of Australia Pty. Limited, *Sydney*
Prentice-Hall Canada Inc., *Toronto*
Prentice-Hall Hispanoamericana, S.A., *Mexico*
Prentice-Hall of India Private Limited, *New Delhi*
Prentice-Hall of Japan, Inc., *Tokyo*
Simon & Schuster Asia Pte. Ltd., *Singapore*
Editora Prentice-Hall do Brasil, Ltda., *Rio de Janeiro*

Contents

Foreword

Background and Purpose

In the 1980s, bridges were deployed to connect disparate LAN segments in a simple and inexpensive manner. Routers were also introduced—to create structure and to add functions—but these often turned out to be complex or expensive. Network managers struggled to learn how to design optimal networks using this new routing technology, as well as how to choose among differing approaches to routing. In addition, some vendors who did very well selling bridges did not adjust to the demand for routers, and lost significant market share.

A similar phenomenon is in progress with Layer 2 (L2) and Layer 3 (L3) switching today. From a technology perspective, L2 switches are similar to bridges and have similar characteristics; i.e., they are low-cost and easy to use. Over the last three years the L2 switch market has grown from nonexistent to one worth multiple billions of dollars. Routing functions, though, are still required in our networks. L3 switches promise to fulfill these requirements, but in a manner that is faster, easier, and less expensive than routers of the past.

Your authors believe that the industry will struggle to deploy L3 switches in the same way it struggled with routers. Network Professionals will have to contend with four problems:

1. It is a lot more difficult to get approval and funding for upgrades to an existing network than for initial deployment.
2. There are several different approaches to designing networks using L3 switches.
3. Vendors have implemented L3 switching in a myriad of ways. As a general rule, multiple alternatives in a marketplace confuse buyers, who often react by not purchasing the new products.
4. People are often suspicious about the introduction of new technology. There is too much history in our industry of hyped technology that ultimately fails in the marketplace (e.g., 100VG-AnyLAN, ATM-25).

As long as prospective buyers struggle, vendors will not prosper. In particular, if network professionals can *not* distinguish among L3 approaches, design their networks with L3 products, and justify network upgrades to management, then vendors cannot sell products to them. In addition, we see vendors often totally self-absorbed in their own approaches to the marketplace, when they really need to be able to place their approaches in a broader context of what network managers need and what competitors are offering.

Our goal in this book is to cut through the intellectual pollution that surrounds the introduction of new technology in general, and the introduction of Layer 3 switching in particular. We provide buyers with the context for evaluating how L3 switching applies to their unique situations. We also provide details about the technology and about selected vendor implementations and products. For vendors, the book provides context in which to better understand the issues faced by potential customers in buying and deploying products. It also provides vendors with a framework for positioning their products relative to the broader marketplace.

Scope and Coverage

Today's society is characterized by some as "information-based" and by others as "knowledge-based." We see today's economy increasingly as "global" rather than regional or national. Coupling these with various "time-is-money" and competitive business pressures, it is hardly surprising that we expect more and more from our communications infrastructure in terms of providing timely access to critical information. Computers and networks have become central to the functional and competitive character of many diverse businesses and organizations. From automated factories to electronic storefronts, from Enterprise Resource Planning (ERP) to on-line reservations, from digital libraries to personal web sites, reliable and effective networks are becoming fundamental to how we work and live. "The more we have the more we want" is turning into "the more we have the more we need." As your authors have traveled over the past year, we have not met anyone from a viable business or organization who was expecting his or her network to shrink over the next year or so. More powerful computers in the hands of more skilled people using them for more, simple and sophisticated applications continue to drive up demands for capacity, performance, and reliability. The impact of all these ramifications is discussed further in Chapters 2, 3, and 8.

Have you ever worked in an environment where new technology was "pushed" by advocates, sometimes for its own sake, rather than being "pulled" by business requirements? Have you ever worked for a company where product development was driven by engineering interest without regard for market potential? Have you ever worked with people who absolutely needed the latest computer hardware or software, but only because someone else had it? If so, you may be keenly aware of how inflated technology promises often are, whether positive or negative. Word processing tools did not really eliminate many secretarial positions and automated tellers have not eliminated the need for traditional bank offices. Nor have television and computers revolutionized how we educate the majority of students, and most people know how to use only a small fraction of the functional capabilities of their application programs. Computing, and networking in particular, have often been accused of over-promising and under-delivering. Yet there are well-know examples of dramatic successes, too—American Hospital Supply, American Airlines, and Frito-Lay, to name a few. While this book provides a lot of coverage for a particular new technology (Layer 3 switching is covered in depth in Chapters 4–6), you may find the *criteria* in Chapter 2 for assessing fundamentally new technologies to be valuable in a much broader context (Table 2.5.1).

Chapter 7 provides several network designs using Layer 3 products in response to a particular case study developed by Strategic Networks. While the case may not resemble your own or your customers' environments, you may find the *process* laid out in Chapter 2 for evaluating the appropriateness of a new technology (Table 2.7.1) to be quite relevant to understanding which pieces of the study apply to your situation. Formalizing some of these steps and involving network stakeholders can help minimize the risks of introducing new technology into a network that has become critical to the successful operation of an enterprise.

Finally, Chapter 9 draws everything together with our suggestions for the "top ten" issues one umust address in order to be successful in the deployment or sale of Layer 3 switching products. We also point out which ones generalize well to a larger context. With any luck, some of these ideas will help to minimize the risks of applying Layer 3 technology today, as well as other new technologies in the future.

Guidelines for Readers

This book is aimed primarily at people in organizations who are struggling to upgrade their LAN infrastructures. We think you can get value from the following:

- Planning methodologies and evaluation criteria that apply not only to L3 switching, but also to successful evaluation and deployment of virtually any new technology;
- Explanations in depth of the spectrum of approaches to Layer 3 switching;
- Suggestions for how the various L3 approaches address three common networking problems: evolving the collapsed backbone, evolving the server farm, and migrating beyond FDDI.

This book is also useful for vendor personnel who are tasked with positioning their products in the marketplace. It can help identify their opportunities and challenges in the customer environment: what is in place today, what is driving or inhibiting change, and what criteria are being used to evaluate L3 technology. It can also provide the background necessary to position their own products relative to the myriad of technologies and other products in the marketplace.

No introduction would truly be complete without some notes of caution. The pace of change in computer and networking technology is not likely to slow, although we do sometimes wonder if it can continue to accelerate forever. Consequently, it is important to note that the product details covered in this book, and to some extent, the information on Layer 3 technologies, represent a snapshot in time that may be accurate for a relatively short period. The technology will evolve; the products will be enhanced or new versions will supplant the ones discussed. We are quite confident, however, that the methodology the book presents for evaluating new technologies will continue to be useful. You can test this for yourself as vendors begin to discuss their approaches to "Layer 4 switching."

It is also worth mentioning that we did not even attempt to cover *all* L3 switching approaches or *all* available products in this book. Our selection of *major* vendors in terms of market leadership and *interesting* products from start-up companies could not possibly please or agree with everyone else's choices. We do think that our selection represents a good diversity and our analysis will help you to evaluate others if you are a prospective buyer. For vendors not covered here, you get a glimpse of who we think your major competition is today.

We do not consider this to be a technical book, despite the fact that it is about a particular technology. We may have provided more technical detail than some of you ever want to know about Layer 3 switching, for others we probably have not provided enough. Our goal is to provide some structure for how to think about L3 and a framework which you can use to evaluate this and other new technologies. It has been a challenging project, and we invite you to share the enthusiasm and concerns we have incorporated here.

Acknowledgments

This book is the result of input and support from many people. Nick Lippis influenced us to segment Layer 3 switches into one of two general categories—packet-by-packet or flow management. Rolf McClellan provided an immense amount of guidance relative to both switch functionality in general and the relevant test methodology in particular. Ellen Quackenbush continually encouraged us to keep focused on a piece of work that would be useful to the industry. Rob Strechay worked closely with us to conduct some of the primary market research. Lucy Ashton provided continuous input on a number of topics. James F. was always there for support.

A number of industry players came together to write chapter 8. These include Geoff Haviland (Cisco), Jeff Aaron (Newbridge Networks), Gordon Saussy (Torrent), Scott Wieder (3Com), Jason Caley and Deb Alford (Digital), Michael Banic and George Prodan (Extreme Networks), Keith Higgins (Xylan), and Bob Yee and Basil Alwan (Bay Networks).

However, the ultimate support for writing this book came from Sarah and Jay.

About the Authors

Dr. Jim Metzler is widely recognized as an authority on both network technology and its business applications. In over 28 years of professional experience, Jim has assisted tens of vendors to refine their product strategies and simultaneously helped over a hundred enterprises evolve their network infrastructure.

Jim's current interests include the evaluation and deployment of Layer 3 switching, the evaluation and deployment of converged IT infrastructures, as well as the deployment of service management. Jim has recently helped several enterprises to establish processes for network baselining, capacity and budget planning, as well as network chargeback. He has assisted a major CLEC plan and design both its network as well as its service offerings.

Dr. Metzler has worked in many positions in the networking industry. This includes creating software tools to design networks; being an engineering manager for high speed data services for a major Telco; being a product manager for network hardware; managing networks at two Fortune 500 companies; directing and performing market research at a major industry analyst firm; and running a consulting organization.

Jim holds a Ph.D. in Numerical Analysis from Boston University. He is a columnist in InternetWeek and a member of the Networld + Interop Planning Committee. Jim conducts tutorials on both local and wide area networking at ComNet in Washington, D.C. and San Francisco as well as at Networld + Interop, both in the United States and Europe. Dr. Metzler is both a faculty member and an advisor to Northeastern University's State of the Art Program in Networking.

Dr. Lynn DeNoia is well known for matching appropriate network and computing technology to the current and future business needs of enterprises. Over more than 27 years in the IT industry, she has facilitated development of strategies, architectures, and implementation plans for end-users, as well as business, product, and marketing plans for equipment vendors.

Lynn is interested in making technology accessible to people who can use it to solve business problems. She is a regular speaker at industry seminars, covering trends and how networks can incorporate new technology, such as Layer 3 switching, to advantage. Her tutorial on high-speed LANs at NetWorld+Interop is increasingly popular because it covers planning, design issues, and network management in addition to technology. Recent consulting assignments have included translation of business requirements into network objectives, development of network architectures, network design, and implementation planning, as well as product features analysis and market introduction planning.

Lynn received her Ph.D. in Computer Science from Brown University, and has held a variety of positions that contribute to her breadth of perspective. These range from systems administrator to network management architect to chief information officer, and include a stint as Motorola's voting representative to the T1M1 national standards committee on management of telecommunication networks. She has also held various consulting positions and served on the faculty as associate and assistant professor at Boston University and Bentley College, respectively.

1 *Introduction and Context*

1.1 The Excitement of New Technology

This book is intended to reduce some of the confusion generated by the frenzy of technology and product announcements as well as the amount of recent press coverage about a new class of technology we call "Layer 3 switching." To set the stage for this discussion, think back over your experience. Do you remember 100VG-AnyLAN? How about ATM25? Until recently, each of these was being advocated as technology that would make a major impact in the world of Local Area Networking. Neither one has done so, however.

The story of 100VG-AnyLAN and ATM25 is hardly unique. Both are sophisticated network technologies that have failed to fulfill their marketplace expectations. Of course, such failure is not a new phenomenon. Consider the three primary LAN technologies of the early 1980s; i.e., Ethernet, Token Ring, and Wangnet. For readers who do not remember Wangnet, it was a broadband, coaxial cable-based LAN capable of supporting voice, data, and video. As shown in Table 1.1, the marketplace acceptance of these three technologies was inversely proportional to their level of technical sophistication.

Table 1.1   1980s LAN Technologies

LAN Technology	Level of Technical Sophistication	Marketplace Acceptance
Ethernet	Low	High
Token Ring	Medium	Medium
Wangnet	High	Low

Principle: *Because a technology allows for a new way of doing business does not mean that people will adopt either the technology or the new way of doing business.*

Principle: *Some technologies will fail in the marketplace. Being the most technically sophisticated technology does not protect a technology from marketplace failure.*

The above principal should cause network professionals to look at their jobs somewhat differently. In particular, it is not a central component of their jobs to choose the most sophisticated technology. As previously demonstrated, some very sophisticated technologies fail in the marketplace. It is also not necessarily central to their jobs to enable new styles of doing work. For example, for several years the technologies have been in place to enable desktop video conferencing. However, few companies to date have found that this new style of doing work has been worth the effort. What *is* central to the jobs of network professionals is captured in the following:

Principle: *One of the primary responsibilities of network professionals is to match appropriate technologies to resolve issues their companies are willing to spend money to resolve.*

As network professionals evaluate networking technologies, they need to be cognizant of the fact that the network industry has seen an often-repeated cycle of hyperbole surrounding the introduction of any new networking technology (e.g., 100VG-AnyLAN, ATM25, ISDN, SMDS, and ATM). This cycle is depicted in Figure 1.1.

The cycle of technology hype begins early in the technology's life cycle. It typically starts with the first major article in the trade press that describes the benefits, in somewhat abstract terms, of the new technology. Because there are no products shipping at this time, it is easy to see only the advantages that the new technology will bring. Also, it is human nature to believe that there is a new technology coming soon that will solve many, if not all, networking problems.

The hyperbole continues, enhanced by the First Customer Shipment (FCS) of products from multiple vendors. The next series of articles in the trade magazines often brings the networking

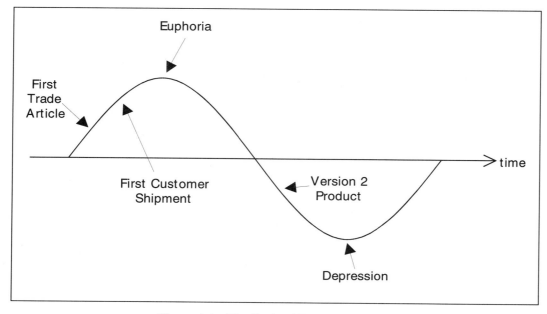

Figure 1.1   The Cycle of Technology Hype

community to a state of euphoria. These articles describe the initial trials of the new products, usually in glowing terms, accompanied by an interview of a network professional who is using the new technology. The slant of the article is that this person had the foresight to try out a new technology and has now either solved some major networking issue or allowed the company to function much more efficiently.

However, in many cases it is not long after these articles appear that the first negative news about limitations of the Version 1 products hits the press. These articles are often published about the time that the next new technology is beginning to work its way up the Cycle of Technology Hype. The appearance of these articles, combined with the untested promise of yet another new technology, tends to drive a cycle of negativity from which some technologies never regain a positive market position. However, for many technologies, stories about the improvements in Version 2 products, combined with more realistic expectations of their usefulness, counteracts the negativity.

Will Layer 3 switching go through a similar cycle of hype? Absolutely. In fact, the hype has already begun. Multiple vendors are claiming that Layer 3 switching will increase your network's performance by a factor of ten while simultaneously cutting cost by a factor of ten—a.k.a., a hundred-fold price/performance improvement! Are these claims merely a smokescreen to mask another technology that will fail in the marketplace? For reasons that will be detailed throughout this book, your authors assert that the answer to this question is absolutely not! In fact, we believe that Layer 3 switching will be a key technology for most, if not all, mid- to large-sized corporations. However, there currently are many approaches to Layer 3 switching that are being either discussed or deployed. We also assert that some of these approaches, like previous network technologies, will fail in the marketplace.

1.2 What's Driving the Need for New Technology?

Network Traffic

If anything characterizes the current Information Technology (IT) environment, surely it is the deployment of new and differing styles of computing. It was only a few years ago that companies began moving away from mainframe-based applications to deploy client-server applications. While the movement to client-server computing has had a notable impact on volumes and patterns of network traffic, it has had an equally significant impact on systems development. In a mainframe environment, the systems development process is typically lengthy and well documented, complete with prescribed review points and deliverables. Such formality usually includes opportunities for a network organization to get involved, understand what's being developed, and quantify the resultant network requirements.

In contrast, alternative styles of computing such as client-server, are typically characterized by both a shorter development cycle and increased use of off-the-shelf software. The irony here is that just as it is becoming increasingly important for network professionals to plan and manage their future capacity and budgetary requirements better, it is also much more difficult to do.

Principle: *The movement away from mainframe-style computing makes it notably more difficult to quantify future network requirements at the same time that budgeting properly for these requirements is gaining added importance.*

While it is clearly premature to refer to client-server applications as legacies, most network professionals have moved from worrying about them to worrying about intranet-style applications. In particular, the vast majority of companies your authors see either already are, or will soon be, deploying major intranet applications. This is occurring at the same time that most companies are also centralizing their servers in order to reduce the cost of distributed administration. Together, these factors invariably lead to both a significant increase in LAN traffic and a notable shift in the patterns of traffic across their networks.

Part of the conventional wisdom of the networking industry is that LAN traffic patterns traditionally follow an 80/20 rule, meaning that 80% of the traffic stays within a subnet and 20% of the traffic goes between subnets. Your authors are finding that the 80/20 rule no longer applies for most company networks. We think it is too early to say whether the new LAN paradigm will be 50/50 or 20/80. However, it is quite clear that an increasing percentage of LAN traffic will cross subnet boundaries, creating a corresponding increase in the need for routing functions across the LAN.

Principle: *LAN traffic has two distinguishing characteristics: it is increasing in total volume, and the amount of inter-subnet traffic is also increasing.*

To illustrate the concept, assume that a given network goes from an 80/20 flow of traffic to 20/80 without any increase in traffic volume. This means four times as much traffic needs to be routed across subnets. Does that mean the network needs four times as many routers? Actually the answer is no—*more* than four times as many routers are needed, because a growing percentage of router capacity is lost to inter-router connectivity and coordination as more are added.

Principle: *As the amount of inter-subnet traffic increases, there is a corresponding increase in the need for routing capacity.*

For the sake of example, let's assume that providing four times as much routing capacity requires six times as many routers. If the volume of traffic happens to double at the same time as patterns shift, then our new network will require *twelve* times as many routers as the original. Given the cost of traditional routing products, this creates an incredible challenge for most IT budget managers.

Principle: *Even a moderate increase in inter-subnet traffic accompanied by a moderate increase in traffic volume will eliminate traditional routers as an economically viable solution to providing required routing capacity in the LAN.*

Network Resources

Another characteristic of the current IT environment is the dramatic gap between the growth of network demands and the network resources (both people and budgets) available for support (Figure 1.2). In your authors' experience, it is rather common to have network traffic growing in the range of 40% per year while network resources are growing at a rate of approximately 5% per year. Please note that if data traffic grows at 40% per year, then the total traffic volume doubles roughly every two years.

Furthermore, we see nothing in the business or network environment to indicate that the situation depicted in Figure 1.2 will change in the near term. It is important to recognize that such average growth rates mask a high degree of variability among companies. Some networks are likely to be growing more slowly, but we have worked with some whose network traffic was growing at close to 100% per year. From a budget perspective, about 10% of the companies with which we are familiar are enjoying double-digit budget increases, while another 10% are actually having their budgets cut.

Principle: *To be successful, network professionals must continually make their networks more cost-effective. The primary quantification of this improved cost-effectiveness should be continually lower unit cost metrics.*

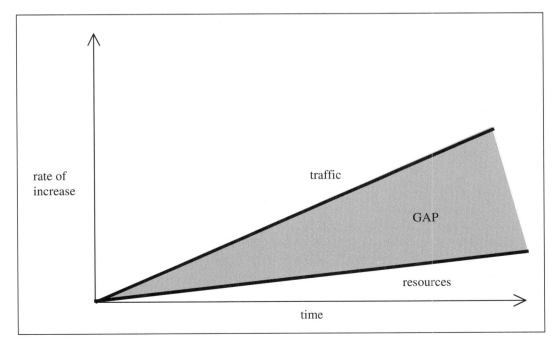

Figure 1.2   The Gap Between Network Demands and Available Resources

As we will discuss later in the book, your authors believe that Layer 3 switching technology will be successful in the marketplace because it allows network professionals to operate their existing networks in a notably more cost-effective manner.

1.3 Criteria for Evaluating Fundamentally New Technology

Remember that some new networking technologies die in the marketplace. This presents a dilemma, particularly for network professionals at leading-edge companies, where networking technologies are often adopted early in their life cycle in order to maintain or gain competitive advantage. The challenge such professionals face is to minimize the risk by only choosing technologies that have a high probability of success in the marketplace. We suggest that the criteria in Table 1.2 can be used to judge the likely market future of new networking technologies.

Table 1.2   Criteria for Evaluating Fundamentally New Technology

Does the technology solve a problem people want to solve?
Is the technology the first solution to the problem?
If the technology is not the first solution, is it notably better than the alternatives?
Is the level of technical sophistication appropriate for the problem being solved?
Does the technology represent a long-term solution?
Are all the relevant technological pieces in place?
Will the technology require a major effort to implement?
Are there any significant non-technical risks?

As an example, let's use these criteria to evaluate the marketplace viability of Layer 3 switching.

1. *Does the technology solve a problem people want to solve?* The problem that L3 switching addresses is to provide a significant increase in routing performance while significantly decreasing the cost of routing. This is a problem that network professionals must solve continually as their network needs change and grow.

2. *Is the technology the first solution to the problem?* L3 switching is clearly *not* the first way to provide routing functions. Routers have been doing that for a decade. However, L3 switching is the first technology to provide simultaneously a significant increase in routing performance and a significant decrease in the cost of routing.

3. *If the technology is not the first solution, is it notably better than the alternatives?* Because L3 switching is the first, the criterion does not apply in this case.

4. *Is the level of technical sophistication appropriate for the problem being solved?* As will be discussed later in this book, the approaches to L3 switching vary in terms of their technical sophistication. One of the challenges for network professionals is to ensure that the approach they choose to deploy has the appropriate level of technical sophistication.

5. *Does the technology represent a long-term solution?* The requirement to offer continually more routing function while simultaneously controlling costs will not go away. In addition, a fundamental characteristic of L3 switching—providing more function in hardware—is indeed a long-term design trend. Consequently, we believe that L3 switching is a long-term solution.

6. *Are all the relevant technological pieces in place?* As a general statement, the answer to this question is no. Some vendors are not even shipping products yet. Other vendors are shipping products with severe limitations, such as low port density or lack of performance. In addition, standards to facilitate value-added functions (such as Quality of Service) are still under development. However, we feel confident that there are viable products currently being shipped and that the market will mature quickly.

7. *Will the technology require a major effort to implement?* While the general answer to this is no, the level of effort will depend on your choice of approaches to L3 switching. For example, some equipment can be deployed in a network with a minimum of effort, because the equipment automatically learns about the rest of the network. Other equipment will require installation and configuration efforts similar to those for existing routers.

8. *Are there any significant non-technical risks?* The risks that we usually include in this category are organizational. However, because L3 switching will typically be deployed by the same organization that currently deploys routers, we do not see any significant non-technical risks.

1.4 The Definitions for Layer 3 Technology

In preparing our material, your authors found many different terms used to represent the same thing, and the same term used to represent different things. To provide clarity for our readers, we must begin with some background and a set of standard definitions that will be used throughout our discussions in this book. Layer 3, remember, refers to the Network Layer and Layer 2 (L2) to the Data Link Layer, as shown in Table 1.3.

Table 1.3   Open Systems Interconnection (OSI) Reference Model

Layer	Name
7	Application
6	Presentation
5	Session
4	Transport
3	Network
2	Data Link
1	Physical

First we need to distinguish the key **internetworking functions** that are fundamental to Layer 3 switching and routing, from switches and routers that are terms we reserve for internetworking products. In fact, there are three fundamental types of **internetworking devices**: bridges, routers, and gateways. A switch is a fancy bridge, routers are routers, and gateways (which operate at Layer 7, the Application Layer) are not relevant to our discussions in this book.

The basic function of **switching** is to forward traffic, by mapping what comes through an input port to an output port. Switch product architectures and implementations (e.g., crossbar matrix or TDM bus) determine when and how the mapping occurs. We are typically most familiar with packet switching at Layer 2, where the destination MAC (i.e., L2 Media Access Control, such as Ethernet) address from an incoming packet is used to determine which output port should transmit the packet for the next stage of its journey toward that destination.

The basic functions of **routing** are:

- Route Processing (path determination, table maintenance); and
- Traffic Forwarding (address resolution, counter maintenance, header rewrite).

Address resolution is usually implemented with some portion (or all) of the Layer 3 destination address used as an index into a table to look up the corresponding Layer 2 MAC address. (We will pay special attention to table look-up as a key component that distinguishes among certain types of Layer 3 switches.) Routing has a much larger (i.e., Layer 3) view of a network than switching (typically Layer 2) does.

Special Services are what we call the other functions that are performed by various switch and router products. These may include a variety of functions, such as:

- Translation into a format suitable for WAN transmission;
- Authentication of source identity;
- Packet filtering (e.g., for security purposes);
- Translation from one frame format into another (e.g., Token Ring to Ethernet); and
- Protocol encapsulation or tunneling.

The first internetworking device, the **bridge**, was designed to connect two LAN segments together. It was slightly better than a repeater that just copied *all* traffic from one port to another, because the bridge could "learn" the L2 addresses of devices in each segment. This means the bridge *switched* traffic from one segment to the other according to its knowledge of the destination's location. You may want to think of switches as "bridges on steroids." Next we look at how the marketplace has come to distinguish routers from switches:

- **Switches** provide switching functions, and may provide Special Services (e.g., packet filtering).

- **Routers** provide routing functions, switching functions, and Special Services.

In the particular perspective of this book, we find it useful to distinguish between:

- **Layer 2 switches**, which:
  - forward traffic based on the Layer 2 (L2) address,
  - perform switching, and
  - may perform Special Services (such as packet filtering); and

- **Layer 3 switches**, which:
  - forward traffic based on the Layer 3 (L3) address,
  - perform switching,
  - may perform Special Services (such as authentication), and
  - may or may not perform route processing.

As an aside, you are more likely to get L3 Special Services from an L3 switch than from an L2 switch.

With this background, our next step is to develop categories of L3 switches. Our approach is based on an early 1997 insight of Nick Lippis, founder and president of Strategic Networks, that basically there are only two types of L3 switches: those that process every packet at Layer 3, and those that don't. The former we call packet-by-packet L3 switches and the latter, L3 flow switches (see Chapter 4).

Among packet-by-packet L3 switches, it is useful to distinguish the following categories:

- Classical Routers (products developed prior to 1995, with most functions implemented in software, although newer ones may use hardware caching to get better performance for packet forwarding);

- Learning Bridges (forward traffic based on the L3 address, but do **not** perform route processing);

- Routing Switches (forward traffic based on the L3 address, and **do** perform route processing); and

- Modern Internet Routers (where "modern" implies breaking through the performance limitations of classical routers, i.e., throughput, latency, and latency variation).

Classical routers, then, are the products we have been using for internetworking among LANs (e.g., Ethernet and Token Ring), to connect different IP subnets, and more recently, to connect distinct virtual LANs (VLANs). Learning bridges is a term we have adapted for a small class of products that provide only one more routing function than Layer 2 switches. Their passive capability to learn L3 address mappings is rapidly becoming a software-controlled option of products in other categories and is not terribly interesting on its own. Our job in this book is to show you what is new and exciting about products in the remaining two categories, and how you can use them to advantage in your organization's network. We have chosen them as our focus because we see them poised to provide one or two orders of magnitude improvement in price/performance over classical routers. Additional detail to characterize routing switches and modern Internet routers is presented in Chapter 4, with sample products and approaches covered in Chapters 5 and 7. We have not tried to provide an encyclopedia of vendors or products, but have selected some that are representative of what's available from market leaders and from innovative start-up companies.

Classifying flow switches further is more difficult because the diversity of approaches is so great, extending beyond the packet realm and even encompassing the cell world of ATM. In addition, these approaches involve far more than moving functions from software to hardware—they are fundamentally new ways of processing the data that are being transferred. Consequently, we discuss these as architectures rather than as specific products. Two categories seem useful: end-system-centric and network-centric. End-system-centric approaches require software to be installed or modified at every participating end-system. Network-centric approaches do not. They provide functions and capabilities within the network equipment itself. Additional detail to characterize these is presented in Chapter 4, with sample approaches and products covered in Chapters 6 and 7. Again, we have selected examples rather than try to provide exhaustive coverage.

1.5 Other Enabling Technologies

In addition to switching and routing, the success of new Layer 3 technology is associated with other developing technologies. We briefly describe these below.

Virtual LANs

Virtual LANs, or VLANs, were developed in response to the broadcast problems of large, switched networks. Such networks are called flat—they do not have any routing, and each constitutes a single broadcast domain. The more devices, the more likely there will be excessive broadcasts throughout the network that drain off network capacity unproductively, or that a broadcast storm will propagate to every corner of the network. Broadcast containment typically occurs at Layer 3, where the network address distinguishes among broadcast domains. The first VLANs were logical groupings of devices at Layer 2 that were used to simulate an L3 broadcast domain. Thus, traffic could flow between different VLANs only if it was routed. It may be convenient to think of a VLAN as a Closed User Group (CUG) for which the L2 switches act as traffic cops. Only routing has the information and power to connect them. Subsequently, VLANs has become a much more general mechanism, with membership defined on various L2, L3, or other policy characteristics. VLANs are especially useful in conjunction with L3 switching to:

- Prevent broadcasts from non-routable protocols (such as NetBEUI) from burdening an entire network; and

- Isolate legacy protocols (such as IPX) to be handled by classical routers instead of L3 switches.

There are two important standards being developed by the IEEE for VLANs. 802.1p is designed to expedite time-critical data and to limit the extent of high-bandwidth multicast traffic, both across switched LANs. This is usually referred to as the VLAN tagging protocol. 802.1Q is known as the VLAN trunking protocol. Its purpose is to avoid the need for one physical link directly from each switch supporting VLANs to a router in order to connect those VLANs. Without these standards, all VLAN schemes are largely proprietary and cannot be expected to interoperate. All major vendors have said their products will support the standards when they are ready, but we urge readers to be cautious in their expectations before then.

NHRP

The Next-Hop Resolution Protocol (NHRP) is a new routing protocol being developed by the Internet Engineering Task Force (IETF) to handle the problems of routing in very large networks. NHRP is being designed to allow a source station (host or router) to determine the network layer and MAC addresses of suitable next hops along the way to a destination, when the network between them is *not* a broadcast network. Figure 1.3 demonstrates the concept of a logically independent IP subnet (LIS), where:

- All members of a LIS have the same IP network/subnet number and address mask;

- All members of a LIS are directly connected to the same subnet;

- All hosts and routers outside the LIS are accessed via a router; and

- All members of a LIS access each other directly (without routers).

In classical IP routing, host "a" can only access host "b" by sending packets through a router that belongs to both subnets. Traversing this router is called a **hop**. In a larger internetwork, multiple IP hops may be required to reach the intended IP destination.

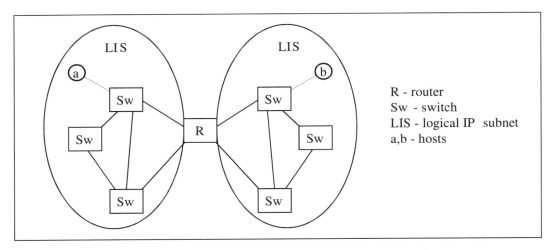

Figure 1.3   Logical IP Subnets make up an Internetwork

NHRP is based on a Local Address Group (LAG) model instead of the LIS model. In the LIS approach, the decision to forward local or remote is based only on the IP address information. The LAG model decouples the outcome of the local-or-remote decision from the addressing information and couples it instead with Quality of Service and/or traffic characteristics. Consequently, any two stations in the whole network can establish direct communication, independent of their addresses. Such a situation requires that any host or router in the network can resolve IP to MAC addresses for any other entity in the whole network. NHRP provides such a mechanism using a client-server approach, and is an integral element of MPOA (Multi-Protocol over ATM).

RSVP

ATM advocates have long promoted the benefits of assigning different Quality of Service (QoS) parameters (such as bandwidth allocation and priority) to different types of network traffic so they could receive different levels of service across the network. As interest in transporting voice and video traffic over the LAN grew, people began to wonder if something similar could be designed for the frame-based, IP environment. The IETF is developing the Resource reSerVation Protocol (RSVP) to facilitate such capabilities. RSVP sees network traffic as a set of **flows**, where each flow is a single stream of data from a single source application to one or more destination applications. Flows may be aggregated into "sessions" that share the same resource characteristics (e.g., multiple voice conversations). RSVP service requests are issued by applications to tell the network what resources it would like to see allocated (e.g., bit rate or burst size). Two classes of service are currently defined: Guaranteed Service for connection-oriented traffic and Controlled Load Service, which offers the best-effort equivalent of an unloaded network. The underlying link layer is responsible for delivering the appropriate level of service. In the case of ATM, the RSVP information is mapped directly to ATM classes of service; other data link technologies (such as Ethernet) use buffering and special queuing mechanisms to achieve similar results. It's important to remember that RSVP is just the signaling protocol—it can allocate no resources at all.

IP Multicast

Basically, IP multicast is a way of saving bandwidth when the same exact information needs to be sent from a single source to multiple destinations, but not to every destination, in an internetwork. The trick is to do it without broadcasting the traffic everywhere at Layer 2. What is needed are mechanisms to join and leave a multicast group, and to keep track of each one. Then, smart routers can forward traffic only toward intended destinations and smart switches can repeat traffic only onto those ports where intended destinations sit. The most important protocols involved are:

- IGMP (Internet Group Management Protocol), which provides for establishment and update of group membership;

- DVMRP (Distance Vector Multicast Routing Protocol), which lets routers find efficient multicast pathways through the network, but has some scalability limitations;

- PIM (Protocol-Independent Multicast), which improves on DVMRP and works with all unicast routing protocols. It has two modes, *dense* (similar to DVMRP and best for stable, concentrated groups) and *sparse* (better for often-changing and widely scattered groups).

With this background in mind, you should now be prepared to investigate what Layer 3 technology is all about.

2 A Framework for Technology Evaluation

2.1 Introduction

This book focuses largely on a leading edge LAN technology—Layer 3 switching. However, this chapter will cover a variety of other factors that influence the successful evolution of a LAN infrastructure. For example, it is the author's experience that in most cases when an organization is looking to upgrade its LAN infrastructure, the choice of leading edge technology is usually not the dominant decision criteria. In addition, the authors have worked with multiple organizations that have a corporate strategy of not using a technology until it has been deployed for over a year. These organizations are choosing not to implement leading edge technology in order to reduce the risk associated with a LAN upgrade. In addition to minimizing risk, there are several other criteria that organizations use to choose between technologies. These criteria will be discussed in detail in section 2.2.

One of the primary criteria used by network professionals when choosing any new technology is cost. It might appear that cost is a well-understood concept. However, there is some confusion relative to cost given the disparate use by LAN equipment vendors of the phrase Return on Investment (RoI). In section 2.3, the authors will define what they mean by RoI and will show how, given their definition, it is seldom possible to actually compute an RoI for a LAN upgrade. The authors will also suggest other financial metrics that network professionals can use to quantify the cost of providing network services.

The authors have been involved in several projects to upgrade a LAN infrastructure in which there was a significant disconnect between the work of the project team and the desires of senior management. In the best cases, this disconnect has resulted in a major delay in the project. In the worst cases, it has resulted in the project ending in failure. In section 2.4, the authors present a business model that network professionals can use to manage the relationship between what senior management expects and what is possible, from the standpoint of the embedded infrastructure as well as new vendor products.

Finally, even in those cases in which there is agreement within an enterprise on both the technology and the vendor for a LAN upgrade, a lingering question often remains—What are the triggers that would indicate the appropriate time to upgrade the LAN infrastructure? In section 2.5, the authors will discuss how a capacity planning process can be used to provide these triggers.

2.2 Decision Criteria

The authors have worked with a number of organizations to help them identify which decision criteria to use when choosing between alternative network technologies. We typically do this by a combination of:

- A brainstorming session in which the network organization creates a set of decision criteria;
- A sanity check in which the criteria are fully defined and duplicate criteria are combined;
- A weighting exercise in which representative members of the network organization identify the criteria of most importance to them; and
- A combination of similar criteria into affinity groups.

In most situations, the affinity groups that emerge are Serviceability and Manageability, Technology and Architecture, as well as Vendor and Price.

Table 2.1 lists the most common criteria that have been identified at these brainstorming sessions as well as the affinity groups into which they were most typically assigned.

Table 2.1   Typical Decision Criteria and Affinity Groupings

Criteria	Affinity Group
Support (defined as "tell us problems before they hit us")	Serviceability and Manageability
Operational simplicity	Serviceability and Manageability
Chargeback (defined as the ability to turn usage data into bills)	Serviceability and Manageability
Low cost of ownership	Serviceability and Manageability
Manageability	Serviceability and Manageability
Performance (defined as both high throughput and low delay)	Technology and Architecture
Open standards	Technology and Architecture
Value-added (a.k.a., proprietary) features	Technology and Architecture
Accounting (defined as the ability to measure usage)	Technology and Architecture

Table 2.1   Typical Decision Criteria and Affinity Groupings (Continued)

Criteria	Affinity Group
Reliability (this had multiple definitions, including "don't fail", "low MTBF (Mean Time Between Failures)", and low "MTTR" (Mean Time to Repair))	Technology and Architecture
Interoperability	Technology and Architecture
Interfaces	Technology and Architecture
Multi-protocol	Technology and Architecture
Architecture	Technology and Architecture
Fault tolerance	Technology and Architecture
Scalability (this had many characteristics including modularity, number and types of interfaces, technologies supported)	Technology and Architecture
Components (defined as the upgradability of the box)	Technology and Architecture
Future direction of the product	Technology and Architecture
Initial price	Vendor and Price
Vendor viability (defined as "will they be around in 5 years?")	Vendor and Price
Relative positioning (defined as "how important is Company E to the vendor?")	Vendor and Price
Is this part of a family of products?	Vendor and Price
What is the vendor's track record for time to market for new products?	Vendor and Price
Is the vendor a niche player or a major player?	Vendor and Price

Below are some of the key conclusions, by affinity group, that the authors have drawn relative to the criteria listed in Table 2.1.

A. Vendor and Price

This affinity group is seldom rated even close to the other two in terms of its importance as a decision criterion. However, that does not mean these are not important issues. There is a somewhat subtle distinction between an important issue and a decision criteria. For example, many companies do not place a high weight on the choice of vendor as a decision criterion because they already have a short list of acceptable vendors. Hence, it is not that the choice of vendor is unimportant. In a sense it is just the opposite. The choice of a vendor is so important that oftentimes companies have already determined a short list of acceptable vendors.

Low initial price is seldom a key decision criterion for network professionals. In a somewhat analogous fashion, this does not mean that low cost is not important. What is does mean is that network professionals often do not expect that there will be a large difference in the initial cost of the equipment from the vendors on their short list. What was also curious is how network professionals typically respond to a Low Lifecycle Cost of Network Ownership as a decision criterion. While many of them mention it as a decision criterion during the brainstorming session, it is rarely weighted highly. The reasons for this vary. One common reason is that network professionals usually find little substance in the universal vendor claims that their products lower the cost of network ownership relative to similar products from their competitors.

Principle: Most network professionals do not place much credence in vendor's claims that their technology lowers the total cost of network ownership.

B. Serviceability and Manageability

This is the affinity group that receives the highest weight the majority of times. There are two factors that drive the importance of this affinity group. The first is the perception of the poor or highly varied service currently available. This poor service takes many forms, including lack of information on new products, misinformation on the capabilities and requirements of products, and sometimes a smugness or arrogance on the part of the account team. One university that the authors have worked with referred to their two existing vendors as "Vendor Night" and "Vendor Day." They stated that the account was Vendor Night's to loose. Vendor Night did manage to loose the account based entirely on their terrible service, particularly when compared to the exemplary service provided by Vendor Day. What is most interesting is that subsequent to this conversation, a large insurance company also explained to the authors the bad service they were getting from their primary vendor. This vendor who was giving such bad service to the insurance company was the same vendor who had given such exemplary service to the university, i.e., Vendor Day.

Principle: The quality of support that a vendor provides to a client can be highly varied based on factors such as the make up of the account team as well as how important that account is to the vendor.

The second factor that tends to drive the importance of Service and Manageability is the overall increase in the importance of network management. We state this because we have recently either talked to or surveyed hundreds of network professionals. In eighty to ninety percent of the time, network professionals report that network management is significantly more important to them than it was just 18 months ago. The reasons they give for this are more evolutionary than revolutionary. They report that the network is truly central to their company's businesses and they are being told to manage more with highly constrained budgets. They are currently viewing network management as critical to their success in this environment.

Principle: The effective use of network management has become a critical success factor for network professionals.

However, while the authors do not have any statistically valid data to substantiate their claim, they do believe that even with the increased importance of network management, most network management tools that are acquired are either not installed or installed but not used.

Principle: There is a significant gap between the importance of network management and how impactful the discipline has been to date.

C. Technology and Architecture

This affinity group is sometimes rated higher than Serviceability and Manageability and is seldom rated much lower than it. The organizations that rate Technology and Architecture higher than Serviceability and Manageability tend to have well defined, short term requirements. For example, one client of the authors intends to make an immediate implementation of Layer 3 switching. This organization feels that over time there will be few, if any, significant technological differences between vendor products. However, due to the immaturity of the current set of products, they are resigned to choosing a product with the fewest technological deficiencies.

One of the interesting insights the authors have gained from interviewing network professionals is how they intend to use the performance claims to differentiate between competing products. We found that when it comes to choosing network equipment, customers want sufficient performance to meet their needs. Most network professionals, however, are not terribly impressed by performance that is notably more than they foresee themselves needing. As such, performance is a more likely to be a requirement (a.k.a., a check off item) than a differentiator.

2.3 Money

The current business environment is best summed up by the title of the August 12, 1996 Time magazine cover story—"Work is Hell." More specifically, every industry segment has been, and will continue to be, under relentless pressure to become increasingly efficient. Within an organization, this pressure is typically felt more intensely by those functions and departments that are not revenue-generating. In almost every case, this includes the networking function. In particular, depending upon the industry sector, the networking function represents an expense that typically ranges from 0.5% to 2% of a company's total revenues. Industries such as forestry and pharmaceuticals tend to be on the low end of this range, while the computer and financial industries tend to be on the high end.

Given the current business environment and the corresponding corporate pressure to become increasingly cost efficient, network professionals need to become ever more facile with understanding both the major cost components and the cost drivers of their LAN infrastructure. This understanding will equip network professionals to better perform two critical tasks. The first of these is to compare network alternatives based on the total cost of networking. The second task is to explain to a variety of constituents the necessity of making investments in technologies such as Layer 3 switching.

As detailed in Table 2.2, the cost of LAN ownership is comprised of three primary components. They are:

- Capital Equipment (the cost of the hardware and software purchases directly related to operating the network);

- People (the total cost (salary plus benefits) of the people assigned to plan, design, implement, and manage the network); and

- Facilities (the costs of the cable plant, office space, hardware and software maintenance and utilities necessary to operate the network).

Table 2.2   Primary Components of the Cost of LAN Ownership

Capital	People	Facilities
Hubs	Network Design	Wiring/Cabling
Routers	Network Configuration	Equipment Maintenance
Servers	Help Desk	Software Maintenance
Network Interface Cards	Operational Support	Floor Space
Layer 3 Switches	Address Management	Power
Network Management Hardware and Software	Implementation	Air Conditioning
Remote Access Hardware and Software	Moves/Adds/Changes	Wide Area Network circuits (if applicable)

Figure 2.1 details what percentage of the total cost of LAN ownership is attributable to capital, people, and facilities. Note that for a LAN, there are no costs attributable to Wide Area Network Circuits. As Figure 2.1 indicates, the people cost is the dominant contributor to the cost of a traditional LAN. The capital equipment cost is the second most important component of the total LAN cost while the facilities costs are relatively insignificant.

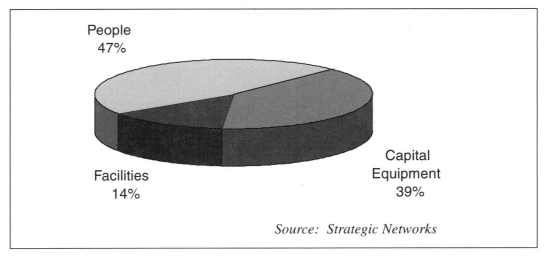

People
47%

Facilities
14%

Capital
Equipment
39%

Source: Strategic Networks

Figure 2.1   LAN Cost Components

Principle: *In order to offer more cost-effective LAN services, network professionals must pay at least as much attention to the people costs as to the cost of the equipment. In part, this translates to the requirement to choose equipment that can demonstrate ease of both implementation and ongoing operations. It also speaks to the need to better leverage network management.*

One financial analysis that is often used to analyze alternative investments is a Return on Investment (ROI) analysis. To the authors, the general premise of an ROI analysis is that if a network professional makes an investment, typically in some new network hardware, there will be a quantifiable reduction of expense dollars. In the optimum situation, within a short period of time (i.e., the Payback Period) the expense savings equals the investment. Also, at the end of the study period (typically chosen to be three years to coincide with the depreciation of the hardware), it is possible to calculate the annualized rate of return that the company earned on its initial investment.

While calculating an ROI is highly desirous, it is difficult to do this for a LAN upgrade. In particular, the typical LAN upgrade will increase the capital costs and will rarely make any measurable reduction in either the people or the facilities costs. For example, one common attempt to develop an ROI for a LAN upgrade identifies some percentage of a LAN administrator's time that will be freed up as a result of deploying some new hardware. For the sake of example, assume that the analysis shows that by deploying some new hardware 10% of a LAN administrator's time is freed up and that there are currently 30 LAN administrators. This analysis typically concludes that deploying the hardware will allow the company to save three Full Time Equivalent (FTE) employees. The flaw in this analysis as seen by the CFO is that usually nobody leaves the system. As such, while there may be cost avoidance, there is no actual cost reduction. Another analysis that the authors often see referred to as an ROI analysis is a comparison of the cost of alternative LAN solutions. While this is an important analysis, it is not what the authors refer to as a Return on Investment analysis.

Principle: *As a general rule, it will be difficult, if not impossible, to compute a true ROI on a LAN upgrade.*

Since calculating an ROI for LAN upgrades is not typically possible, the authors recommend that network professionals look to develop some other form of financial analysis. In particular, we recommend that network professionals develop a small set of key Unit Cost Metrics. The authors suggest four criteria for choosing a Unit Cost Metric. It must be:

- End user focused;
- Easy to understand;
- Closely aligned to the cost drivers of the network; and
- Under the influence of the network professionals.

Principle: *Network professionals should identify and manage a small set of Unit Cost Metrics.*

For example, consider a voice network. Unlike a Local Area Network (LAN), voice networks have a well-understood unit cost; i.e., the cost per minute of a call. For the sake of example, consider a hypothetical company, Call Centers, Inc., that was spending ten cents a minute on voice calls and made one million calls a month. This would result in a cost of $100,000 per month for voice communications.

In most cases, network professionals have little control over the number of minutes of voice traffic. However, they do have some control over the unit cost of voice traffic. They can drive down this cost through techniques such as contract re-negotiation with their service providers, network redesign, as well as the deployment of newer, more cost effective services.

Again consider the hypothetical company, Call Centers, Inc., and assume that the Director of Telecommunications instituted a project that drove the unit cost of voice networking down from ten cents a minute to eight cents a minute. On just the issue of cost, the director has done a good job and should, in theory, receive a positive year-end performance review. However, further assume that at the same time that the Director was driving down the cost of voice networking the number of monthly minutes of voice calling actually doubled. The monthly cost for voice would then rise to $160,000; i.e., a 60% increase in the bottom line cost of networking. If the Director's year-end review is impacted by the bottom line cost of networking, it is highly unlikely that he or she will receive a very positive review.

Regrettably, in the LAN environment there is not a single unit cost metric that is well understood and meaningful. The LAN cost metric that is used most often is the annual cost to support a desktop. It has the advantage that it is easy to understand, at least at the conceptual level. This metric is a good one to use in a company where the set of programs running on the desktop is relatively static, there are no significant changes in the traffic, and the number of networked desktops is increasing. In this case, it is truly the number of desktops that is the primary driver of cost. If this is the case, then the network professional can potentially drive down the cost per desktop, and hence be perceived as being successful.

Principle: *In those environments in which the set of applications running on the desktop are relatively static and there are no significant changes in the traffic, the annual cost to support a desktop is a viable Unit Cost Metric.*

However, in most environments new applications are continually being added to the desktop. These applications increase the traffic on the network as well as the overall support costs. In these cases, it is likely that the best the network professional can do is to reduce the rate of growth in the cost per desktop. In many cases, reducing the rate of growth is not going to lead to the network professional being regarded as successful. In these situations, another possible LAN cost metric is the cost to carry a megabyte of information across the LAN. This metric better reflects one of the cost drivers in these networks; i.e., increasing traffic. Also, the network professional often has the ability to reduce the cost per megabyte metric by techniques such as redesigning the network, deploying new technology, and using network management to become more efficient.

The authors would like to suggest that it is important to include all the cost elements shown in Table 2.2 into the calculation of cost per megabyte. The authors would also like to point out that there is a significant difference between a cost per megabyte metric and a cost per megabit per second metric (Cost/Mbps). The former metric measures what it costs to carry a company's traffic. As such, it is end-user focused. The latter metric measures what it costs to provide the network capacity. It is usually possible to reduce the Cost/Mbps metric by building a larger network independent of the need for that network. As such, while Cost/Mbps can be an insightful metric to compare differing technologies, it is not a useful measure of the cost effectiveness of an operational network.

Principle: *In those environments in which applications are continually being added and/or the traffic volumes are changing significantly, the cost to carry a megabyte of traffic over the LAN better reflects the network cost drivers than does the annual cost to support a desktop.*

Note that the above principal does not state that in rapidly changing environments the annual cost to support a desktop is not an important metric. It is. What the principal does say is that in these dynamically changing situations, the annual cost to support a desktop does not satisfy one of the criteria to be a Unit Cost Metric; i.e., it is not easily influenced by the network professionals.

2.4 A Three Step IT Business Model

As previously mentioned, there is often a disconnection between network professionals working on a LAN upgrade and other key members of the organization. The authors have developed a management model called Managing for Success that is intended to eliminate this disconnect. The model identifies the three major functions that network professionals must focus on—stakeholder management, network optimization, and vendor management.

Broadly defined, a stakeholder is anyone who exerts significant influence over the decisions being made in the network organization. This could include the Chief Financial Officer, the Chief Information Officer, or the Business Unit Managers (BUMs). The purpose of stakeholder management is to ensure that periodic, effective communications exist between the network organization and its primary stakeholders. This dialogue allows the network professional to better understand the business direction and to apply both traditional and emerging technologies to facilitate the company's achieving its goals. In addition, this communication should ensure that few surprises, if any, occur in terms of both the expectations that the stakeholders have on the network professional as well as their support for the network professional's initiatives; i.e., the deployment of Layer 3 switching. Table 2.3 details the primary components of stakeholder management.

Table 2.3   Components of Stakeholder Management

Component	Description/Purpose
An Account Management Function	This is intended to help network professionals market the existing network services, gather business requirements that drive the evolution of network services, and quantify the affordability of the business requirements.
A Capacity and Budget Planning Process	The output of a capacity plan is a quantification of what point in time individual components of the network reach exhaust. The budget planning process turns the capacity requirements into budgetary requirements. This information positions network professionals to gain approval from the appropriate stakeholders.
A Service Catalog	The purpose of the service catalog is to describe to key stakeholders what services the network provides to them. A service is defined from the vantage point of the user and could include: • conferencing (room, desktop, audio); • Internet access; • voice mail; • e-mail; and • file transfer.
Service Level Agreements (SLAs)	The function of an SLA is to describe the quality parameters of each service as seen by the stakeholder. For example, the e-mail service may specify that 99% of all e-mail messages up to one megabyte will be delivered within 30 minutes.
Chargeback	As a minimum, this involves the creation of reports to allow user organizations to understand the network cost for which they are responsible. More broadly, this involves the development of the processes and procedures to charge back for these network costs.
Financial Analysis	As a minimum, this involves the identification, measurement, and reporting on a few unit cost metrics; e.g., the cost per megabyte in the LAN.
Benchmarking	The comparison of your network to those of similar companies. The comparison should be relative to both the key financial, operational, and performance metrics.

Network professionals have historically focused on network optimization. Typically, network optimization involves planning, designing, implementing, and managing network hardware. However, the role of network optimization is steadily changing. In the Wide Area Network, for example, there is a steadily growing reliance on outsourced services such as Managed Frame Relay, and Virtual Private Networks (VPNs). At the logical conclusion of this trend, corporations will own little, if any, WAN hardware.

Principle: *As companies outsource an increasing amount of their network functions, the role of the network professional is increasingly to serve as the interface between the vendor community and the network organization's stakeholders.*

Most companies are not outsourcing quite as much of their LAN infrastructure as they are their WAN infrastructure. However, whether outsourcing is a major activity or not, the role of LAN optimization has to change for two reasons. The first change driver is that network professionals must support a significant increase in network traffic with only a modest increase in resources. This will be difficult, if not impossible, with the traditional approaches to network optimization. The second change driver is the enhanced requirement for network professionals to perform stakeholder management.

Functions that need to be added to the network optimization function include network baselining, network cost analysis, and in some cases, applications modeling. Table 2.4 contains a list of the primary components of network optimization.

Table 2.4   Components of Network Optimization

Component	Description/Purpose
Network Baselining	A network baseline quantifies both the current status of the network as well as trends in parameters such as utilization and delay.
Network Cost Analysis	The analysis can be done at a variety of levels, including: • the unit cost for running the network (i.e., cost/megabyte); • the unit cost for providing a service such as messaging or conferencing; and • the unit cost to perform a function such as moves/adds/ changes, or a hardware installation.
Technology Evaluation	One purpose of this function is to determine the appropriateness of an existing or emerging technology in a company's network. Another purpose is to determine the marketplace viability of emerging technologies.
Applications Modeling	Typically this involves running simulations to quantify the impact a given application will have on a corporation's network.
Network Design	The purpose of network design is to ensure that the network is meeting the SLAs at the lowest unit cost. A design works within well-defined boundaries that are established in the network architecture. For example, a design could look at the viability of re-segmenting an Ethernet LAN.

Table 2.4   Components of Network Optimization (Continued)

Component	Description/Purpose
Network Architecture	The purpose of a network technology architecture is to: • ensure that emerging business requirements can be satisfied; • limit the uncoordinated purchasing of network products and services in conjunction with a vendor management plan; and • ensure a progressive improvement in the cost effectiveness of the network. It accomplishes this by: • identifying the optimal mix of technologies in a network; • describing a set of rules for network design.
Network Management Architecture	There are three primary components of this architecture. They are: • tools to gather traffic statistics; • platforms and tools to process the traffic statistics; and • a set of processes that indicate what happens to the processed data. Part of the processes is a determination of the optimum organizational structure.
Evaluation of Outsourcing	This function involves the determination of what activities (e.g., time of day, geography), are best handled by an external vendor.
Policies for Network Usage	This function involves the creation of any of a variety of policies surrounding the use of the network. Examples include policies that detail: • what is appropriate use of the Internet; and • who has access to what corporate data.

Similar to the way that network professionals need to broaden their approach to network optimization, they also need to broaden their view of vendor management. One component of vendor management that takes increased importance in the new environment is the development of product and service acceptance plans. The reason this is of increased importance is that there is a spate of new products currently hitting the marketplace. New products are typically accompanied by unsubstantiated claims of notably increased performance. Table 2.5 details the other primary components of vendor management.

An example of this spate of new products is all of the Layer 3 switching products being introduced into the marketplace. Associated with each of these devices are claims of how many millions of packets per second these devices can switch. Network professionals need some assurance of how these devices will actually perform in their networks running their application mix, with the appropriate routing functionality enabled, prior to exposing both themselves and their company to the vagaries of vendor slideware.

Table 2.5 Components of Vendor Management

Component	Description/Purpose
Product and Service Acceptance Plans	The purpose of these plans is to ensure that the products and services that a company acquires perform in accordance with the vendor's proposals.
Product and Service Prototyping	The purpose of this function is to try a product or service, typically in a laboratory environment, prior to deploying it in either a trial or a production network.
Creation and Evaluation of RFPs	The purpose of this function is to: • identify and prioritize a company's requirements; • communicate those requirements to a select number of vendors; and • evaluate the responses from those vendors.
Negotiation and Management of Contracts	One purpose of this function is to ensure that any contract that a company signs protects the company, particularly when acquiring new technology. One area to focus on is to minimize the impact on the company of a vendor's changing its direction relative to the deployment of new technology.
Creation of a Vendor Strategy	One purpose of this function is to identify for a company the appropriate number of vendors to have in its local and wide area networks. This is driven by the need to ensure that the network professional is never locked into a given technology or vendor.
The Creation of SLAs	While this function is analogous to the creation of SLAs that network professionals offer to their stakeholders, the focus is different. In particular, the purpose of these SLAs is to outline the quality parameters of the products and services that a company acquires from external vendors.

2.5 A Three Step Model of Network Management

One of the many purposes of network management is to allow network professionals to identify events that would trigger a network upgrade. However, the discipline of network management has been a moderate failure. The evidence that supports that assertion is the gap between the importance that network professionals place on network management contrasted with their ability to answer simple questions about the performance of their networks. For example, the great majority of network professionals that we talk to at all levels in the organization assert that network management is either very important or extremely important to them. However, at most one out of twenty of these same professionals have even a moderately good estimate of the annualized rate of growth of their data traffic.

This lack of information on the rate of growth of data traffic makes it difficult if not impossible to project the need for added network capacity. It also exacerbates the difficulty of getting management signoff for the capital to perform a network upgrade. The purpose of this section is to outline some processes that network professionals can use to improve network management within their organizations.

2.5.1 Three Step Network Management Model

As shown in Figure 2.2, The Three-Step Network Management Model identifies the major functions that network professionals must focus on—Gathering Traffic Data, Processing Traffic Data into Information, and Acting on the Information.

A. Gather Traffic Data

RMON II is an extension of the RMON (Remote Monitoring) MIB (Management Information Database). RMON II adds statistics at the network and application layers of the protocol stacks. It provides information to see beyond the segment and to get an end-to-end view of who is talking to whom and what application(s) are being used. With the shipment of RMON II standardized products, the authors feel that network professionals have the capacity to gather a significant amount of traffic data. The primary issue relative to capturing traffic data is cost. By cost, the authors are referring to the cost of the people and instrumentation required to gather the data, the memory required to store the data, and the impact on the network from transferring the traffic data.

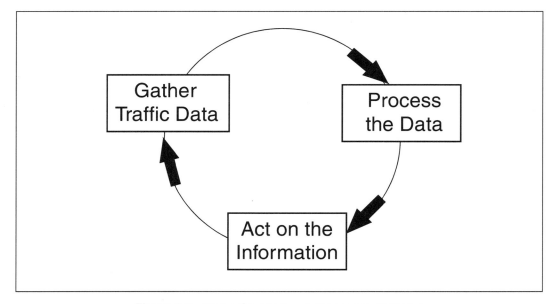

Figure 2.2   Three-Step Network Management Model

B. Process the Raw Traffic Data into Information

After capturing traffic data, network professionals need tools to process the data into actionable information relative to the status of their network. The good news is that there is a lot of activity in the industry in terms of the development of tools to do a variety of network management functions. However, these tools often suffer from two significant limitations. The first of these limitations is that they are not tightly integrated. For example, it is highly desirous to take the output of a baselining tool and export it into a network design tool. As a general rule, this is not possible. The second key limitation is that most of these tools do not give network professionals much ability to customize their reports. As such, many network professionals find themselves in the position of having captured data that is of importance to them but they are unable to generate reports that highlight the data in the format they need. In spite of these limitations, the authors feel that there are tools in the marketplace that can provide a broad range of functionality.

C. Act on the Information

There are clearly limitations to a network professional's ability to gather traffic data as well as to process this data into information. However, it is the author's experience that the area that gives network organizations the most difficulty is implementing effective procedures to act on the data. However, without these procedures, the previous two steps are useless.

Principle: *In order to be successful, network professionals must do at least a good job on each step of the Three-Step Network Management Model.*

It is the authors' experience that the way most network organizations implement network management is from the bottom up. By that we mean that it is common to deploy a new network management tool and then develop either formalized or ad hoc procedures around the use of the tool. In order to be successful, this approach must change.

Principle: *To provide the most benefit, a network management architecture must be designed to focus on the problems to be solved and not on the tool de jour.*

The authors recommend that network professionals implement a service management function. The authors further suggest that network professionals should concurrently redesign network management to ensure the success of service management. Examples of what the authors refer to as services would be Internet access, conferencing services (room and desktop), as well as messaging services.

Below are some of the key steps that network professionals should take to ensure that network management supports service management.

- For each service, determine what functions must be performed in order to ensure that the service conforms to the parameters of the Service Level Agreement (SLA).

- For each function so identified, determine what data is needed to perform the function.
- For each piece of data so identified, determine the optimum source(s) of that data.
- Define the new workflow; i.e., who gets the data, what they do with it, how the data moves between groups.

2.5.2   Model of a Capacity Planning Process (The Model)

Because of our belief that an effective capacity planning process is central to the successful deployment of Layer 3 switching, the authors have developed a model (The Model) of how to perform capacity planning. The Model is based on the following principal.

Principle: *Most corporate networks are too large and complex to allow network managers to thoroughly examine each component; i.e., every NIC, LAN segment, switch port, router port, Frame Relay circuit.*

The Model overcomes this obstacle by systematically looking at increasingly granular levels of information about an increasingly shrinking number of network elements. The Model is comprised of a four-step process, where the outcomes of each step provide input for the next step. Figure 2.3 depicts The Model and representative outcomes of each step.

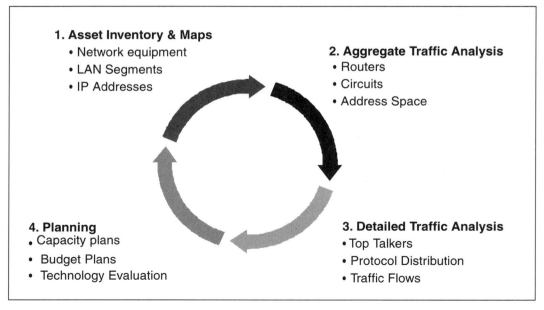

Figure 2.3   Model of Capacity Planning

2.5.2.1 Maps and Asset Inventory

The primary purpose of this step is to identify the current network by documenting a corporation's physical and non-physical network assets. Physical assets include entities such as routers, bridges, switches, and hubs. Non-physical network assets are entities such as a company's registered IP networks and domain names.

2.5.2.2 Aggregate Traffic Analysis

The primary purpose of this step is to quantify the usage on the network assets that were identified in Step 1. This quantification provides a corporation with insight into the utilization of its network. It also helps the corporation to identify network elements that warrant Detailed Traffic Analysis.

When the authors use the phrase "Aggregate Traffic Analysis," we are referring to analysis that can be performed on MAC (i.e., Layer 2 of the OSI Model) layer traffic data. Aggregate traffic analysis would identify situations such as a Frame Relay circuit that was running at 80% utilization for several hours a day, or an Ethernet segment that was experiencing unacceptable rates of collisions.

2.5.2.3 Detailed Traffic Analysis

The purpose of detailed traffic analysis is to determine the root causes of the traffic patterns discovered in Step 2. Hence, the input to this Step is the identification of some number of network elements that warrant detailed traffic analysis. Typically, a network element is deemed to warrant detailed traffic analysis when it either currently exceeds, or is trending to exceed, thresholds of acceptable usage. However, in the particular case of planning for a LAN upgrade, a network professional might well decide to perform detailed traffic analysis on a broader set of network elements.

2.5.2.4 Capacity, Budget, and Technology Planning

Three processes that are enabled by the use of this model are capacity, budget, and technology planning. Capacity planning is the process of determining the likely future requirements of a corporation's network assets. Budget planning takes the output of capacity planning and assigns a cost to the change in capacity requirements. Technology planning is the quantification of when increased capacity requirements justify the deployment of a new technology; e.g., Layer 3 switching.

As shown in Figure 2.4, there are three major inputs to capacity planning. The first of these inputs is the mathematical projection of historical usage trends. This can usually be accomplished with the assistance of a tool to perform network baselining. The second component of input is the result of applications forecasting. By the term "applications forecasting" the authors mean two things. The first is the identification of the new applications that will make a significant impact on the network. The second is the quantification of what that impact will be. The third input is the quantification of the impact of any significant business changes. By the term "significant business changes" the authors mean either changes in the way that a corporation operates its business or the way the IT organization functions inside the corporation. An example of the former would be the acquisition of a new company. An example of the latter would be the decision to centralize servers.

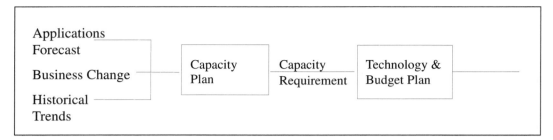

Figure 2.4   Capacity and Budget Planning

3 *Traditional Network Design*

3.1 LAN Technology is Retro

In the early 1980s, bridging technology was introduced both as a way to connect LAN segments and to extend the geographic extent of a LAN. In the late 1980s, routers were introduced, in part, to also interconnect LAN segments and to interface into a variety of WAN technologies. In the last ten years, much has been written about the relative strengths and weaknesses of designing LANs using both bridging and routing technologies. This chapter will briefly summarize some of the key strengths and weaknesses of these technologies. The chapter will also discuss the two key new LAN interconnect technologies of the 1990s, along with a detailed explanation of Layer 2 switching.

The discussion of bridging and routing is not intended merely to provide a history of networking. Rather, this discussion is intended to identify the key aspects of bridging and routing that impact LAN design. This is important because bridging and routing have been re-invented, or merely re-named, for the 1990s. In particular, Layer 2 switching is a direct descendent of bridging; i.e., switches are really sons of bridges. Also, the case can clearly be made that a Layer 3 switch is nothing more than a fast, inexpensive, and in some cases a stripped down router. Hence, many of the same concepts and issues that applied to designing LANs with bridging and routing will now apply to designing LANs with Layer 2 and Layer 3 switching.

3.2 Shared Ethernet Networks

In the early 1980s, many network professionals deployed Ethernet LANs of the type shown in Figure 3.1. The usual purpose of the first Ethernet LANs was to allow a small group of users to share a printer. The physical media for most of these early LANs was coaxial cable that was snaked

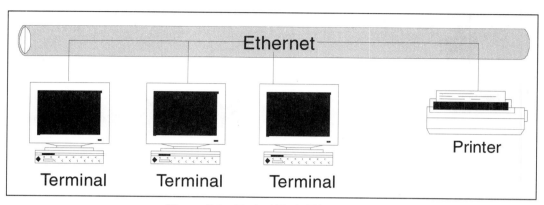

Figure 3.1   Typical Early Ethernet LAN

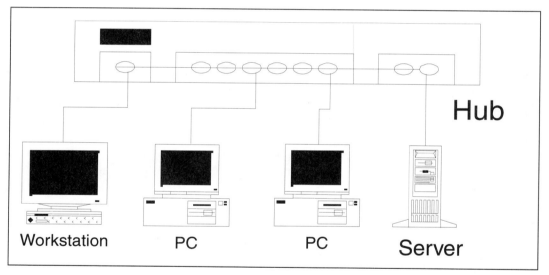

Figure 3.2   Typical Hub-Based Ethernet LAN

through the work area. Since coaxial cable was not common within office buildings, LAN deployment at this time was typically associated with a custom, expensive installation of coaxial cable. LAN design quickly evolved to the point where Unshielded Twisted Pair (UTP) replaced coaxial cable as the common physical media. As shown in Figure 3.2, most contemporary LAN installations run over UTP that is star wired into a hub.

One important characteristic of both of the Ethernet LANs depicted in Figures 3.1 and 3.2 is that each station on the LAN shares the total capacity of the LAN. An individual station's ability to use this shared capacity is controlled by the Carrier Sense Multiple Access with Collision Detection (CSMA/CD) protocol. Also, because of how the CSMA/CD protocol works, the delay on the LAN starts to increase notably as the LAN utilization increases. One of the primary reasons for deploying Layer 2 switching is to reduce or even eliminate the phenomena of having the delay in the network increase as traffic load increases.

Principle: *In spite of the movement to Layer 2 and Layer 3 switching, shared media networks will be a common form of networking into the next century.*

A characteristic typically associated with an IP based network is the concept of a broadcast storm. A broadcast storm is usually caused by either a bug in the implementation of a protocol or by ambiguities in the protocol specification. The storm can last from a few seconds to an indefinite period of time. During a broadcast storm, the network is flooded with packets. In addition to degrading the performance of a shared Ethernet LAN, these storms also consume support resources and degrade applications processing. Support resources are consumed because they are required to identify the problem and resolve it. Applications processing is degraded because each computer that receives a network packet has to spend cycles processing the extraneous traffic instead of processing applications. In extreme cases, computers would not be able to do any applications processing because of the huge number of broadcast packets they had to process.

Also in the 1980s, network professionals deployed bridges to connect disparate LANs simply and inexpensively. A simple two port, bridged LAN is depicted in Figure 3.3. While some bridges provide an array of advanced features, such as packet filtering, the basic purpose of a bridge is quite simple. Referring to Figure 3.3, the bridge listens to all frames on LAN segment A. If there is a frame on LAN segment A with a destination address that resides on LAN segment B, the bridge forwards the frame to segment B. Otherwise the frame stays on segment A. The bridge performs the equivalent function as it monitors LAN segment B.

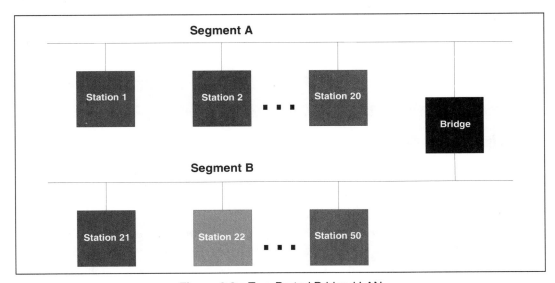

Figure 3.3   Two-Ported Bridged LAN

Bridged networks are often referred to as being flat. The term flat means that all the users share a common broadcast domain. Because of this, bridged networks have something in common with the networks depicted in Figures 3.1 and 3.2. All three networks are vulnerable to broadcast storms.

Principle: Broadcast storms consume scarce resources; i.e., network, computer, and people.

One of the design issues associated with building large, bridged networks is the issue of eliminating loops. If there are loops in a network, it is possible that data will traverse the same path forever, and never reach the intended destination. The standards based technique to avoid loops is to implement the Spanning Tree Algorithm. One purpose of the spanning tree algorithm is to have bridges dynamically discover a subset of the topology that is loop free. This is referred to by mathematicians as a tree. A second purpose of the spanning tree algorithm is to ensure that there is logical connectivity whenever there is physical connectivity. This means that there is a path between every source and destination pair on the LANs. Mathematicians would refer to such a tree structure as being a spanning tree. Note that as a result of the spanning tree algorithm, if there are multiple links between bridges, only one of them can be active at any point in time. Any other link could function as a hot standby.

Principle: There are two significant limitations of bridging relative to the implementation of large networks. The first limitation is that bridges often do not control broadcast storms. The second limitation is that there is not currently a standards based technique to provide multiple active links between bridges.

3.3 Hierarchical Routed Networks

3.3.1 Routing Functionality

Until the development of Layer 3 switching, there was little need to distinguish routing functionality from routers. It was a tautology: providing routing functionality was what routers did. However, now that Layer 3 switches can perform most if not all of the functionality of what we used to call a router, it is important to more precisely identify what are the primary components of routing functionality. In particular, the authors believe that you will need routing functionality in your networks for the foreseeable future. However, the authors also believe that over time an increasing percentage of routing functionality within your network will not be provided by a classical router, but by a Layer 3 switch.

Principle: Routing functionality will be a network requirement for the foreseeable future. That does not necessarily translate to a requirement for traditional routers.

The authors distinguish two classes of routing functionality. As shown in Table 3.1, these classes are core routing functions and Layer 3 special services. The two primary core routing functions are packet forwarding and route processing. Packet forwarding is the minimum functionality a device, either a router or a Layer 3 switch, can perform and still move packets between subnets. Route processing sub-functions include routing table construction and maintenance. This is accomplished using routing protocols such as RIP and OSPF to learn about and create a view of the network's topology. Once route processing has been accomplished, it is the role of packet forwarding to send the packets to their destination address. Packet forwarding sub-functions include decrimenting the Time to Live (TTL) parameter, Media Access Control (MAC) resolution, and calculation of the IP checksum.

Table 3.1   Classification of Routing Functionality

Core Routing Functions	Layer 3 Special Services
Route Processing	Packet Translation
+ Routing Table Construction	Encapsulation
+ Routing Table Maintenance	Traffic Prioritization
Packet Forwarding	Security
+ TTL Modification	Accounting
+ Media Access Control Resolution	Address Management
+ IP Checksum Calculation	WAN Interface

Layer 3 special services refers to a broad range of value-added functionality that traditional router vendors have put into their products. The most common components of this functionality are:

- Packet translation from one LAN technology such as Ethernet, to a disparate LAN technology such as FDDI;
- Encapsulation of one protocol such as IPX within another protocol such as IP;
- Queuing or traffic prioritization to allow one traffic stream such as SAP traffic to have priority over a second traffic stream, e.g., e-mail;
- Security services such as authentication of users and packet filtering;
- Capturing of traffic accounting data;
- IP address management such as DHCP; and
- Translation between LAN protocols such as Ethernet and WAN protocols such as Frame Relay.

However, for all the advantages that traditional routers bring to internetworking, they do extract a price. For example, many of the author's clients complain bitterly about the degraded performance they experience with their routers if they actually turn on one or more of the Layer 3 special services. Table 3.2 contains the author's characterization of a classical router.

Table 3.2   Characteristics of a Traditional Router

Software intensive
Complex to configure and manage
Expensive
Relatively low throughput
Relatively high throughput variation

3.3.2   The Motivation for Router Centric Networks

As previously mentioned, in the late 1980s routers were introduced into corporate LANs. Routing is a requirement to facilitate inter-subnet communications. However there were additional reasons why routers were introduced. One of the key reasons was that routers have the capability to contain and control the broadcast storms that were described in the previous section. Another key reason was to facilitate the deployment of separate administrative domains.

The goal of having separate administrative domains was to eliminate the need to tightly coordinate the activities of multiple LAN administrators. This desire to eliminate the need to coordinate the activities of the LAN administrators had two primary drivers. The first driver was that as networks grow in size, the number of LAN administrators often increased. As such, any requirement for tight coordination between the LAN administrators was an administrative burden that had the potential to limit the growth of the network. The second driver was that for reasons of local control, many organizations did not want to have their activities closely coordinated with those of other organizations within their corporation.

Principle: The business need to compartmentalize a corporate network into separate domains does not go away merely because technology exists to support a single flat network.

Figure 3.4 depicts the type of router centric, multiple administrative LAN that many of the author's clients have implemented. For example, the authors have worked with multiple universities where the central IT group operates a LAN backbone. In Figure 3.4, that LAN backbone is based on FDDI technology. In each case, the individual departments and/or colleges within the universities operated their own network. It is the author's experience that the ability of the central organization to influence the individual colleges and departments is highly varied.

3.4 Layer 2 Switching

3.4.1   Introduction

This section will provide detail on Layer 2 switching, outline the functionality typically found in Layer 2 switches, describe the available network management capabilities, and recom-

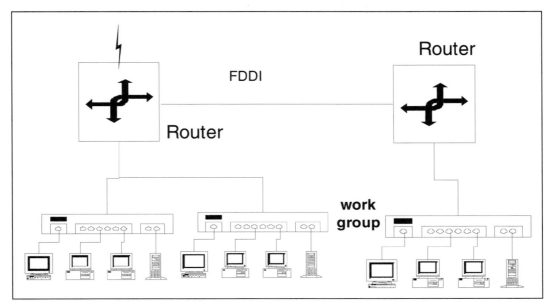

Figure 3.4   Hierarchical Routed Network

mend switch functionality based on the network topology. The section will also summarize testing of Layer 2 Fast Ethernet switches recently completed by Strategic Networks. These test results are contained in Appendix I. Additional results can be found at www.snci.com.

As LAN traffic and performance requirements grew, Layer 2 (L2) switches were introduced in the mid 1990s. Compared to alternative methods of upgrading performance, Layer 2 switching:

- Builds on and preserves the utility of most of the earlier investment in shared media networking;
- Allows an appropriate increase in bandwidth to be added to the network wherever it is needed; and
- Costs less to deploy, operate, and administer than competing approaches.

As the name implies, Layer 2 switches process the MAC header of data packets. This is in contrast to routers that process at the network layer. Layer 2 switches deliver more than an order of magnitude increase in network performance when compared to shared LANs. They are able to deliver this increased performance because L2 switches are bridges with one exception—they provide multiple simultaneous wire speed connections between ports. Layer 2 switches further speed up traffic flow by terminating Ethernet's CSMA/CD protocol on each port, thereby reducing potential collisions.

The authors believe that Layer 2 switch deployment at 10 Mbps, 100 Mbps, and potentially 1000 Mbps will continue at a fast pace over the next several years. One of the factors driving this deployment is that, as shown in Table 3.3, Layer 2 switches are both network and network-professional friendly.

Table 3.3   Characteristics of a Layer 2 Switch

Hardware intensive
Simple to configure and manage
Relatively inexpensive
Relatively high throughput
Relatively low throughput variation

Another factor driving Layer 2 switch deployment is the rapidly diminishing cost of the technology. At the low end of the market, Switched Ethernet (10 Mbps) ports cost less than $100 today and the authors predict they will drop below $50/port by year-end 1998. Today's low end Fast Ethernet (100 Mbps) switch ports currently cost less than $200 and will cost about $100 in the same timeframe. The third factor driving the deployment of Layer 2 switching is the changing Network Interface Card (NIC) market. Due to competition between vendors such as 3Com and Intel, it is possible to buy 10/100 Mbps NICs today for around $55. This is one of the factors that has caused the great growth in the deployment of 10/100 Mbps NICs. As can be seen in Figure 3.5, the sale of 10/100 NICs has surpassed the sale of 10 Mbps NICs. Hence, the majority of new Ethernet desktops and servers are Fast Ethernet ready!

Principle: *Companies will continue their deployment of Layer 2 switching to provide a low cost, easy to implement performance boost.*

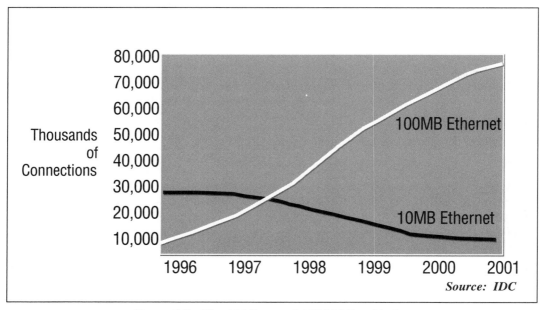

Figure 3.5   The 10 Mbps and 10/100 Mbps Market

3.4.2   Switch Functionality

Layer 2 switches come with a broad array of functionality and hence price. A switch that is appropriate to support a small workgroup is generally not an appropriate switch to support a collapsed backbone. For example, a switch for a small workgroup may only support a single technology (i.e., Ethernet), have only a small number of ports, and fault tolerance is not cost justified. A switch for a collapsed backbone will typically support multiple LAN technologies (i.e., Ethernet, Fast Ethernet, FDDI, and ATM), have a large number of ports, and be highly fault tolerant.

This section will outline Layer 2 switch functionality and section 3.4.4 will make recommendations as to when this functionality is a requirement.

Principle: *Layer 2 switches are rapidly becoming a commodity. However, there still are differences in switches, notably early versions of high-end switches, that potential buyers need to be aware of.*

Switch Fabric

Most switch architectures can be classified as either cross-point matrix, shared memory, or shared media. Cross-point matrix switches employ an array of switching elements to provide parallel-switched paths between distinct pairs of input and output ports. This design approach has yielded fairly attractive price per port in Ethernet switches with relatively few ports. Shared memory architectures are also very common for low cost, small scale switches and have the advantage of easily accommodating mixed LAN types and speeds within a single switch. Shared media switches use a high-speed backplane to interconnect switching elements, which may consist of an individual bridge per port or a multiport switch module. The latter may use shared media or shared memory as an internal architecture. Shared media architectures are frequently used to build modular switches that can scale to high port densities.

Bandwidth of Switch Fabric

For switches in all three architectural classifications, bandwidth of the switch fabric provides an overall measure of the theoretical capacity of the switch to support multiple simultaneous streams of data traffic. This specification is closely related to the ability of the switch to achieve high aggregate throughput.

Internal Data Format

Internally, the switch can use either the native Ethernet frame format or it can convert the frames into fixed length cells, typically ATM cells. Fixed length cells can simplify the design of buffering and facilitate the addition of higher speed ports, including ATM. However, the frame-to-cell and cell-to-frame conversion for Ethernet-to-Ethernet switching can incur some cost overhead versus simpler frame switches.

Forwarding Mode

Switches can forward packets in either store-and-forward, cut-through, or fragment-free modes. Store-and-forward allows for full error checking, packet filtering, and LAN speed conversions at the cost of higher transit delay, especially for large packets. Cut-through minimizes transit delay by foregoing the possibility of error checking, packet filtering, and speed conversion. Fragment-free mode is cut-through switching in which runt packets (collision by-products of less than the minimum legal packet size) are discarded.

Buffering per Port

Buffer space can be allocated in a number of ways. Three of the possibilities are: 1) to dedicate a fixed amount to each input port; 2) to dedicate a fixed amount to each output port; or 3) to allocate space as needed from a common pool shared by input or output ports within a switch module. While these approaches have differing degrees of complexity, the authors believe that the best measure of their effectiveness is found in the results of third party tests of congestion control.

Congestion Control Mechanism

Congestion control involves the ability of the switch to deal with oversubscribed output ports, i.e., a number of input ports contending simultaneously for a single output port. Passive congestion avoidance is based on buffers holding packets in queues until the output port becomes free. Active congestion control techniques apply back pressure to the traffic sources by using the Ethernet jam signals to spoof the occurrence of collisions or raising the carrier sense signal to delay transmission.

Switch Configuration

Ethernet switches are available in expandable, stackable, modular, or fixed configuration formats. Most of the expandable and stackable switches currently available in the marketplace have the ability to accommodate a very limited number of expansion modules for additional Ethernet or individual high-speed ports. Some of the smaller switches can also be used as modules in enterprise hubs. Such a switch may function as a collapsed backbone switch connecting shared media segments within the hub or as a means of converting the hub into a modular Ethernet switch. Analogously, a modular switching hub may accommodate shared media modules and/or high-speed modules to assume the role of a high performance enterprise hub.

The authors suggest that expandable, stackable, and fixed configuration switches are generally most appropriate for small workgroup and small collapsed backbone configurations. Modular and hub module switches are most appropriate for larger workgroup and backbone applications.

Maximum Number of Ethernet Ports

The maximum number of Ethernet and Fast Ethernet ports that can be configured is an important consideration for switches that will be used in larger workgroup applications. Analogously, the maximum number of Fast Ethernet and Gigabit ports that can be configured is an important consideration for switches that will be used in concentration points such as a collapsed backbone. As a general rule, the authors strongly advise against trying to build a concentration point from multiple small switches.

Full Duplex Ethernet

Full duplex Ethernet is an interesting option for increasing the bandwidth per port of Ethernet switches. Full duplex Ethernet eliminates collisions in dedicated Ethernet connections and can essentially double the bandwidth for links that support symmetrical traffic flow. The authors believe that full duplex Ethernet offers some reasonable benefits for switch-to-switch connections. However, since client/server interactions do not often involve symmetrical traffic flows, full duplex does not have as much impact on the effective bandwidth in end system-to-switch connections.

High-Speed Ports Available Today and in the Future

FDDI, Fast Ethernet, Gigabit Ethernet, and ATM all constitute faster, more flexible options as "fat pipes" for connecting switches to servers and/or to high-speed backbones. All these LAN technologies feature at least ten times the bandwidth of Ethernet and are also capable of full duplex operation. The availability of high-speed ports is becoming increasingly important for both workgroup and backbone applications.

Number of MAC Addresses per Ethernet Port

The amount of memory devoted to address tables can limit the number of MAC addresses that can be stored per port. If the switch is limited to a small number of MACs per port, it cannot be used in any sort of collapsed backbone configuration involving the interconnection of segments that are shared by a number of stations.

Fault Tolerance

Fault tolerance presents perhaps the clearest tradeoff of functionality versus money. That follows because fault tolerance is usually provided in the form of redundant power supplies and/or hot swappable modules in the case of modular devices. These extra power supplies and/or modules cost money. Switches that have been designed as modules for chassis-based enterprise hubs can themselves be hot swappable units within the hub chassis and can draw their power from the hub's redundant power supply. In other words, the switch module essentially inherits the fault tolerant features of the host hub. Fault tolerance becomes an important issue where a large number of users would lose use of the network in the event of a switch failure. Therefore, most of the switches with high port count or those intended for use in network concentration points can be expected to have native or inherited fault tolerant features.

Packet Filtering

Most store-and-forward switches have the capability to do some form of packet filtering beyond the simple discarding of damaged (runt) or misaligned packets. Packet filtering based on source or destination address or protocol type can be used as a security measure or to exclude unwanted traffic from being forwarded over the backbone or other secure LAN segments. Some measure of protection from broadcast storms can be achieved with a switch that is capable of filtering out broadcast and multicast packets that exceed some threshold level that the network manager can control. Packet filtering is obviously more important for backbone applications, but many workgroup switches include this capability as a means of preventing unwanted traffic from crossing the boundary, in either direction, between the workgroup and the backbone.

Protocol Support

Most Ethernet switches include support for the IEEE 802.1d Spanning Tree protocol. This allows interoperability of switches with conventional bridge routers and other switches to prevent the formation of active loops within the network. Support for the spanning tree algorithm also allows the network manager to install switches in parallel in order to build redundant network connections to key resources. However, as described previously, the spanning tree algorithm does not allow for multiple active paths between switches.

3.4.3   Network Management

This section will detail some of the relevant network management functionality for Layer 2 switches and will also briefly discuss the role of network management applications.

Below is a description of the primary components of network management for Layer 2 switches.

Port Mirroring

Port mirroring allows traffic on any port of the switch to be replicated on a designated port, so that a single protocol analyzer or RMON probe can be switched to any port on the switch or network of interconnected switches under network management software control.

In-Band CLI and Out-of-Band Management

An in-band Command Line Interface (CLI) via TELNET is complementary to SNMP management and facilitates software reconfiguration, software installation, and remote management of the switch. An out-of-band CLI or SNMP/serial line IP (SLIP) interface allows the switch to be managed even during periods when the network is down.

Support for MIB II and the Bridge MIB

Support for MIB II and the Bridge MIB, as well as additional MIB coverage, facilitates the gathering of aggregate traffic statistics.

RMON Agent Support

Internal support for the RMON agent defined in RFC 1271 allows the traffic through the switch to be monitored based on nine classes of network data. With an RMON agent integral to the switch, traffic can be monitored more efficiently than with an external RMON probe and port mirroring.

Virtual LAN (VLAN) Support

VLAN functionality allows the network manager to define logical groups of users without regard to the location of their physical connections to the network. This functionality offers the potential benefits of easing the administrative burden of moves, adds, and changes, as well as confining broadcast traffic within the boundaries of the VLAN. Ethernet switches can offer VLAN support to a single switch or across multiple switches.

Many vendors offer a network management application that is optimized for the management of their switch. In many cases, the cost of the management application is not bundled with the price of the switch. If a network management application is not offered, a third-party application would be needed or the switch could be managed via browsing the standard MIBs from any SNMP management station.

Where a switch management application is offered, the authors believe that an important consideration is whether the application is compatible with the enterprise management systems and operating system platforms already deployed for management of the site network. In the ideal situation, management of switched internetworking would be well integrated with management of shared media network infrastructure. This is ideal because in the author's experience an application that is compatible with the existing platforms is much more likely to be used than yet another stand alone product.

3.4.4. Switched Layer 2 Applications

This section describes some common scenarios in which network professionals can use Layer 2 switches to relieve bandwidth constraints. For each scenario, a checklist of desirable features and characteristics is provided to help guide network professionals through the switch selection process.

3.4.4.1 Small Workgroup LAN—Local Servers

The simplest scenario in which bandwidth limitations are encountered is in small workgroups where congestion is caused by local peer-to-peer traffic sharing the same segment as local client/ server traffic. In many cases, the server also functions as a router connecting the workgroup to the department or site backbone as shown in Figure 3.6.

One potential solution is to microsegment the LAN by multi-homing the server with additional LAN connections and dividing the client connections among these segments. Although straightforward, this approach has the disadvantages of burdening the server with additional route computation and of introducing router latency among segments or to the backbone that could hamper throughput, particularly for non-windowed protocols such as non-Burst-Mode NetWare.

A better approach is to replace the shared media hub with a LAN switch that expands the bandwidth of the LAN by several times, while segregating peer-to-peer from client/server traffic. In

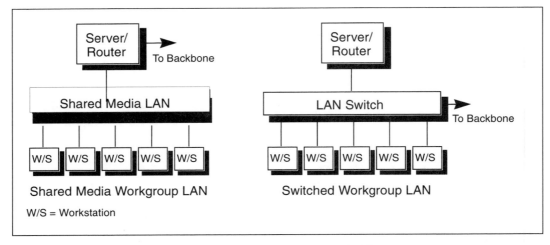

Figure 3.6   Small Workgroup LAN

this scenario, an Ethernet to Fast Ethernet (10/100) or Fast Ethernet to Fast Ethernet (100/100) switch is appropriate as long as demand on the server and/or server throughput are low enough to preclude any significant benefit from higher speed server connections. However, when the server is upgraded, it may also be advisable to upgrade to a switch with higher speed ports for server connections, e.g., Gigabit Ethernet or ATM at OC-12.

The switch in Figure 3.6 can also provide the backbone connection for the workgroup, offloading this task from the server. For workgroup scenarios similar to this one, the following switch characteristics are usually sufficient:

- small number of media access control (MAC) addresses per port;
- primarily a single LAN speed, possibly with one or more high speed, full duplex ports for connectivity to the router or server;
- high throughput, low latency for non-windowed protocols;
- minimal modularity or fault tolerance;
- simple network management; and
- low cost per port.

3.4.4.2   Larger Workgroup—Local Servers

Another common scenario involves a sizable number of client systems that need simultaneous access to one or more high performance departmental or workgroup servers, as shown in Figure 3.7. Again in this scenario, bandwidth is scaled up by replacing shared media hubbing with switching hubs or switching modules. This scenario differs from the previous one in that the number of client systems in the group is significantly larger. This means that fixed configuration and

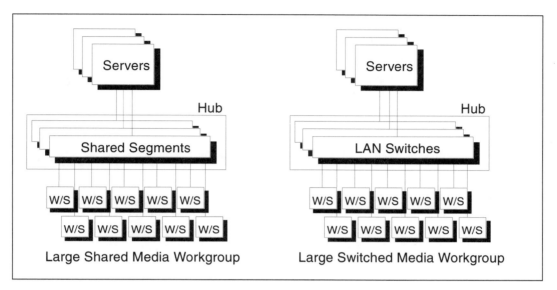

Figure 3.7   Large Workgroup LAN

stackable 10/100 and 100/100 switches are less appropriate. Enterprise hubs with switching modules or chassis-based switching hubs, on the other hand, generally have more than adequate backplane bandwidth for interconnection of a larger number of switched ports. If there is a large number of dedicated Fast Ethernet desktop ports and a relatively small number of local servers, the likelihood of congestion on the server ports is much higher than in the small workgroup scenario.

For large workgroup networks, the following switch characteristics are typically sufficient:

- intermediate number of MAC addresses per port;
- auto-sensing 10/100 ports;
- expandability to one or more higher speed ports for server "fat pipes" and backbone access, e.g., Gigabit Ethernet, ATM;
- high aggregate throughput;
- low latency, especially for non-windowed protocols;
- active congestion control or good congestion tolerance;
- modularity and fault tolerance;
- low cost per port; and
- more sophisticated network management.

3.4.4.3 Small Site/Departmental Collapsed Backbone

In most organizations, the performance crisis that is the most critical is in the site or campus backbone itself. This is because more and more of the traffic from feeder LANs aggregates in the backbone as distributed computing becomes less localized. Collapsed backbone routers and distributed high-speed, shared-media LANs have been used successfully in the past to effectively expand the bandwidth of the site backbone. In many instances, however, the bandwidth demands of the microsegmented feeder networks have exceeded the limits posed by shared backplane capacity or the speed of shared LAN media.

It is possible to upgrade the collapsed backbone using either Layer 2 or Layer 3 switches. A Layer 2 switch has the advantage of generally costing less than a Layer 3 switch. However, a Layer 3 switch has additional functionality that is particularly important in the collapsed backbone. For example, a Layer 3 switch often has more ability to manage broadcast storms than a Layer 2 switch. A Layer 3 switch also provides added reliability and faster network reconfiguration because of running robust routing protocols such as OSPF.

As shown in Figure 3.8, LAN switches can provide bandwidth relief for both of these prevailing backbone paradigms. In the case of the collapsed backbone, the LAN switch can be deployed as a direct one-for-one displacement of a conventional bridge/router. In a similar fashion, a small shared Fast Ethernet backbone, for example, can be collapsed into a LAN switch. In either case, there can be minimal disruption of server connections or feeder networks based on shared media hubs or LAN switches.

Site backbone applications generally require a more robust and flexible category of LAN switch with the following features:

- large number of MAC addresses per port;
- advanced bridging to filter unwanted broadcasts and other traffic from the backbone;
- routing as an option where additional firewalling is required;
- expandability to one or more high-speed ports for connection to central servers and the campus backbone;
- runt filtering for data integrity;
- active congestion control or good congestion tolerance to deal with contention for servers or backbone access;
- high aggregate throughput;
- fixed configuration or expandable/stackable packaging and moderate cost per port; and
- management application offering platform-level integration with other network management tools.

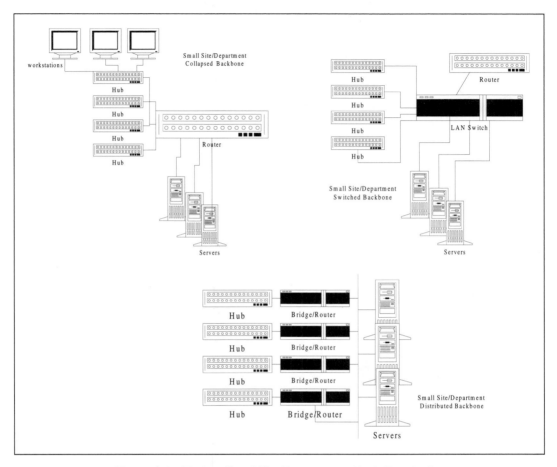

Figure 3.8   Typical Small Site/Departmental LAN Topologies

3.4.4.4   Large Site/Departmental Collapsed Backbones

As site or departmental collapsed backbone networks scale up to accommodate larger numbers of shared and dedicated segments, the topology shown in Figure 3.8 does not change. However, as the network scales to serve more desktop and server connections, high-speed server and backbone ports, Layer 3 routing, and modular packaging, network management features and fault tolerance become increasingly important. In some cases, the need for higher speed will prevent Fast Ethernet-to-Fast Ethernet switches from playing the role of campus or larger site collapsed backbone.

Collapsed backbone switches for larger sites need:

- additional robustness and manageability;

- large number of MAC addresses per port;

- advanced bridging to isolate broadcasts and unwanted traffic from the backbone;

- routing as an option where additional firewalling is required;

- expandability to one or more high-speed ports for connection to central servers and the campus backbone;

- runt filtering for data integrity;

- active congestion control or passive congestion avoidance to deal with contention for servers or backbone access;

- high aggregate throughput;

- network management enhancements, and integration with management of shared media hubbing;

- modular packaging for flexibility and expandability; and

- redundant power and hot modules that can be swapped for fault tolerance.

3.4.5 Summary of Test Results

One of the major limitations of most of the early Ethernet Layer 2 switch products was the lack of high-speed ports as a means of connecting local high performance servers, a high-speed backbone or as switch-to-switch connection. This made it difficult for workgroup configurations to scale beyond a relatively small number of users. Therefore, a common theme in second-generation Layer 2 Ethernet switches was the addition of one or two Fast Ethernet ports—resulting in the 10/100 Ethernet switch. We are currently well into the third-generation of Layer 2 Ethernet switches - the Fast Ethernet-to-Fast Ethernet (100/100) switch for interconnecting multiple 10/100 switches in departmental and site backbones. This generation of switches is being followed by the first members of a generation of 100/1000 and 1000/1000 switches made possible through the development of standards based, Gigabit Ethernet.

Strategic Networks evaluated a number of Fast Ethernet-to-Fast Ethernet switches. The test results are contained in Appendix X. Below is a summary of the findings.

- Fast Ethernet switches are available in a range of port densities from 12 ports per switch or less to over 50 ports per switch. In some of these configurations the switch may be blocking in the sense that the aggregate bandwidth of the ports exceeds the bandwidth of the switch fabric.

- Modular and expandable Fast Ethernet switches make provisions for high-speed ports for down links and server connections. Often, choices of Gigabit Ethernet and ATM OC-12c are either available or planned.

- Throughput, at or near wire speed, was measured for up to ten parallel streams of traffic (1,488,090 pps). For a number of switches, throughput fell slightly short of theoretical rates for small packet traffic. In general, increasing packet size to 128 or 256 bytes resulted in throughput at 100% of theoretical rates. The authors believe that as switch fabric and forwarding engine performance improves, Fast Ethernet-to-Fast Ethernet switch throughput at theoretical rates for 64-byte packets will become as commonplace as it is with Ethernet-to Ethernet switching.

- Store-and-forward latencies were as low as 7 microseconds independent of packet size. For the most part, latency variation was less than 3.5 microseconds.

- Approaches to dealing with congestion constitute an area of significant differentiation among Fast Ethernet switches. Flow control mechanisms can completely eliminate packet loss due to buffer overflow. For switches that rely on buffering to prevent packet loss, buffer sizes can vary widely. Where Fast Ethernet switches are deployed in a departmental or site backbone, aggregated traffic can be expected to result in frequent congestion of switch ports.

- Rich features and functionality improvements include advanced bridging, active congestion control, and fault tolerance.

- Network management can be performed via graphical applications that are compatible with popular enterprise management systems and platforms. Network management enhancements, including Virtual LANs (VLANs) and internal Remote Monitoring (RMON) agents, are available to help make switched networks easier to operate, configure, and manage.

- Switch packaging options include models with fixed configurations, as well as expandable, stackable, and modular chassis enclosures. In addition, switches are available as modules for popular enterprise hubs. A wide choice of vendors is available, including switch specialists, all the major hub and router vendors, and specialists in low-end networking products.

4 Two Basic Types of Layer 3 Technology

4.1 Introduction

In Chapter 1 we provided a set of definitions to serve as a foundation for our discussions of Layer 3 switching. In particular, we characterized Layer 3 switches as internetworking devices that:

- Forward traffic based on the Layer 3 address;
- Perform switching;
- May perform special services (such as packet filtering or authentication); and
- May or may not perform route processing.

In Chapter 3 we saw how networks have evolved, from the use of Layer 2 switches and classical routers to the introduction of Layer 3 switches. We have suggested that L3 switches might be used to advantage primarily at aggregation points in a network, such as in server farms, for collapsed backbones, and for campus backbones. In this chapter we delve into Layer 3 switching technology, including the architecture and design of L3 switches, to help us understand in more detail what benefits might be expected of particular products. After discussing some products in detail in Chapters 5 and 6, you will see how particular vendors suggest using their products to solve the problems of a specific case study presented in Chapter 7.

The first distinction to be made in understanding Layer 3 technology is based on whether every packet undergoes Layer 3 processing (i.e., at least route processing) and traffic forwarding based on the L3 address. If the answer is yes, we call the approach Packet-by-Packet (PxP). Those approaches that do not process all packets at Layer 3 we characterize as Flow-Switching (FS).

Figure 4.1 shows the Packet-by-Packet flow of activity. Packets enter the system at Layer 1 of the OSI reference model, i.e., at the physical interface. The packets are then examined at Layer 2 (e.g., for the MAC address of the intended destination) and pushed on to Layer 3 if they cannot be switched. At Layer 3, packets undergo processing for path determination (i.e., route calculation),

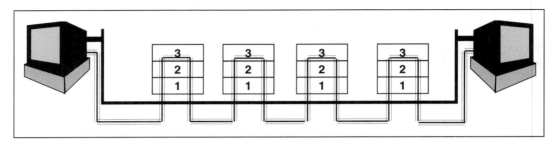

Figure 4.1   Routed Packets Are Processed at Layer 3 Everywhere

address resolution (i.e., table look-up or other mechanism to determine the L2 address correspond-ing to the L3 destination), and any special services (e.g., authentication, capture of accounting data, translation to another L2 format). By the time L3 processing is complete, the packet has been updated (header rewritten, counters adjusted, etc.) and is ready to be passed back to Layer 2, where the appropriate output port is determined, and the packet is physically transmitted on the medium through Layer 1.

Principle: Layer 3 Packet-by-Packet techniques perform route processing on every packet and forward all packets based on the Layer 3 address.

In flow switching, the first packet is analyzed to determine whether it identifies a "flow" or a set of packets from the same source to the same destination, such as the packets belonging to a par-ticular TCP session, for example. If that first packet has the right characteristics, then subsequent packets in the identified flow will receive all the same privileges, such as access rights, and the flow switch saves processing time that would be spent examining each packet. In addition, subsequent packets in the same flow are *switched* to their destination on the basis of Layer 2 (Figure 4.2) or even Layer 3 address, depending on the particular FS implementation. The first trick is to identify which characteristics of the first packet identify a flow that will qualify the rest to take the short cut, L2 path. The second trick is to have flows long enough to benefit from the short cut once the path across the network is set up. Flow-switching approaches have also been called "cut-through routing" tech-niques because the subsequent packets shortcut the need for routing and get switched instead.

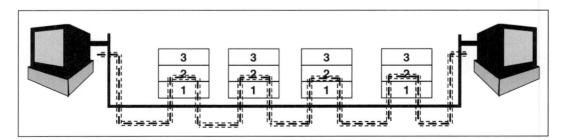

Figure 4.2   Subsequent Packets in a Flow Are Switched at Layer 2

The concept of a stream or flow of packets between a particular source and destination is thus at the heart of all flow-switching schemes. How flows are detected, how packets are recognized as belonging to a particular flow, and how flow paths are set up through the network may be different among the various schemes. Meanwhile, the ability to track and properly manage large numbers of flows remains to be seen.

Principle: *Layer 3 flow-switching techniques analyze the first packet in a flow in order to both perform route processing as well as forward the packet based on its Layer 3 address. Subsequent packets in the flow are processed via one or more short cut techniques whose design goal is to facilitate wire speed routing.*

The second distinguishing characteristic of packet-by-packet approaches is adaptability to changes in routing topology. Because they run standard routing protocols and maintain routing tables, PxP devices can dynamically reroute packets around network failures and congestion without waiting for higher layer protocols to detect packet loss and without adding new protocols to exchange information about topology. Flow-switching approaches do not have these options, because packets after the first take a short cut through Layer 3 processing and consequently do not "see" routing table changes made by standard protocols. Consequently, FS approaches may need additional protocols to get information about topology changes or congestion to the right places in the switching systems.

A third difference in Layer 3 approaches is that packet-by-packet approaches are inherently applicable only to the world of frame-based switches—they are designed around, and handle, packets. Flow-switching techniques, on the other hand, have been developed for both packet (i.e., frame-based) networks and for cell-based networks, such as ATM. Individual products to date, however, have implemented flows only over one or the other, not both.

4.2 Packet-by-Packet Approaches

Classical Routers

Classical routers are the oldest class of devices that fit our definition of a Layer 3 packet-by-packet switch. They certainly perform switching, routing, and special services. Products developed prior to 1995 used software engines to provide the scope and flexibility desirable for handling multiple underlying technologies (i.e., different L2 frame formats) and L3 protocols (e.g., IP, IPX, DECnet, AppleTalk), and for allowing functional enhancement through software upgrades (typically for additional special services). Cisco's IOS is a well-known example of router software undergoing a continual process of enhancement to provide additional capabilities. Classical routers were usually built as complete stand-alone devices, such as the Cisco 7500 family or the BCN from Bay Networks.

Classical routers run routing protocols such as RIP (Routing Information Protocol) or OSPF (Open Shortest Path First) in order to exchange information about topology, congestion, etc. Because they were implemented with so much software, classical routers have earned a reputation for being complex (to set up, configure, and maintain), expensive (especially for additional functions or upgrades), and slow. The assessment of slow came from two areas. First, the more "features" that are enabled, the more software processing is required, and the longer it takes for a packet to get through the router (Figure 4.3). Second is the comparison with more recently developed L2 switches, especially when the router becomes an aggregation point for packet streams from multiple switches. These are what led us to characterize new L3 switches as attempts to bring the cost of routing down, and the performance of routing up, to match what we have come to expect for L2 switches.

When the majority of network traffic was confined to a workgroup or LAN segment rather than traversing subnets, classical routers were easily able to keep up with the flow of traffic they needed to handle. As today's total volume of traffic continues to increase and the patterns have shifted so that more traffic crosses subnet boundaries, much more traffic must traverse that router. As more special features are invoked, more processing time is required, and the processing path through the classical software router becomes slower and slower. Equipment vendors have thus begun to apply alternative product design strategies, often learned in the Layer 2 switching arena, to routers. Some of the approaches being used are:

- reducing the number of protocols handled, often to IP only;

- performing only switching and routing functions, limiting the special services; and

- building more functions with application-specific integrated circuits (ASICs) rather than running them in software on RISC processors.

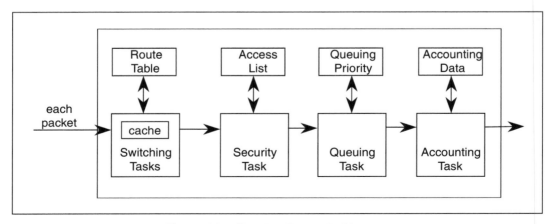

Figure 4.3   Classical Router Architecture

It is just these approaches that have led to some of the Layer 3 switching products known as routing switches and modern Internet routers. New routing products have various implementations, with vendors making different choices about:

- what is put in software (typically running on a RISC chip);
- what is put in hardware (ASICs or even Digital Signal Processing (DSP) chips); and
- whether information is kept centrally for the whole device, distributed fully, or cached.

For example, if only IP will be routed, then the position in the frame and the format of the destination L3 address are well known. Address bits may thus be extracted by hardware, which then performs fast route calculation or address table look-up to resolve the L3 to an L2 address. Routing table construction and maintenance, on the other hand, might continue to be performed in software on a RISC chip. Representative vendor approaches to these new products are presented in detail in Chapter 5.

Classical routers and their follow-on designs have also been packaged in a "router on a card" format. Some vendors have inserted such cards into a chassis slot to add routing to existing Layer 2 switches. This approach gave rise to the moniker "switch blade." Early versions had the same performance characteristics as the classical routers from which they were derived (typically 100-200Kpps or less), and the same configuration complexities. However, they were often less costly than adding a stand-alone router to an existing network. Newer blades are taking advantage of the same ASIC approaches as stand-alone routers, and continue to offer performance improvements, making them of much more interest as L3 switches.

Learning Bridges

Layer 3 switches have been developed not only from the router side down, so to speak, but also from the Layer 2 switch side up. Learning bridges, for example, take one step from L2 switches toward routers by incorporating the capability of forwarding traffic based on the L3 address, but not going on to perform route processing. That is, they do not run routing protocols such as RIP or OSPF, but rather take advantage of routing information that is already available in the network. These L3 devices are analogous to L2 devices with advanced bridging features. Learning bridges listen for Address Resolution Protocol (ARP) traffic broadcast by routers in the network and build their own tables to hold the mapping between L3 and L2 addresses. This is strictly passive "snooping," as they do not issue or respond to ARP requests themselves. When the learning bridge looks up a destination L3 address and finds it in its table, the associated packet is forwarded directly to the destination instead of being passed to a router. Forwarding for particular L3 protocols (e.g., usually IP and sometimes IPX) is supported in hardware; others are typically bridged and must continue to be handled by a router. This type of L3 switch is limited by the L3 protocols that are handled, the modest size of the address table, and the inability to update that table dynamically as topology changes occur. Advantages of learning bridges include ease of installation (routing table is learned, not configured), interoperability with existing routers, and higher performance at lower cost than classical routers.

We will not discuss learning bridges any further because this approach is rapidly becoming subsumed into routing switches as an optional mode of operation. Even the first product announced in this category, Bay's Switch Node, had both "IP AutoLearn" and full routing modes of operation.

Routing Switches

Another way to develop L3 products may also have started from the switching perspective, but its emphasis has been to integrate routing and switching right from design inception. Design techniques include:

- reducing the number of protocols handled at L3 (often to IP only), and often at L2 as well (e.g., Ethernet only);
- limiting the L3 special services supported; and
- building as much as possible into hardware, e.g., with application-specific integrated circuits (ASICs), rather than in software.

We call this category of products that perform switching, route processing, and L3 traffic forwarding, routing switches. All are intended to bring the cost of routing down and the performance of routing up to match what we've come to expect of L2 switches.

The variety of designs for routing switches is probably as great as the number of companies building them. Some support only Ethernet and IP as dominant technologies in the LAN, resulting in significant design economies. Of course, few LANs of any size today are actually limited to these. In most LANs, routers and routing switches will have to coexist until extraneous protocols are eliminated. One of our clients, for example, created a policy direction to minimize the number of protocols supported in their network. A full year later, well after all Macintosh desktops had been replaced with PCs, they found AppleTalk still running. It took a little sleuthing to discover the highly reliable, quite functional Apple LaserWriter printers that had been retained for use and were still chatting away. In another situation, Novell servers were gradually being replaced with Windows NT servers—yet the amount of IPX traffic observed did not diminish. It turned out that one Novell server was still providing master software copies for downloading to initialize newly installed desktop equipment. The targets for the downloads, that is, the new PCs, had been moved from a single, central, setup bench to multiple locations distributed across the enterprise. Consequently, Novell traffic that had originally been local began traveling across the enterprise backbone.

Routing switches typically support only a limited number of routing protocols, i.e., the ones needed to support their chosen technologies. A switch that routes only IP, for example, need only support RIP and OSPF to interoperate successfully with other routers in the same network. This again leads to design economy and enhances the potential for building more functions with hardware instead of software. Remember, the goal for these products is to bring the cost of routing down and the performance up.

Modern Internet Routers

Your authors are forced to admit a certain struggle over whether this last class, called modern internet routers, should really be classified separately from the routing switches. We've finally agreed that it should be, and also that it bears distinguishing from classical routers simply reincarnated. The key characteristics of this type of Layer 3 switch are:

- it is typically not multi-protocol, but focuses on IP only (hence the "internet" descriptor);
- it is definitely not software-based, but builds as much function into hardware as sensible;
- no packets fall back to slow-path processing, either for table look-up failure or cache misses; and
- routing tables are large enough to handle the number of destinations likely to be needed for operation within, or at the edge of, the Internet (i.e., multiple tens of thousands rather than the few thousand more typical of implementations using cached information local to each interface card or port).

Modern internet routers are discussed further in the next chapter.

4.3 Flow-Switching Approaches

Because they have been developed for both frame-based and cell-based networks, there may seem to be more diversity in flow-switching approaches than for packet-by-packet. However, we feel they can be classified into only two primary types: end-system-driven and network-centric.

End-system-driven schemes typically require no changes to the switching infrastructure of a network, while network-centric approaches must usually be installed or supported by switches throughout a network in order to achieve major performance improvements. Remember that flow switching has often been called cut-through because once a flow has been identified, subsequent packets take a shortcut through, or avoid, routing to be switched at Layer 2. Your authors have found that people get confused between cut-through Layer 2 switches (which begin to process and output bits before the entire packet has been received) and cut-through routing at Layer 3 (which route the first and switch the rest of whole packets in a stream).

The first agreement on any standard for flow switching came from the ATM (Asynchronous Transfer Mode) Forum when they ratified MPOA (Multi-Protocol over ATM) in July 1997. Other techniques have been published and some have been submitted to the IETF (Internet Engineering Task Force) for consideration as standards. Examples include Ipsilon's IP Switching protocols, Cabletron's SecureFast Virtual Networking, IBM's ARIS, Cisco's tag switching, etc.

Principle: MPOA is the first standard for flow switching.

End-System-Driven Flow Switching

In this category, end-systems examine packets for characteristics that would identify flows that could benefit from switching subsequent packets at Layer 2. This means that the flow would generally have to be long enough so that time saved switching at Layer 2 would exceed the time spent to set up the flow path across the network. The first packet is always sent to a routing device somewhere in the network. Then the source and destination systems coordinate discovery of whether a shortcut, Layer 2 path is available between them. If it is, subsequent packets are switched at Layer 2 rather than being routed (Figure 4.4).

There is currently no standard way of defining or identifying flows, or of establishing the shortcut paths for end-system flow switching. Other concerns you should have include where the processing is done on the end-system to negotiate the shortcut (e.g., in the processor, on the NIC), and how the capability gets there. To load software on every server and desktop, for example, could require someone to visit every machine if automated downloads are not supported. Even with auto-mation, downloading software to every node in a large network could be a very time-consuming, high-traffic process, especially if any characteristic must be individualized to each machine (such as network address). Another option would be to load the software only on new equipment and gradually roll out the capability only as older machines are replaced.

Principle: Schemes requiring every desktop to be touched will be expensive or take a long time to implement.

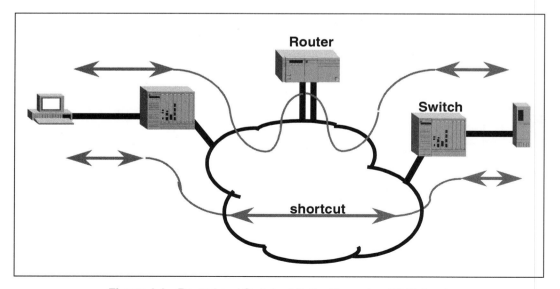

Figure 4.4 Routed and Switched Paths Through a FS Network

Network-Centric Flow Switching

Network-centric approaches require the cooperation of multiple switches throughout a network in order to set up a shortcut path once a flow has been identified and the destination is understood. If flow identification and routing are centralized, any packet not belonging to an established flow is forwarded to a route server somewhere in the network (Figure 4.5). The server decides whether the packet represents a new flow, calculates the appropriate path to the intended destination, and communicates throughout the network the information required for switching subsequent packets. The server must also forward the first packet toward its destination. A central route server constitutes a single point of failure in the network, thus requiring duplication and a fail-over protocol to be fault-tolerant.

Principle: *Distributed mechanisms are more robust but may require new protocols to coordinate information sharing and failure recovery.*

Consequently, most vendors have used distributed techniques to implement network-centric flow switching (Figure 4.6). All of these approaches require mechanisms to coordinate or synchronize the activities of the various distributed elements. MPOA, for example, defines how fail-over works among redundant servers. Other implementations use proprietary protocols.

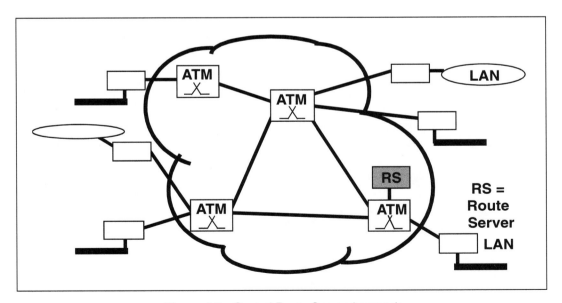

Figure 4.5 Central Route Server Approach

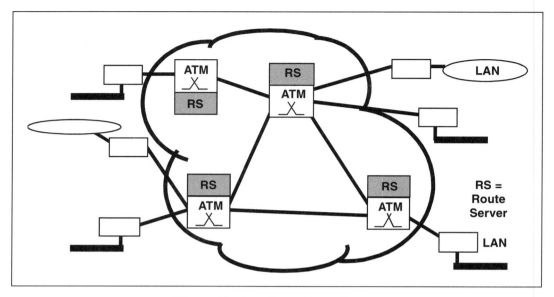

Figure 4.6   Distributed Route Servers

4.4 Positioning of Layer 3 Switches

Layer 3 switches offer a good deal of flexibility for designing networks. They may be used to aggregate traffic from segments within a building for example, keeping local traffic within the sub-net while forwarding cross-subnet traffic at wire speeds as well. They may be used to front-end shared resources such as server farms, providing high-speed switched connections while protecting those servers from extraneous broadcast traffic that eats up processing time. They may also be used to offload IP traffic processing from legacy routers, forestalling further expansion or investment in older technology while improving performance for all L3 protocols.

With packet-by-packet L3 switches, you can put routing wherever you did in a network design, but remember that not all are multi-protocol. If your network requires routing of multiple protocols, the L3 switch may not be able to *replace* existing routers, so you would put them in *new* places. PxP switches will, however, work with those existing routers and improve overall network performance by offloading IP from the routers and handling it really fast. This leaves the routers with capacity to improve their performance in routing all the other protocols. In fact, PxP switch performance is determined by the same characteristics well understood for classical routers: chip speeds, fabric bandwidth, table sizes, and buffering. Consequently, their performance would be measured and pre-sented the same way as well, in terms of throughput, latency, and latency variation.

Principle: *PxP switches require no new learning or staff skills—they are configured, deployed, and managed virtually the same way as routers are.*

With flow switches, it is more difficult to predict performance improvements. If new software must be installed in every end-system, large organizations may do it gradually and take a long time to realize performance improvements for the network as a whole. Where new L3 flow switches are installed, network performance still depends on detailed traffic characteristics, such as how much of the traffic is made up of flows long enough to benefit from shortcut paths. Path setup times are not well known and little is available for test data. According to Scott Bradner of the Harvard Device Test Laboratory (HDTL) and Strategic Networks, the average length of a flow on the Internet is only eight packets. If this is also characteristic of your LAN, flow switching may not provide much improvement over classical routing.

In general, FS methods are more complicated to understand and probably require more vendor support for designing customer networks than PxP products. It is not yet clear what will be required to identify, set up, manage, and tear down large numbers of flows successfully in a dynamic network environment, or how large the address caches need to be to hold information for the number of flows likely to be active at any one time. Meanwhile, new protocols and mechanisms for coordinating distributed elements are still under development and testing. Remember that MPOA is the only agreed-upon standard, and its complexities may not be well understood until vendor implementations are farther along.

Principle: *It remains to be proven how well various FS approaches will perform in given LAN environments, and how well they scale to very large networks. Path set-up times and average flow lengths depend on the detailed characteristics of individual networks.*

Regardless of whether equipment vendors use PxP or FS techniques, a design issue relevant to all L3 switches is the size of their address tables. You will see in the next chapters that storing the correspondence between L3 and L2 destination addresses is handled in different ways and places by various products: central routing tables, distributed routing tables, local caches for each interface module or port, forwarding information bases, etc. The performance question is: How large is that table? Within an enterprise LAN, it may be quite adequate to store information for only a few tens of thousands of destinations. In the Internet, one or more hundred thousand destination addresses are far more likely to be appropriate. To get best performance from any L3 switch (including classical routers), the table size should be large enough to limit the probability of a table search failure.

4.5 Summary of Functional Characteristics

In addition to the difference between PxP and FS techniques, there are numerous features that distinguish one Layer 3 switch from another. In this chapter we have discussed the following as important ones:

- what protocols are routed (most often IP);
- what underlying Layer 2 technologies are supported (often Ethernet only);
- which routing protocols are used to share information with other routers; and
- what Layer 3 special services are performed (tunneling, filtering, WAN interfaces, etc.).

Additional characteristics for evaluating switches were discussed in Chapter 3 for Layer 2 switches. All of those that are not L2-specific are relevant to L3 switches as well.

5 Packet-by-Packet Layer 3 Switches

5.1 Introduction

Chapter 4 distinguished packet-by-packet Layer 3 switching from Layer 3 flow switching. It is the purpose of this chapter to provide a detailed analysis of packet-by-packet switches from a variety of vendors. However, due to limitations of both space and time, the number of vendors whose switches we analyzed had to be limited to a relatively small number. Realizing this limitation, the authors have deliberately included a cross section of vendors. As shown in Table 5.1, this cross section includes both large established companies as well as small, newer companies. It also includes products that are focused on the Enterprise as well as those focused on the Internet. The reader should note that this switch analysis is a snapshot in time. By that the authors mean that, while the information we present is accurate to the best of our knowledge, it will change in time.

Table 5.1 The Marketplace Focus of the Analyzed Products

Enterprise	Internet
Bay Networks: Accelar™ 1000 Series	Torrent: IP9000
3Com: CoreBuilder 3500	Ascend: GRF 400
Extreme Networks: Summit1™, Summit2™	

The reader also must be aware of the fact that given the newness of the technology, the authors were forced to rely heavily on information provided to them by the vendors. In those few instances where we have test data or we have anecdotal feedback from users of the technology, we mention it.

Two of the primary ways that Layer 3 switches designed for the Internet differ from those designed for the Enterprise are the generic scalability of the switch as well as the routing table search process that the switch uses. Generic scalability covers a variety of parameters including the number and type of interfaces supported, the aggregate throughput of the L3 switch, as well as the degradation in switch performance under heavy traffic loads.

The routing table search process is a key component of traffic forwarding, with traffic forwarding being one of the two basic functions of routing as previously described. While it is not usually discussed, the route search operation is often the single most time-consuming operation that must be performed in a Layer 3 device. As such, the efficiency of this process establishes a limit on the Layer 3 device's ability to route traffic. Note that a Layer 3 switch intended for use within the Internet must have a notably more sophisticated routing table search process than a Layer 3 switch intended for use within the typical enterprise.

In the route search process, an L3 switch receives a packet with a Destination Address (DA). Given current IP Version 4 implementations, this DA is identified by a 32-bit field. The L3 device searches a forwarding table using the IP destination address as its key. The purpose of this search is to determine which entry in the table represents the best route for the packet to take as it traverses the network to its destination.

In the current network environment, this search process is complicated by the fact that entries in the forwarding table have variable lengths. In addition, it is possible that multiple entries represent valid routes to the DA. Unlike a simple search that seeks to find an exact match within a table, a routing table search algorithm must select the most specific route from a number of entries. This is the route that represents the longest network prefix for the given DA.

The complexity of the route search process will continue to increase significantly over the next few years. For example, data links now operate routinely at 100 Mbits/second. At this speed, these links can generate approximately 150,000 packets-per-second that require routing. New protocols, such as RSVP, will require route selection based not only on destination address, but potentially also on Protocol Number, Source Address, Destination Port, and Source Port. If IP Version 6 becomes mainstream, it will increase the size of the address field from 32 bits to 128 bits, with network prefixes up to 64 bits in length. In addition, many companies are making increased use of IP Multicasting. IP Multicasting requires that searches include large numbers of Class D (Multicast Group) addresses with large numbers of users.

Vendors of Layer 3 devices have a variety of approaches to improving the efficiency of the route table search process. Many of these vendors use a two phased process. The first phase is a fast path process that performs an exact-match search for the DA in a relatively small address cache. If the DA is not found in the cache, the device defaults to a full table search, i.e., the second phase. Not surprisingly, this approach tends to perform well when a match is found in the cache and less well when the device has to do a full table search.

There are other approaches to improving the efficiency of the route table search process. Torrent, one of the vendors whose products will be analyzed in this chapter, has developed a new algorithm called the ASIK algorithm. Torrent's claim is that this new algorithm can be readily implemented in hardware and adapted to various link speeds. Unfortunately, Torrent has not released any details of the ASIK algorithm.

Given that an inefficient or inappropriate route table search process can significantly limit the throughput of a Layer 3 switch, the author's advise the readers to get information from prospective vendors as to the process they use. However, while it is certainly helpful to review details of arcane search algorithms, it is more important that potential buyers of Layer 3 switches review test data. In particular, we suggest that potential buyers of Layer 3 switches review data that reflects how the vendor's route table search process performs in environments similar to that of the potential buyer.

As was previously discussed, classical routers typically perform all or most of the basic routing functionality in software. This is why classical routers were described as:

- Being complex to configure and manage;

- Being expensive;

- Providing relatively low throughput; and

- Providing relatively high throughput variation.

This software centric nature of classical routers is what gave rise to the conventional wisdom in the networking industry that it is not possible to perform routing at wire speeds. Given that assumption, Layer 3 flow switching can be viewed as a workaround.

However, now that Layer 3 switches are being deployed, it is possible to test that conventional wisdom. Appendix II contains the results of tests that were performed on the Bay Accelar 1200 by Strategic Networks (www.snci.com) and the Harvard Device Test Laboratory. These tests clearly indicate that, under the conditions of the tests, it is possible to do wire speed routing.

Some of the key findings of those tests were:

- The distributed forwarding/shared memory architecture of the Accelar 1200 delivered throughput at full theoretical media rates for both Layer 2 and Layer 3 traffic. The maximum load applied to the switch was forty-eight parallel streams of Fast Ethernet traffic. Forty-eight streams of Fast Ethernet traffic equates to 4.8 Gbps of aggregate bandwidth and forwarding performance of 7,142,832 pps for 64-byte packets. No packets were lost in any of these tests.

- The average LIFO latency was nearly identical for both Layer 2 and Layer 3 traffic at less than 7 microseconds over the range of packet sizes under all test conditions. These results show that the efficiency of forwarding table lookups performed by the Accelar 1200 is the same for both Layer 2 and Layer 3 packets. Latency was also found to be almost completely independent of background load on the switch.

- Latency variation with no background load was extremely low at 100–400 nanoseconds (0.1-0.4 microseconds) in both Layer 2 and Layer 3 tests. Latency variation was quite comparable to the tester's time resolution of 100 nanoseconds. With a sizable background load of up to 39 Fast Ethernet streams (3.9 Gbps), latency variation increased only slightly (to 1–2 microseconds for the various packet sizes).

5.2 Bay Networks

The Bay Networks Accelar™ 1000 series consists of the Accelar 1200, the 1250 and the 1100. As can be seen in Figure 5.1, Bay is positioning the Accelar™ 1000 series as being deployable either entirely as a Layer 2 switch or as any combination of routed and switched ports.

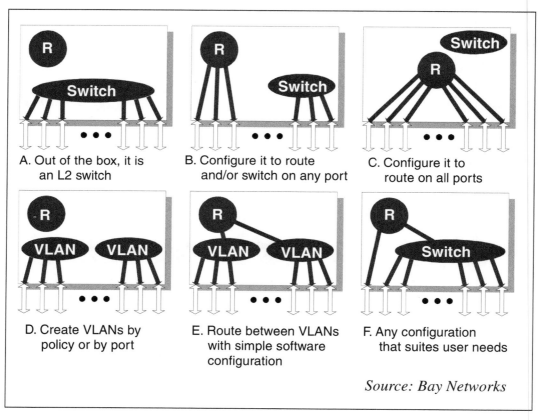

A. Out of the box, it is an L2 switch

B. Configure it to route and/or switch on any port

C. Configure it to route on all ports

D. Create VLANs by policy or by port

E. Route between VLANs with simple software configuration

F. Any configuration that suites user needs

Source: Bay Networks

Figure 5.1   Deployment Options for the Bay Networks Accelar™ 1000 Series

5.2.1   Hardware Architecture

As seen in Figure 5.2, the Accelar™ 1000 switches are comprised of two main hardware components, the Silicon Switch Fabric((SSF) and I/O port modules.

Silicon Switch Fabric CPU module

The center of the Accelar™ 1000 architecture is the Silicon Switch Fabric (SSF) CPU module. This CPU performs all protocol functions including spanning tree, bridge learning functions, RIPv2, OSPF, DVMRP, and PIM. Routing and bridging tables computed by the CPU are stored in up to 16Mbytes of main memory. Packet forwarding information is derived from the routing tables and distributed to the forwarding engine ASICs on all I/O port modules. The packet forwarding decision is made independently on every port module through multiple, distributed sets of forwarding engines. The authors believe that this distribution of packet forwarding to ASICs on each I/O port is a key component that allows the switch to achieve wire speed IP routing.

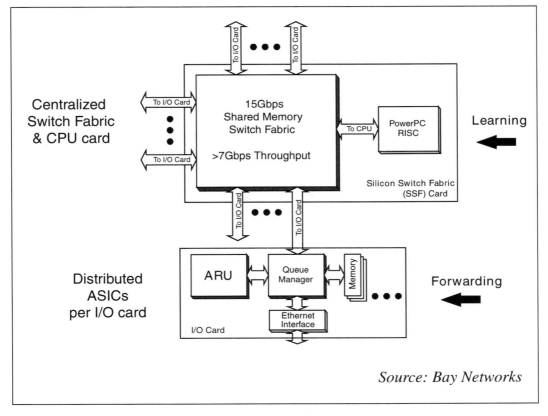

Figure 5.2   The Accelar™ 1000 Hardware Architecture

The Accelar™ 1000's Silicon Switch Fabric uses a 15Gbps shared memory architecture. As is shown in Appendix II, full-duplex throughput of 7Gbps can be sustained, providing a forwarding rate of over 7 million packets per second, for 64 byte packets. 4MB of shared memory is dynamically allocated to priority queues. High and low priority queues exist for multicast traffic, as well as for each output port.

I/O Port Modules

The I/O port modules contain the physical layer, Media Access Control (MAC) layer, and forwarding engine and output queues. Each forwarding engine maintains its own forwarding information base for both routed and bridged traffic. This forwarding information base contains up to 24,000 entries to service either one Gigabit Ethernet port or four Fast Ethernet ports.

With forwarding data stored locally, the forwarding engine can resolve addresses and forward packets through the silicon switch fabric independent of the CPU. This architectural feature yields both a higher performing as well as a more resilient switch. The forwarding engine also checks each packet against current prioritization policies and sets prioritization information in the internal packet header if appropriate. Priority policies can be based on physical port, VLAN ID, multicast destination, or RSVP flow.

Unicast Packet Forwarding

When a packet arrives, the forwarding engine performs an address lookup, determines which port will output the packet, and if necessary updates the Cyclical Redundancy Check (CRC), MAC, and Time To Live (TTL) fields. A header is created containing the internal address of the input and output ports, and priority information in the header is set if the packet meets configured priority policies. Each packet is fragmented at wirespeed into blocks and written into a prioritized unicast queue in the switch. From the switch fabric, the blocks are then forwarded to the destination output port based on the internal output port address in the header. Note that these blocks are not ATM cells. While awaiting transmission the packet is buffered in either the low or high priority queue depending upon the priority bit in the header.

Multicast and Broadcast Packet Forwarding

Upon packet arrival, the forwarding engine looks up the multicast record in the forwarding table and creates an internal multicast label pointing to the list of ports belonging to the multicast group. Port lists are stored at distributed locations within the switch. In the switch fabric, the label points to the list identifying port modules that belong to the multicast group. Simultaneously, the label points to the list that identifies individual output ports that belong to the multicast group on the port modules. Using the multicast label in conjunction with the group membership lists, packet forwarding decisions can be distributed within the switch to maintain wirespeed operation.

Broadcast packet forwarding is similar to multicast. Broadcast packets are forwarded to all ports belonging to the same VLAN.

Redundancy

As is the case with any Layer 3 switch, the convergence properties of standard routing protocols provides infrastructure redundancy should the system fail. For maximum network availability, Accelar™ 1000 routing switches also provide redundant, distributed management, and switching functionality. For example, all Accelar™ 1000 modules are hot swappable. The Accelar™ 1200 and 1100 routing switches provide hot swappable redundant power supplies. In addition, redundant SSFs are supported in the Accelar™ 1200.

A process that Bay Networks refers to as LinkSafe provides physical interface redundancy for Gigabit Ethernet (GE) links. If the primary physical interface fails, the secondary interface comes up. Bay Networks claims that this happens in less than one second and without connection loss.

5.2.2   Software Architecture

Routing and VLANs

The Accelar™ 1000 switches support RIPv1, RIPv2, and OSPF. They also support up to 127 port-based, protocol-based, or subnet-based VLANs.

Trunking (802.1Q)

Trunks or links between switches keep the traffic of each VLAN separate by associating tags with each packet in compliance with the IEEE 802.1Q standard. Accelar™ 1000 routing switches also allow for creation of multiple spanning tree groups across links between switches by associating separate tags with bridge protocol data units (BPDUs).

QoS

There is significant interest among network professionals in deploying Quality of Service (QoS). RSVP is a QoS technique that was developed to provide deterministic mechanisms for applications to request bandwidth allocation in Ethernet, similar to what is planned for ATM. As shown in Table 5.2, the Accelar™ 1000 supports RSVP as well as a variety of other QoS techniques.

Table 5.2   The Accelar™ 1000 QoS Mechanisms

Port	Prioritizes traffic entering through the port. Used for server or inter-switch connection.
VLAN	Assigns priority to particular workgroups or mission critical data in specific protocols.
MAC Address	Prioritizes traffic for a particular device.
Multicast Destination	Multimedia traffic destined for a group address, representing a group of workstations.
RSVP	Prioritization of RSVP data. End station must support.
IP Flow	Provides maximum bandwidth to data requesting priority through RSVP or static configuration. IP flow prioritization applies to both routed and L2 switched traffic.

Accelar™ 1000 routing switches prioritize traffic using queues and headers. As each packet is transmitted through the switch fabric, a header is attached. The header contains prioritization information set by the forwarding engine on the ingress port when the packet is received. Each time the packet moves in the switch, it is placed in either a high or low priority queue depending on the priority information in the internal packet header. At each stage within the switch, packets in high priority queues are sent before packets in low priority queues.

5.3 3Com

5.3.1   The FIRE Architecture

3Com is positioning the Flexible Intelligent Routing Engine (FIRE) as its third generation Layer 3 switching architecture. In particular, 3Com is positioning FIRE as a delivery mechanism for 3Com's TranscendWare™ software. Their intention is to provide an end-to-end, policy-based networking framework that enables IT professionals to offer service level agreements (SLAs) to their user base. In their definition of SLA functionality, 3Com includes security, traffic prioritization, bandwidth reservation, and quality of service (QoS).

The FIRE architecture is depicted in Figure 5.3. The FIRE architecture attempts to build upon the advancements made in developing and deploying Layer 2 switching. The goal is to also support wire-speed performance levels for Layer 3 routing, multicast forwarding, and user-selectable policy. 3Com claims that there is no disparity between Layer 2 and Layer 3 performance.

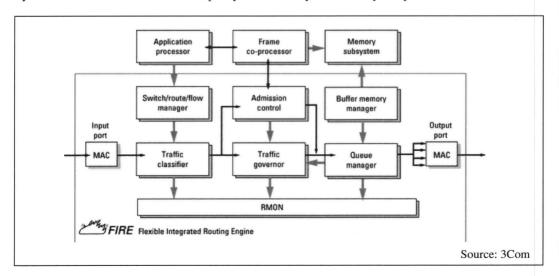

Figure 5.3   FIRE Architecture Detail

3Com's performance claim is supported by a review of the CoreBuilder 3500 written by Pankaj Chowdhry in a December 22, 1997 edition of PC Week. Chowdhry's review comments very favorably on the CoreBuilder 3500's performance, but advised readers that they would have to wait for a future release of the product before it had much Layer 3 functionality such as QoS. In addition to this review, one of the author's clients told us that they have tested the CoreBuilder 3500 and that it "never skipped a beat."

One truly interesting aspect of the FIRE architecture is that 3Com has extended ASIC capabilities by embedding a processor in the silicon. The result is a concept that the authors once thought was an oxymoron—a programmable ASIC. This innovation has the potential to provide all of the performance expected of an ASIC, but makes it extensible as well. This means that it should be possible to add features such as IP version 6 without a product upgrade or a sacrifice in performance. However, the authors need to point out that until this has been done, the capability remains in the realm of the theoretical.

Distributed Packet Pipelining

The FIRE architecture introduces a concept referred to as distributed packet pipelining (DPP). With DPP, multiple distributed forwarding engines independently transfer packets through the system. As a packet works its way through the pipeline, the system performs the following tasks:

- Verifies frame integrity
- Captures statistics for relevant MIBs, including RMON
- Determines VLANs
- Distinguishes bridged and routed frames
- Classifies specific data flows
- Polices data rates on flows and reservations
- Applies filters
- Modifies packet headers if routing or tagging
- Applies priorities
- Transmits the packet

Within an individual pipeline, several ASICs simultaneously handle multiple frames. This parallelism and pipelining has the potential to support forwarding performance at Layer 2 and Layer 3 that is wire speed on all ports for unicast, multi-cast, and broadcast traffic. In addition, all buffering is done on the output port because all the necessary checking and updates are complete by the time a packet arrives at the output stage. This avoids accessing a packet in memory.

Dynamically Scalable Memory

Within the FIRE architecture, a portion of the buffer memory is associated directly with the forwarding engines. As interface modules are added with their respective forwarding engines, memory scales accordingly. Memory is not statically coupled with the forwarding engines, but is made available to all forwarding engines in the system.

3Com states that the FIRE architecture allocates buffers in relation to the size of received frames and does so dynamically. This means that large packets get large buffers and small packets get small buffers. The authors believe that this has the potential to use memory more efficiently and increases the system's ability to handle large traffic bursts without losing a packet. These dynamically constructed buffers are then allocated in a two-level hierarchy, on a per-port basis and a common pool. 3Com claims that this arrangement allows FIRE to guarantee a fixed amount of buffering for each interface, yet handle large bursts of data without depleting resources.

Advanced Queuing Mechanisms

Many LAN switches buffer output traffic on a single queue. Traffic is then served on a first-in, first-out manner, with excess traffic discarded when the queue became full. In addition to discarding traffic, another issue with this approach is that if the single queue size is increased in order to handle large volumes of traffic, the time that the data spends in the queue tends to grow. These characteristics made deploying real-time and multimedia applications very difficult in a single queue system.

In an attempt to eliminate these characteristics of a single queue system, 3Com introduced PACE technology. PACE is intended to allow for different classes of service over the same Ethernet LAN and to control latency and jitter. The FIRE architecture builds on PACE technology and introduces four levels of output queuing. Packets associated with real-time flows and multimedia are placed in higher-priority queues. Weighted Fair Queuing (WFQ) services the higher-priority queues more frequently, while ensuring that some attention is given to the lower-priority queues. Note that this approach (WFQ) is different than the approach used in the Accelar™ 1000 series.

Automatic Flow Classification (AutoClass)

FIRE can instruct its packet pipeline to discriminate among user-specified traffic flows. The priorities are established by system administrators and are implemented in silicon. This should result in decreased latencies, high-priority transmissions, and congestion avoidance. AutoClass instructs the pipeline to classify data flows and assign them a queue-based priority. The process is media independent, working over all Ethernet, FDDI, and ATM media.

AutoClass can also recognize data link encapsulation such as SNAP types and LLC, as well as protocol types. Unicast, multicast, and broadcast traffic can be distinguished, as well as IP UDP, TCP source, destination addresses, and well-known ports. Mappings of 802.1p and 802.1Q services are provided as well as default classifiers. One example of using AutoClass is prioritizing FTP traffic during large file backups to ensure timely completion. Another is wire-speed firewalls, where certain flows are allocated zero bandwidth.

5.3.2   The CoreBuilder 3500

The CoreBuilder 3500 (the 3500) is built around an architecture whose key element is the FIRE ASIC. This ASIC is further illustrated in Figure 5.4. As previously mentioned, 3Com claims that with the 3500 there is no longer a disparity between Layer 2 and Layer 3 performance.

5.3.2.1   CoreBuilder 3500 Features

VLANs

The CoreBuilder 3500 supports three basic types of VLANs:

- Port-based VLANs. An arbitrary group of ports within a bridge group.
- Protocol-based VLANs. A collection of ports designated as a VLAN interface for packets belonging to a specific Layer 3 protocol family.
- Network-based VLANs. A collection of ports designated as a VLAN interface for packets belonging to a specified Layer 3 network address.

The 3500 also supports IEEE 802.1Q tagging as well as a 3Com proprietary tagging and Layer 3 address tagging mechanism.

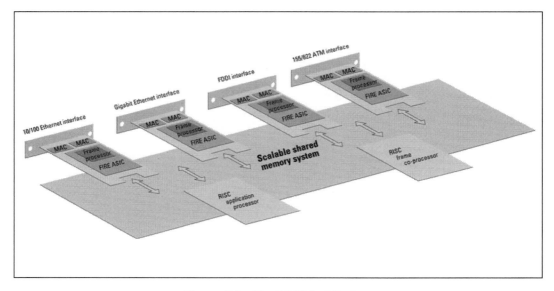

Figure 5.4   The FIRE Architecture

Traffic Control Mechanisms

The purpose of these mechanisms is to prevent the propagation of certain traffic. Packet filtering allows the user to define filters that cause blocking of traffic to or from the designated source or destination address. Protocol filtering prevents certain protocols from being processed on particular ports. Route filtering defines the prevention of routes from being advertised on selected interfaces. This type of filtering is mainly a security feature.

Multicast Packet Firewalls

The primary purpose of these firewalls is to limit the rate at which multicast packets are forwarded.

5.3.2.2   Internetworking

As was previously discussed, the authors view LAN technology as being retro. In particular, while most enterprises have deployed Layer 2 switches (a.k.a., bridges), we feel that these same enterprises will want to deploy additional routing functionality, given the price/performance of Layer 3 switches.

Below is a listing of the internetworking functionality that the 3500 supports that will allow users to deploy it as a router supplement.

IP

This includes TCP, UDP, RIP, OSPF, DVMRP, and all RFCs defined for the routing of IP. Both unicast and multicast traffic types are supported.

IPX

This includes IPX RIP, SAP, NLSP, and all IPX Ethernet encapsulation types.

AppleTalk

The CoreBuilder 3500 supports AppleTalk SNAP, AARP, DDP, RTMP, ZIP, AEP, and NBP.

PACE technology

As previously described, PACE technology works in conjunction with PACE NICs to provide priority to certain traffic classes and bound latency and jitter in Ethernet networks.

Policy-Based Services

The 3500 supports multiple output queues, AutoClass of traffic types, and Weighted Fair Queuing (WFQ) of priority-queued traffic.

Fast IP

As will be described in the next chapter, Fast IP is one instance of Layer 3 flow switching. Working in conjunction with intelligent NICs, Fast IP uses the Next Hop Routing Protocol (NHRP) to map MAC and IP addresses so Layer 2 paths can be used for high speed and low latency. The first packet is routed and all packets following are switched. The CoreBuilder 3500 Layer 3 switch can act as the NHRP device for a Fast IP network segment.

5.3.2.3   CoreBuilder 3500 Interfaces

Ethernet

There are three Ethernet modules for the CoreBuilder 3500 Layer 3 switch. They are the:

- 6-port 10/100BASE- TX
- 6-port 100BASE-FX (MMF)
- 6-port 100BASE-FX (SMF)

Gigabit Ethernet

The single-port Gigabit Ethernet module has a Gigabit Interface Converters (GBICs) interface which supports a variety of media types. This includes 1000BASE-SX (62.5 and 50 micron MMF), 1000BASE-LX (62.5 and 50 micron MMF), 1000BASE-LX SMF, and a future 1000BASE-TX transceiver.

FDDI and ATM

3Com states that the 3500 will support both FDDI and ATM at some time in the future.

5.4   Extreme Networks

5.4.1   Hardware Architecture

Extreme Networks refers to their line of Layer 3 switches as Summit™ switches. As of the time that this book was written, there were two members of this line, the Summit1™ and the Summit2™. All Summit switches share a common architecture based on a 17.5 gigabit per second non-blocking switch fabric. Based on the internally developed Summit Chipset, Extreme claims that this architecture is capable of delivering wire-speed IP routing at Layer 3 and full line-rate switching at Layer 2. Results of tests performed by Strategic Networks on the Summit2™ switch are contained in Appendix III. These tests show that for a broad range of packet sizes, and for 10, 9, or 6 streams of Fast Ethernet, the Summit2™ achieved wire speed with zero packet loss.

Summit switches are designed and optimized for wire-speed IP routing and switching for all other protocols. This optimization allows the Summit switch architecture to take advantage of custom silicon and a 64-byte-wide data path to perform real-time IP routing in hardware. At the same time, Extreme claims that the CPU does not adversely affect performance because it is located out of the data path, where it maintains route tables and determines the policies and resources used by the custom ASICs.

Using hardware-based header processing, Summit switches process and switch packets efficiently because IP routing information is found at exactly the same location within each Ethernet/IP packet. When traffic reaches a port on a Summit switch, each packet is examined and a mask is applied to the header. This mask locates important routing information and real-time processing occurs in the following areas:

- Checks header validation, including length, check sum and version type
- Identifies time-to-live (TTL) information on input
- Identifies the destination address and the next hop
- Creates a new MAC address header
- Decrements the TTL counter and updates check sum information

Parallelism and Pipelining

To enhance performance, Summit switches distribute their hardware-based header processing in parallel to all eight data-path channels. Once packets reach the Summit's ASIC-based hardware routing engine, pipelining takes over. According to Extreme Networks, pipelining allows Summit switches to process up to eight instructions simultaneously.

Data Path and Central Memory

As an additional performance enhancement, the data path to the Summit switch's central memory is 64 bytes wide. This enables a small Ethernet packet to be read or written in a single clock cycle. The Summit1© supports eight full-duplex ports of Gigabit Ethernet. This requires 16 gigabits to sustain wire-speed, full-duplex performance. The central memory in the Summit architecture has 34 gigabits of raw bandwidth.

Forwarding Database

The Summit switch's forwarding database is supported by 1.25 MB of memory and a 21 gigabit-per-second access rate. The forwarding database is a memory store that contains several cross-linked tables. This includes MAC address tables and VLAN tables for Layer 2 switching, IP route and ARP tables for Layer 3 switching, and multicast routing tables. The forwarding database also stores additional packet-filtering information, including session ID tables. These tables contain IP source/destination addresses and TCP/UDP source/destination ports that are necessary to support RSVP and detect policy-based QoS IP flows.

Central Processing Unit (CPU)

The Summit switch's 64-bit, RISC CPU is primarily responsible for controlling the policies and resources needed by ASICs and tables in the Summit switch architecture. Specifically, it provides initialization, handles routing protocols, performs route server functions, supports management interfaces and MIBs, stores bridging/routing tables, and distills QoS policies into hardware parameters.

QoS

Software provided by Extreme Networks, ExtremeWare, supports the IETF industry standard RSVP protocol that allows end-stations to request resources from the network and Integrated Services guidelines for delivering requested bandwidth. ExtremeWare also supports IEEE 802.1p priority levels and 802.1Q frame format for VLAN tagging and priority classification. According to Extreme Networks, ExtremeWare's policy-based QoS builds on these standards to also guarantee greater bandwidth control, enforce traffic prioritization, and deliver QoS to applications without altering end-stations.

In the Extreme Networks schema, setting QoS policy is a combination of identifying traffic groups and defining QoS profiles for those traffic groups. Traffic groups may include all of the manufacturing subnet, for example, or all web servers or a power workgroup or even one particular print server that is under heavy use.

By use of an in-band browser-based (HTML) management tool the network manager decides which traffic groups have priority. Associated with each Summit switch port is a set of queues. The queue length/size is dynamically allocated from the shared central memory switch architecture. Each queue is assigned a priority relative to the other queues on the port. Using these queues, QoS profiles can be defined for each traffic group on every Summit switch.

For each traffic group, the network manager can define a QoS profile that allocates minimum and maximum bandwidth, peak bandwidth, relative priority, and maximum delay. According to Extreme Networks, the queue management system provides a way to prioritize traffic and guarantee bandwidth for identified applications. This system also limits bandwidth and automatically buffers packets based on priority so that no traffic group can monopolize the link.

These traffic classes are then mapped onto the various Summit switch queues so they can be serviced with different bandwidth levels according to policy. Weighted fair queuing is used to determine the delivery schedule of the queued data.

5.4.2 The Summit1™ and Summit2™ Switches

The Summit1™ comes with eight full-duplex switched Gigabit Ethernet ports. The Summit2™ comes with two Gigabit Ethernet ports and sixteen 10/100 Mbps autosensing Ethernet ports. Each Summit system comes pre-installed with ExtremeWare™.

Extreme Networks uses a technique that they refer to as the Summit Virtual Chassis™ to scale the capability of the Summit switches. The Summit Virtual Chassis™ is a high-speed external backplane that interconnects up to eight stacked or distributed Summit switches into one system. The Summit Virtual Chassis™ comes with eight SummitLink™ backplane channels supported by 64 Gbps of non-blocking switch fabric bandwidth. It can support configurations such as 32 full-duplex Gigabit Ethernet ports or 128 full-duplex, autosensing 10/100 Mbps Ethernet ports. The Summit Virtual Chassis™ also features redundant power supplies, hot swappable Summit switches, hot-swappable Summit Virtual Chassis, load-balanced links, environmental sensors, as well as fan failure detectors.

Extreme Networks is targeting the Summit1™ switch to support LAN backbones and server farms. Below is a listing, provided by Extreme Networks, of the key functionality of the Summit1™ switches.

- 17.5 Gbps non-blocking switch fabric bandwidth
- Wire-speed IP routing performance at greater than 11.9 million packets per second
- Fully interoperability with routers using standard IP routing protocols
- Full gigabit and 10/100 Mbps performance with wire-speed Layer 3 and Layer 2 switching
- Eight Gigabit Ethernet ports
- Policy-based QoS, including bandwidth management, prioritization and congestion control
- ExtremeWare with standards-based bandwidth reservation, IP routing, multicast control, and VLAN switching
- Fault-tolerant features, including multiple load-sharing trunks and multiple spanning trees
- Network management through HTML, SNMP, RMON, local and remote CLI (telnet)
- Redundant power supply (RPS) support

Extreme Networks is targeting the Summit2™ switch to support high performance workgroups as well as wiring closets. Below is a listing, provided by Extreme Networks, of the key functionality of the Summit2™ switches.

- 8.5 Gbps non-blocking switch fabric bandwidth
- Wire-speed IP routing performance at 5.4 million packets per second
- Full interoperability with routers using standard IP routing protocols
- Full gigabit and 10/100 Mbps performance with wire-speed IP and Layer 2 switching
- Two Gigabit Ethernet ports, 16 10/100 Mbps Ethernet ports
- Policy-based QoS, including bandwidth management, prioritization and congestion control

- ExtremeWare with standards-based bandwidth reservation, IP routing, multicast control, and VLAN switching
- Fault-tolerant features, including redundant Gigabit Ethernet PHY, multiple load-sharing trunks and multiple spanning trees
- Network management through HTML, SNMP, RMON, local and remote CLI (telnet)
- Redundant power supply (RPS) support

5.5 Torrent

5.5.1 Hardware Architecture

As of the writing of this book, the only Layer 3 switch from Torrent Networking Technologies (Torrent) was the IP9000 Gigabit Router. It is built around three major elements: the Gigabit Switch Fabric, the Forwarding Engines, and the Route Processor.

The Gigabit Switch Fabric

The Gigabit Switch Fabric is packaged in a modular chassis with redundant power supplies. Torrent offers both an 8-slot and a 16-slot version of this chassis, with maximum throughput, according to Torrent, of 10 Gbps and 20 Gbps, respectively. All traffic is forwarded through the fabric, which is a multistage shared-memory network using a per-flow queuing architecture. The Torrent per-flow queuing architecture will be detailed later in this section.

The Forwarding Engines

The Forwarding Engines are modules that plug into the 8 or 16 slots available on the switch fabric chassis. All per-packet routing operations are performed in ASICs on the forwarding engines. This includes route lookup, packet classification, Layer 3 forwarding, and flow policing. Forwarding engines host various interface types with different densities, i.e., eight 10/100 Ethernet ports, four ATM OC-3 ports, one Gigabit Ethernet port. In all cases, the per-packet routing operations are distributed to each port on the module.

The Route Processor

The Route Processor is a stack-on general-purpose computer handling a variety of background operations for the IP9000 system. The IP9000 route processor is not part of the forwarding path for traffic. Its operation is limited to performing background tasks such as routing table maintenance and system configuration. One Fast Ethernet interface on the IP9000 system must be dedicated to the route processor.

5.5.2   Key Processes

The Routing Process

In chapter 3, the authors defined two primary core routing functions—route processing and packet forwarding. In the Torrent model, there are three components of core routing: Developing the Routing Table, Resolving Routes from Addresses, and Layer 3 Packet Forwarding. Basically, Torrent has taken what the authors consider to be one function (packet forwarding) and split it into two functions (resolving routes from addresses and Layer 3 packet forwarding). Torrent has taken this approach because of the high priority they place on resolving routes from addresses.

Developing the Routing Table

Any router must continually communicate with other routers using protocols such as OSPF and BGP and constantly update its routing table. This is a well-defined background operation. It is not done per packet, but must be done with high priority since any change to the routing table may affect packet forwarding. Layer 3 devices must also handle events referred to as route flaps. These are situations when routing table updates arrive with great frequency, and demand rapid handling.

In the IP9000 system, routing table maintenance is fully handled by the route processor. The route processor is dedicated to routing table maintenance and develops a unique per-port table of unicast and multicast routes. It also uses its private channel through the switch fabric to update tables on the forwarding engines, and only issues updates when changes occur.

Resolving Routes from Addresses

As mentioned in section 5.1, the efficiency of resolving routes from addresses (the routing table search process) establishes a limit on a Layer 3 switch's ability to route traffic. Traditional routers have always performed this task by executing a full, longest-prefix matching search in software. Performing this function in software has limited packet-forwarding rates. To overcome this limitation, many router vendors developed different techniques for fast path forwarding. The most common approach is to maintain a cache of frequently used addresses and to perform an exact-match search in hardware within the cache. If a route is found by this search, the packet can be forwarded immediately instead of being sent to the slow path software lookup.

This approach has some disadvantages. First, a process must be used to learn addresses in order to build the cache. This means that some percentage of the traffic will always be sent to the slow path for software handling. Second, when the cache is filled, previously learned entries are flushed out of the cache and must be re-learned later. This makes fast-path performance achievable, but unpredictable.

The IP9000 Gigabit Router combines a new search technique with a single pass through the routing table. So instead of a potentially small cache, the entire routing table is maintained on every port of the IP9000, and a full table search is performed for every packet. The search results include the output port, next-hop router address and also any stored service profiles to be applied to the packet. With a full table search on every packet, route search becomes deterministic, enabling routers to better handle multimedia traffic. Torrent claims that the patent-pending search algorithm, which was developed by Torrent's founding team, is sufficiently simple and compact to be implemented in a per-port forwarding ASIC.

Layer 3 Packet Forwarding

Unlike Layer 2 forwarding (a.k.a. bridging), Layer 3 forwarding requires a number of packet manipulations. For example, the Layer 2 addresses in the packet must be modified, the Time to Live field must be decremented, and the IP header checksum must be re-calculated.

In the IP9000 router, Layer 3 forwarding is fully handled in the forwarding engine port ASIC. With the information obtained from the routing table search, per-port silicon is able to make all the necessary packet modifications on the fly, before presenting the packet to the switch fabric for processing. The ASIC also includes with the packet appropriate queuing and priority information for the switch fabric.

Per-Flow Queuing

Most high-performance routing products use some sort of scalable switch fabric to carry traffic between ports. Packets are transferred from input ports to output ports across this fabric, and are held in queues within the fabric when contention with other traffic prevents a packet from being delivered immediately. There are many different methods and tradeoffs involved in both switching architectures and packet queuing, and each approach has different implications for the overall design.

The IP9000 switch fabric is based on a shared memory system, but uses a multistage network of memory resources rather than a single common pool of buffers. Depending on which queue it belongs to, an incoming packet is transferred to a different region of the interconnected shared memory network. Torrent claims that this approach maintains reasonable access speeds for the shared memory switch while at the same time providing scalability up to a maximum of 20 Gbps of throughput in the IP9000 system.

The IP9000 Gigabit Router uses a per-flow queuing architecture. Per-flow queuing associates a unique queue within the switch fabric with every end-to-end traffic flow, and flows may be as granular as individual applications running between two users. Note that although the IP9000 assigns queues based on traffic flows, this does not make it a Layer 3 flow switch in the author's definition as the IP9000 fully processes each packet at Layer 3.

As packets are received at input ports, they are correlated at line speed with known traffic flows. Flows are matched based on multiple fields of the IP Header, such as the destination address, source address, destination port, source port, and protocol number. Each identified flow is assigned a unique queue through the switch fabric to its output port. Flows may be assigned one of four priorities, and round-robin service is performed among flow queues at the output port to insure fair delivery.

The IP9000 router polices the use of flows to specific pre-set throughput limits. A designated flow is set not only with a priority, but also with a throughput limit. When traffic bursts exceed the throughput limit of a flow, subsequent packets in that flow are directed into best-effort queues. This prevents priority traffic from hogging network bandwidth while preserving per-flow resolution.

A full mesh of input-to-output flows is pre-established for best-effort traffic, giving each input port a unique queue to each output port. Any traffic not belonging to a designated flow will be sent to these default queues and processed at the lowest priority level. This resembles output queuing for best-effort traffic, but has the advantage of not allowing a burst on a single input port to take service away from other input ports targeting the same output.

Multicast traffic is handled independent of unicast traffic. A unique multicast queue is established for every multicast group operating in the system, and packet replication is done within the fabric itself. Thus multicast packets are queued only behind other packets destined for the same group, effectively eliminating any blocking.

Mechanisms for Guaranteed Service

The IP9000 forwarding engines perform wire-speed route lookup, Layer 3 forwarding and packet classification into flows. As described above, each packet is searched against any installed flow filters. If a flow filter is installed, it will have a service profile associated with it and a unique per-flow queue through the switch fabric. If there is no installed flow filter for this packet, it will be applied to the default mesh of best-effort queues.

Service profiles include three parameters:

- The Per-Flow Queue that should be used for packets matching this flow. This queue will be serviced independently from all other queues in the system.

- The Priority at which packets belonging to this flow should be serviced within the fabric. The IP9000 switch fabric supports four levels of priority, and the highest level is reserved for internal traffic, such as routing table updates. At the output ports, higher-priority flows will always receive service ahead of low-priority flows.

- The Throughput that this flow is allowed to use, in bits or bytes per second. This parameter will be used to establish a "credit" level for the flow, and the IP9000 route processor periodically (every 1-2 seconds) refreshes all credits allocated to flows. Policing of flows is designed to insure that priority traffic never hogs all the available bandwidth.

According to Torrent, it is possible to use the mechanisms described above to establish guaranteed service levels for individual flows. For example, flows that are set with a high priority and throughput limit will receive guaranteed minimum bandwidth from the system equal to the throughput limit. At output ports, flows are summed to verify that total priority bandwidth allocated does not exceed a preset threshold. If a priority flow bursts at a rate exceeding its throughput limit, subsequent packets will be forwarded through the fabric with best-effort service. Thus, priority traffic is guaranteed a minimum bandwidth but must contend with other traffic if it exceeds this level.

Alternatively, users may also use the mechanisms above to define policed best-effort flows for background applications. A flow may be established with best-effort, rather than priority, service as well as a throughput limit. In this situation, when traffic arriving for the flow exceeds the preset limit, packets will be dropped. This will force the TCP layers in the transmitting hosts to back down their transmission rates. In effect, flow routes are being used here to establish a maximum allowed throughput for specific applications.

Finally, users may take advantage of the per-flow routing capabilities of the IP9000 Gigabit Router simply for accounting purposes. Each flow maintains a set of counters on its utilization, which may be interrogated via the router's management interface to determine how much traffic is actually traversing a flow. This information can be used as a basis for capacity planning or to make users or business units aware of how much network resources they are consuming.

5.5.3   Additional Functionality

Router and System Configuration

The IP9000 supports three alternatives for configuration. The first of these is a simple Command Line Interface (CLI) and is available either via a directly attached terminal or a Telnet session over the network. According to Torrent, this interface has been designed to use a command structure that is very similar to that used in the Cisco Systems family of routers, and should support command scripts developed for Cisco routers.

The second alternative is that a complete set of standard SNMP MIBs is hosted by an SNMP agent in the IP9000 route processor. The IP9000 also hosts enterprise-specific MIB variables. Existing applications for router management can interrogate these MIB variables and display statistics for the IP9000 router along with statistics for existing routers from other vendors.

As a third alternative, the IP9000 router maintains a set of Java-based applets that it can upload to any Web browser. Using these Java applets, network managers can configure the router's ports, set up routing protocols, and manage any aspect of the system from a set of graphical configuration screens. With this approach, any computer equipped with a browser can be used for graphical configuration of the IP9000 system.

Internetworking

Many routers require that one subnet number bond uniquely with a single physical port. The IP9000 router supports both one to many and many to one associations of subnets and ports. One subnet number, for example, may be assigned to span a large number of ports on the IP9000 router. For example, each server in a server farm can be directly attached to a port on an IP9000. However, the servers could all be in one subnet. Traffic is routed to the appropriate ports even within the subnet, and intra-subnet traffic such as IP multicast and ARP is still selectively delivered.

Conversely, multiple subnets may exist on a single physical port. For example, assume that a Fast Ethernet port is connected to an access concentrator that fans out to many WAN ports. In this example, each WAN port may retain its own subnet number and the IP9000 router will be able to handle inter-subnet routing even when both subnets reside on the same physical interface.

Multipath Routing

It is often desirable to have multiple, identical paths between two routers, either for added capacity or resiliency. The IP9000 Gigabit Router supports parallel, equivalent cost paths between multiple routers and, according to Torrent, manages the traffic so that the offered load is balanced among the parallel paths. If one of the paths fails, traffic is automatically rerouted via the remaining paths. This capability has been built using standard routing protocols, so it will interoperate with routers from other vendors that run the same protocols.

5.6 Ascend

5.6.1 Design Goals and Network Architecture

The GRF 400 is a Layer 3 switch from Ascend. The networking problem that Ascend claims that the GRF 400 addresses is very similar to the networking problem that the other L3 switches that are analyzed in this chapter address. Specifically, traditional routers cannot keep up with the relentless demand for bandwidth. In particular, the way that traditional routers perform both packet forwarding and route determination do not scale to meet user demands.

Ascend refers to its solution as an IP switch. The authors feel that the use of that phrase is confusing. We say that because the term IP switching is more commonly associated with a Layer 3 flow switching technique first made popular by Ipsilon. However, Ascend has a somewhat different definition of an IP switch than the definition that was made popular by Ipsilon and its partners. To Ascend, an IP switch is a full-fledged router that uses a fast internal switching engine that runs over any media, not just ATM, combined with equally fast route table lookup to achieve wire-speed performance.

Ascend established ten essential design objectives for its Layer 3 switch project. They are:

- Compatibility with existing network infrastructures, including interoperability with conventional routers and LAN switches;

- Full compliance with industry standards to eliminate any need for proprietary gateways or special client software;

- IP next-hop address lookup fast enough to take advantage of a switching fabric's low latency and high throughput;

- Sustainable throughput that is independent of traffic characteristics (flows and cache hits);

- Wire-speed performance for all external LAN/WAN ports;

- Support for a wide range of popular LAN and WAN media;

- Support for ATM without an architectural dependence on ATM;

- Linear scalability within each IP switch and in a network of IP switches;

- Packaging in a small chassis, able to fit into the limited space in network points-of-presence (POPs); and

- An order of magnitude improvement in price/performance.

Ascend states that all ten objectives were achieved in GRF 400 (Figure 5.5)

At the core of the GRF 400 is a 4 Gbps crosspoint switch fabric. This switch fabric has four data paths, each with a non-blocking, bi-directional capacity of 1 Gbps. Ascend claims that the high

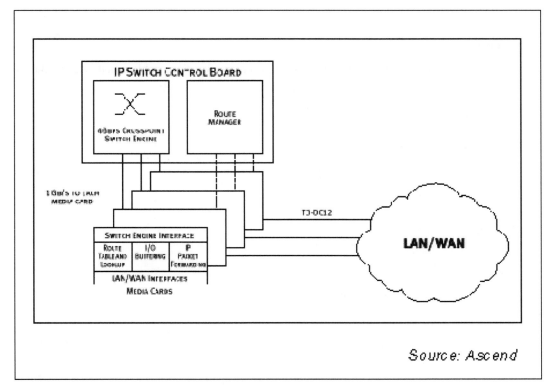

Figure 5.5   GRF 400 Architecture

speed, non-blocking nature of the switch engine permits multiple data paths to operate simultaneously. Path setup time is stated to be less than 250 nanoseconds (0.25

External LAN/WAN interfaces are provided by an assortment of plug-in IP forwarding media cards. Each media card has its own dedicated 1 Gbps path in the crosspoint switch fabric, thereby assuring linear scalability to the switch's capacity of 4 Gbps. Up to four media cards can be inserted into the GRF 400, for a total of up to 32 external LAN/WAN interfaces. Every media card is effectively a full IP router attached to the internal switching engine. Each media card contains 8 MB of input/output buffering, a complete next-hop route table, hardware-assisted route table lookup, and an IP forwarding engine.

Previously we discussed how Torrent claims that its unique technique for doing route table look up distinguishes it in the marketplace. Ascend makes a similar claim for the GRF 400. In particular, Ascend claims that key to the GRF 400's wire-speed performance is Ascend's unique hardware-assist table lookup technology. Ascend states that route lookup times range from 1-3 xt-hop routes in the table. Performance is enhanced even further with parallel processing of table lookups occurring on each media card, another technique that helps assure linear scalability. The route manager on the controller board, which also contains the switch fabric, maintains the master route table and distributes updates simultaneously to all installed media cards.

5.6.2 GRF 400 Functionality

Ascend is positioning the GRF 400 IP switch for large-scale public and private backbone applications. Packaged in a 5" high, rack-mountable chassis, the GRF 400 is configurable with four slots that accept plug-in media cards for external LAN/WAN interfaces. Available IP forwarding media cards include:

- 8-port 10/100 Mbps Ethernet
- 2-port 52 Mbps/45 mbps DS-3 HSSI
- 4-port 100 Mbps FDDI
- 2-port 155 Mbps OC-3 ATM
- 2-port 155 Mbps OC-3 SONET
- 1-port 800 Mbps HIPPI
- 1-port 622 Mbps OC-12 ATM

Ascend claims that the GRF 400 delivers wire-speed performance for any mix of LAN and WAN interfaces. Its full routing capabilities include support for RIPV1, RIPV2, BGP4, EGP, OSPF, IS-IS, and IGMP. The GRF 400 offers a variety of availability features including redundant load-balancing power supplies, hot-swappable media cards and power supplies, and remote SNMP-based management.

5.7 Summary

The Layer 3 switches discussed in this chapter have as many similarities as differences. From a marketing perspective, each one of the vendors is attacking the same weaknesses found in the traditional routers. However, some of the vendors are clearly targeting the enterprise market, i.e., 3Com, Bay, Extreme. Other vendors are targeting both the high end of the enterprise as well as the network service provider marketplace, i.e., Torrent, Ascend.

In terms of technical similarities, they all tend to separate route processing from route forwarding. In addition, they all tend to do route forwarding by a combination of hardware and software. Also, the majority of the Layer 3 switches support a variety of advanced features, such as QoS. However, while most of the products tend to support QoS, they do it in diverse ways. Other significant differences include the port densities as well as the level of resilience provided.

The authors will summarize recommended Layer 3 switch functionality in Chapter 9.

6 Flow Switching Approaches and Products

6.1 Introduction

In Chapter 4, we distinguished Layer 3 flow switching from packet-by-packet Layer 3 switching as not requiring every packet of a flow to be fully processed at Layer 3. Also, flow switching is slightly more general because it can be performed either on packets (for Token Ring or Ethernet environments) or on cells (in an ATM environment). This chapter provides a detailed discussion of a variety of flow-switching techniques. As in Chapter 5, however, we do not have the space or time to present every technique or every vendor's approach, so we have selected examples that are representative of a class of solutions or come from particular market-leading network equipment vendors of interest, as shown in Table 6.1. In contrast to Chapter 5, however, we have presented most in terms of architectures rather than specific products. In some cases, new products have either just begun to ship or have not shipped at all. Thus, it is very difficult to compare hardware, software, and specific features as in Chapter 5. Perhaps we can do that in the next edition of the book.

Table 6.1   Selected Layer 3 Flow-Switching Examples

End-System-Driven Flow Switching	Network-Centric Flow Switching
3Com: Fast IP	Cisco: NetFlow LAN Switching
Cabletron: SecureFast Virtual Networking	Cisco: Tag Switching
	Ipsilon: IP Switching
	ATM Forum: Multi-Protocol Over ATM

For those approaches that are new, your authors have once again relied heavily on information provided by vendors in describing how each one works. In general, we will emphasize the architecture that constitutes the approach rather than specific product implementations, which in most cases are quite new. Remember that MPOA is a relatively new standard and it may take time for products from various vendors to be tested, first for interoperability, and then for conformance to the details of the standard specifications.

6.2 3Com's Fast IP

Fast IP is an element of 3Com's TranscendWare^{TM} architecture. It is an end-system-driven flow-switching approach based on two premises:

- general-purpose routers cannot keep up with the performance demands of today's LANs; and
- only end-systems have enough application knowledge to make informed decisions about the performance requirements of particular communication flows.

From 3Com's perspective, decisions made within the network infrastructure (i.e., by switches and routers) are based more on guesswork than on knowledge of application requirements. Consequently, 3Com proposes that allowing end-systems to investigate and negotiate the potential for flow shortcuts should be a more effective mechanism. Of course it's hardly surprising that the world's market-leading NIC vendor would foster an end-system approach!

Fast IP works by having the source end-system (IP address "a" in Figure 6.1) keep track of where it is sending packets (IP address "b"). After sending some specific number of IP packets to a particular destination in a non-local subnet, the source will begin to look for a shortcut path. Using NHRP, it sends a Fast IP connection request that gets routed through the network just as the data packets have been, preserving all existing router control policies (such as authentication). If the destination end-system is also running Fast IP, it sends an NHRP response containing its own MAC address ("y" in Figure 6.1), directly back to the source station using the MAC address that came in the connection request ("x"). Switches along the return path for the NHRP response forward the packet on the basis of the destination MAC address (now "x"). If the original source end-system receives the NHRP response, it redirects subsequent packets directly to the destination's MAC address ("y"), effectively eliminating the router from the path. If no NHRP response is returned because there is no switched path between the two end-systems, packets continue to be routed as before. Notice that the path determination and thus the performance improvement is only *one-way*. 3Com suggests that this is not a significant limitation, because the bulk of long-lived flow traffic is likely to be from server to clients anyway.

The benefits 3Com claims for Fast IP include:

- provides L3 switching at L2 price/performance;
- runs over any underlying switching topology: ATM, Ethernet, Fast Ethernet, Gigabit Ethernet, FDDI;

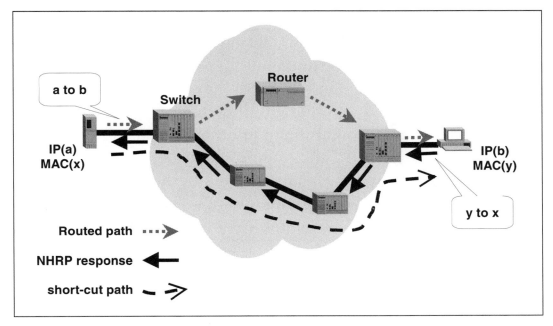

Figure 6.1   Operation of FastIP

- runs over existing switches and routers;
- runs over 3Com's and other vendors' NICs;
- is based on (draft) standard technology, i.e., NHRP; and
- is ready for 802.1Q (to bypass routing between different VLANs).

Fast IP software runs primarily on top of existing driver software for the end-system NIC (Figure 6.2). It interfaces with the end-system IP Stack and the NIC driver to coordinate the results of the NHRP exchange. Eventually 3Com would like to offer Fast IP hooks right into the application software, where the most detail about network performance requirements is seen to reside. How well this will match up with or support enterprise resource allocation policies is an open question as far as your authors are concerned.

Fast IP was made available first for 3Com's own NICs, as an element of their DynamicAccess™ software technology. Thus, it could be installed in a variety of ways, such as:

- using Etherdisk (3Com NIC-specific);
- obtaining self-extracting executables from the web;
- via software download packages (SMS, LANdesk Manager, McAfee, etc.); or
- using a login-based download.

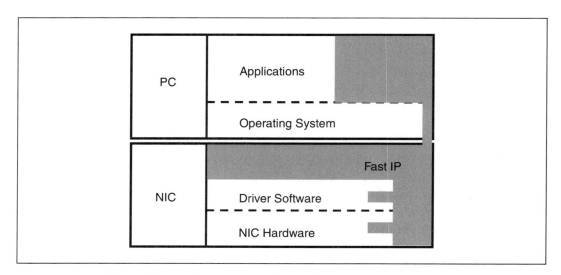

Figure 6.2   Implementation of FastIP Software in an End-System

In later releases, the latter three are also intended to support NICs from vendors other than 3Com.

As an alternative to running Fast IP in every end-station, 3Com offers Asymmetric Fast IP Proxy in their network switches. Switches at the edge of the network can thus negotiate on behalf of their locally attached end-stations. In Figure 6.1 for example, the switch to which IP station "a" is attached would keep track of the number of packets being sent to IP destination "b," and could initiate a Fast IP connection request for "a." If "b" is running Fast IP, it would return its own NHRP response. Otherwise the switch to which "b" is attached would need to be running the Proxy software in order to complete the negotiation.

In summary, Fast IP is intended to provide significant performance improvement when routing is performed over a switched infrastructure. As an end-system-driven approach, Fast IP can accelerate unidirectional IP traffic over existing NICs, switches, and routers—for any switched backbone structure. It is based on the well-known, but draft, standard of NHRP for routing. There is nothing inherently resilient about Fast IP, nor is there any security capability available through packet filtering.

6.3 Cabletron's SecureFast Virtual Networking

SecureFast Virtual Networking from Cabletron is a connection-oriented approach to building large, switched networks without routers. In retrospect, it was the first L3 flow-switching technique, with products first delivered to customers in early 1996. We classify SecureFast as an end-system-driven flow-switching approach because connections are built through the network for each end-to-end conversation, and each participating end-system requires modification.

SecureFast Virtual Networking approaches Layer 3 differently from traditional IP routing—it does not recognize any location restrictions or addressing hierarchy in the assignment of IP addresses. This removes traditional router constraints, such as requiring all hosts attached to a particular router port to have addresses within a single IP subnet. IP addresses can then be treated as unique host identifiers, independent of host location in the network (Figure 6.3). However, if interoperability with traditional IP is required, because there is a router somewhere within the LAN for example, then standard rules for IP networks apply—a single network or subnet cannot span more than one of the router interfaces. Figure 6.4 shows that assignment of the IP address 167.5.3.10 is invalid because the network 167.5 already exists on another router port.

In order for SecureFast to work, every participating end-system must be modified to support the "belief" that all IP destinations throughout the network are on their own local subnet. In standard IP communication, each host has a table entry to the router that acts as a default gateway for non-local destinations. This entry is usually a configuration parameter in each host system's IP software stack. For SecureFast hosts, the default gateway entry must be set to that host's own local IP address instead of the router's. Every source host (IPs) will thus begin each communication to an IP destination (IPd) with an ARP request if it does not already know the destination MAC address (Figure 6.5, step 1). SecureFast intercepts these ARP requests and rather than flooding them out all

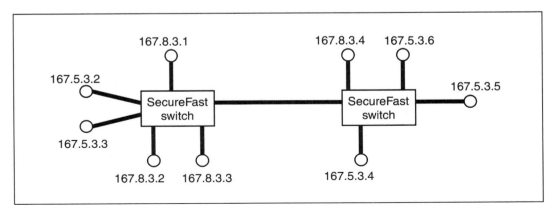

Figure 6.3 A SecureFast Virtual Network

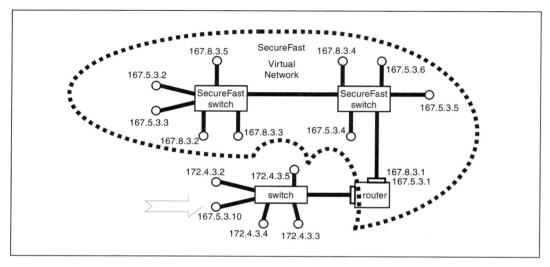

Figure 6.4   SecureFast Interoperability Requirements within a Routed Network

ports, sends a connection request (step 2) to the SecureFast Virtual Network (SFVN) server (which can be centralized or distributed) for the destination IP end-system. The server acts as a route server, resolving the IP destination to a MAC-level address and building a connection or flow pathway across the SecureFast switches (step 3) that sit between the source and destination. Subsequent traffic flows directly between the source and destination hosts (step 4) with all forwarding done at Layer 2. If the source host knows the destination MAC address, it begins communication with a unicast-addressed packet. Again, the local SecureFast Packet Switch (SFPS) understands a connection must be built, issues the connection request (step 2) to the SFVN Server, and all proceeds the same way.

Unfortunately, the ability to reset the address of the default gateway is not inherent to *all* IP protocol stacks. End-systems without this configurable parameter cannot participate in SecureFast Virtual Networks, thus limiting somewhat the applicability of this approach. For any destination that is not within the SecureFast Virtual Network, there must be a router attached to the edge of the SecureFast network in order to forward packets across what the SFVN hosts believe to be the local subnet boundary. In this case, the SFVN server builds a path from the source host to the edge router and returns the router's MAC-level address to the source. The source end-system thus proceeds to forward packets at Layer 2, but now they go only as far as the edge router, where they must be forwarded at Layer 3 as in traditional routing.

In essence, a SecureFast Virtual Network amounts to a single, flat, network-layer address space. This leads to at least three issues of additional concern:

- A centralized SFVN server is a critical resource that could be a single point of failure for the network.

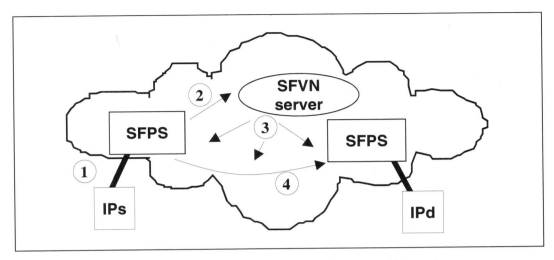

Figure 6.5   Virtual Routing in a SecureFast Virtual Network

- Distributed SFVN servers must have a way of keeping their common information up to date.
- IP subnet distinctions are no longer available to create boundaries between workgroups for security or other policy purposes.

6.4 Cisco's NetFlow LAN Switching

NetFlow LAN Switching is a network-centric flow switching approach for Cisco's Catalyst 5000 family of LAN switches. It is also based on the fundamental concept of flows. A network flow comprises a unidirectional stream of packets between a given source and destination, both defined by IP addresses, with a particular transport layer port number (watch out—here comes Layer 4!). The basic components of NetFlow LAN switching (logically depicted in Figure 6.6) are:

- the NetFlow Feature Card (NFFC), a daughter card to the Supervisor Engine (SE) module; and
- a companion router, either the Route Switch Module (RSM, a locally inserted router-on-a-card) or a locally attached "one-armed" router that gets and returns all its traffic to the local switch.

With these in place, no other changes are required in the LAN, i.e., NetFlow does not have to be implemented in *every* switch in the network to get improved performance. Typically, NetFlow will be used at the edges of a LAN, where the end-systems are attached.

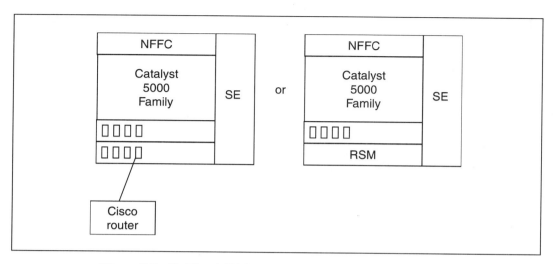

Figure 6.6   NetFlow LAN Switching Supported by a Local Router

All packets arriving at the Catalyst 5000 family switch (step 1 in Figure 6.7) traverse the Supervisor Engine (step 2). If the packet cannot be switched at Layer 2, it is passed to the NetFlow Feature Card (step 3). If no flow has been previously established (i.e., the NFFC does not find an entry in its local cache), the packet is passed to the router (external or RSM) for route processing (step 4). When the packet returns from the router, the SE again passes it to the NFFC (step 5), which caches the L3 address information and proceeds to process the packet through any remaining Layer 3 special service functions, such as authentication or accounting. Additional detail about the identified flow is also cached so that subsequent packets will not have to undergo the special services processing. Thus the first packet is routed by the router, processed by the NFFC, and forwarded by the NFFC on the basis of its L3 address (steps 6, 7, 8). Subsequent packets in the same flow are recognized by the NFFC from the cached L3 information and are forwarded without any router processing (Figure 6.8, steps 4, 5, 6).

The NetFlow Feature Card does not run routing protocols, calculate paths, or keep a routing table up to date. It must depend on the router/RSM for all these functions. Cisco implements a "lightweight" connectionless protocol between their routers and switches so that the routers can inform the Catalyst 5000 family switches of routing topology changes. The NFFC can thus purge stale cache entries to speed up convergence of the routed network. Cisco refers to NetFlow LAN switching as "packet-by-packet" because every packet is forwarded on the basis of the L3 address. We believe this simply adds confusion to the marketplace, when the essential nature of the scheme is so clearly based on flow identification and switching. Consequently, we have included it here rather than in Chapter 5.

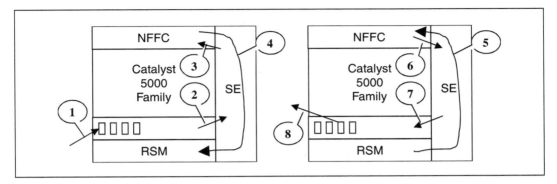

Figure 6.7 NetFlow Processing of the First Packet in a Flow

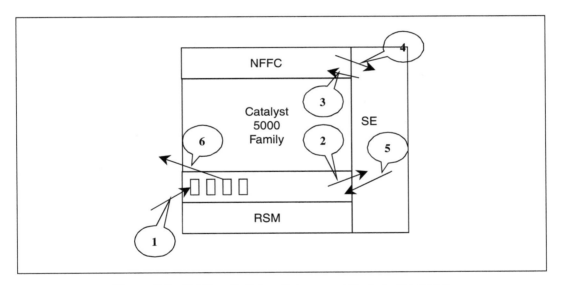

Figure 6.8 NetFlow Switches Subsequent Packets at Layer 3

6.5 Cisco's Tag Switching

Cisco actually has numerous approaches in its repertoire of Layer 3 switching solutions, with the various relationships shown in Table 6.2. As you can see, tag switching is positioned as a technology for Wide Area Networks (WANs). We include it here to make a clear distinction from Net-Flow. Tag switching is designed to blend Layer 2 switching and traffic management capabilities with the flexibility and scalability of Layer 3 routing functions. The basic concept is to associate a "tag" value with routing information that would get the packet or cell to its appropriate destination in the network. The advantage tag switching gains is when large numbers of packets, i.e., flows, can be tagged with the same value. Having a tag attached to individual packets or cells allows network switches to make very fast, efficient forwarding decisions using a technique called label swapping. For ATM networks, tags can be conveniently carried in the Virtual Channel Identifier field, with no modification of the ATM cell format required. For packet networks, the tag must either be placed in an existing frame field or be appended to the frame.

Table 6.2   Cisco's Layer 3 Solution Elements (source: Cisco)

	<- **Cisco IOS** ->		
	Campus	**Enterprise WAN Backbone**	**Service Provider**
NetFlow LAN Switching (L3 switching and services)	<<<<<<<>>>>>>	}	
		}Cisco FUSION	
NetFlow ATM (MPOA: Inter-VLAN L3 switching over ATM)	<<<<<<<>>>>>>	}	
NetFlow (scalable statistics and services)		<<<<<<<<<<<<<	>>>>>>>>>>>
Tag Switching (scalable Internet/ Intranet and advanced services)		<<<<<<<<<<<<<	>>>>>>>>>>>
Gigabit Switch Routing (multi-gigabit L3 performance with carrier-class availability)		<<<<<	>>>>>>>>>>>
Express Forwarding (efficient, full route table lookups)		<<<<<	>>>>>>>>>>>

Tag switching separates routing into two components: forwarding (includes what we have discussed previously as table lookup and forwarding) and control (what we have called route processing). When the forwarding component receives a tagged packet or cell, the tag is used as an index into a Tag Information Base (TIB). If a match is found, the incoming tag and L2 information are replaced by the outgoing tag and L2 information. The packet or cell is then sent to the appropriate outgoing interface port. The essential requirement is a binding between the tag and the routing information. Efficiency is gained by allowing a range of forwarding granularities, such as a group of routes (binding to the reachability information of the routes in the group), an individual application flow (e.g., an RSVP flow), or a multicast tree. It is the job of the control component, called routing function modules, to create the bindings and share information among tag switches. They also keep a hierarchy of routing knowledge for destination-based routing.

Tag switching uses existing routing protocols (e.g., OSPF, EIGRP) to establish reachability to destination networks (step 1a in Figure 6.9), but requires a new protocol, the Tag Distribution Protocol, in order to share information about tags among the network switches (step 1b). Ingress routers at the edge of the WAN receive packets, perform any L3 special services, and tag the packets (step 2). Within the WAN, packets are handled by a new switching mechanism that works on tags instead of addresses (i.e., using label swapping through the heart of the network, step 3) to deliver them across to the other edge. Egress routers then must remove the tag and deliver the packet to its destination LAN (step 4).

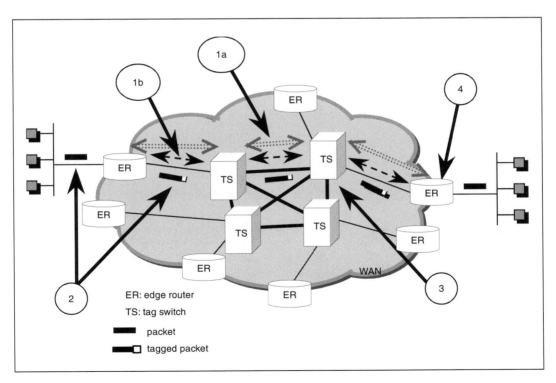

Figure 6.9   Elements and Operation of Tag Switching

Advantages Cisco suggests will accrue from tag switching are:

- It handles multiple protocols inherently.
- The forwarding component is simple enough to be suitable for hardware implementation.
- The forwarding component is flexible enough to support a variety of routing functions.
- The range of forwarding granularities (routes, groups, etc.) contributes to network scalability.

To foster acceptance, Cisco has submitted tag switching to the Internet Engineering Task Force (IETF) for consideration by the Multi-Protocol Label Swapping (MPLS) working group (which Cisco co-chairs with IBM). Appropriate tag switching features and operations will be married to characteristics from other submissions (such as IBM's Aggregate Routing Information Service or Toshiba's Cell Switch Routing) to create a standard definition for MPLS.

6.6 Multi-Protocol Over ATM (MPOA)

Multi-Protocol over ATM (Asynchronous Transfer Mode) is a set of standards first ratified by the ATM Forum in July 1997. The Forum's goals for MPOA included:

- Creating a simple model for migration to ATM from legacy LAN infrastructures;
- Decoupling the logical from the physical network structure (i.e., virtualization of functions such as routing);
- Supporting scalability to increasingly large networks;
- Providing Quality of Service to QoS-aware applications; and
- Developing new internetworking functions that are enabled by the nature of ATM.

MPOA creates a standard way to run end-to-end Layer 3 networking over an ATM infrastructure (Figure 6.10), integrating routing functions without creating any bottlenecks or latency that would inhibit performance. In fact, MPOA is the *only* standard method to date for flow switching. It builds upon or incorporates other standards, such as LAN Emulation (LANE, for bridging of MAC-layer protocols like Ethernet; LANE version 2 is integral to MPOA) and Next-Hop Routing Protocol (NHRP), in order to provide flow switching capabilities in the cell domain.

Figure 6.10 shows several IP hosts connected to an ATM backbone network, either directly (IP host 1) or from other LANs (IP hosts 2 and 3) via an MPOA edge device (designated by the triangle). These hosts can talk to each other via LAN Emulation (LANE) if they are members of a single emulated LAN (ELAN), or must use MPOA if they belong to different ELANs (e.g., IP hosts 2

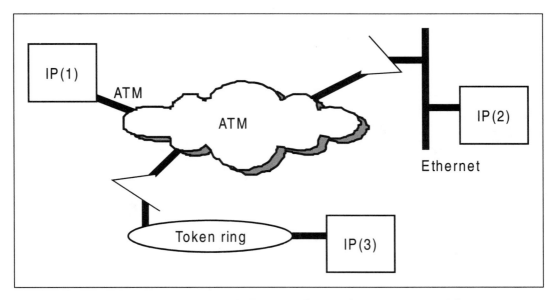

Figure 6.10   Traditional LAN Elements Connected over ATM by MPOA

and 3 are on distinct L2 LANs). This is quite analogous to the need for a router to interconnect VLANs or IP subnets or to translate between Ethernet and Token Ring protocols. MPOA provides virtual routing capabilities across an ATM network. The first version of the standard supports IP traffic; later versions will add other L3 protocols.

MPOA uses a client-server model to separate route processing from packet forwarding and create a flow-switching L3 approach (Figure 6.11). The MPOA Client (MPC) in the edge device or the ATM-attached host examines the L3 destination address of each packet it receives from local host(s). If the L3 destination address can be resolved to an ATM (L2 MAC) address from locally cached information or by contacting the MPOA server, the MPOA client establishes a direct Virtual Channel Connection (VCC) to the destination and all packets in the flow get switched there. If the MPOA server does not know the ATM address of the destination, it propagates the client's query to other servers using NHRP. Thus MPOA clients do only table lookup and packet forwarding (by putting the information into cells, of course), while the MPOA server handles all route processing. MPOA includes mechanisms to coordinate activity among multiple servers to avoid having a single, critical resource and to provide a resilient network.

As an architecture, MPOA lends itself to various questions about operational scalability when it gets implemented, such as:

- How large a cache will be necessary for the MPOA clients to function well?

- Will flows be long enough that time saved by switching will outweigh the VCC setup time?

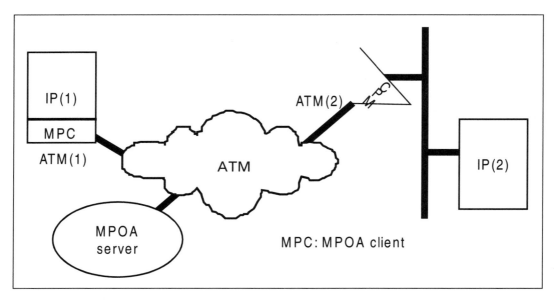

Figure 6.11   MPOA Server and Its Clients in Hosts and Edge Devices

- What will the performance be when many VCCs must be set up at the same time?
- What impact will network convergence have for traffic with various classes of service?

During the development and approval cycle for the MPOA standard, some ATM vendors jumped ahead to implement proprietary extensions to earlier ATM standards like NHRP and LANE version 1. In retrospect, we might think of these as **pre-standard** versions of MPOA. Two notable examples are:

- Multiprotocol Switched Services as a key component of IBM's Switched Virtual Network architecture (MSS is also provided by Xylan under a partnership arrangement with IBM); and
- Switched Routing products from Newbridge Networks (see the case study in Chapter 7).

6.7 Ipsilon's IP Switching

Ipsilon was an early leader in developing methods to route IP traffic across an ATM backbone infrastructure. By keeping to a proprietary approach, Ipsilon was able to deliver IP switching (and license it to other vendors) long before MPOA-standard products could be developed. IP switching is a network-centric flow-switching approach that consists of three main elements:

- The IP switching engine: proprietary code licensed to other vendors such as Digital and Hitachi—responsible for identifying flows and mapping them to ATM circuits;

- IFMP, Ipsilon Flow Management Protocol: a protocol needed to share information about flow labels and to enable flow switching at Layer 2 instead of Layer 3; and

- GSMP, the General Switch Management Protocol: a protocol to control ATM switches internally as they manage switch ports, establish and tear down connections through the switch, etc.

IP switching begins with IP packets being forwarded hop by hop over a well-known virtual channel (VC). At each hop, the IP packets are reassembled from the ATM cells in order to be routed, and then segmented back into ATM cells for forwarding (Figure 6.12, step 1). The IP Switch Controller makes a flow classification decision based on the characteristics of the received packet. If the packet is suitable for flow switching, the IP switch controller sends a redirect message to the upstream node (step 2 in Figure 6.13), telling it to use a specific, different VC for traffic belonging to this particular flow. Subsequent packets are forwarded over the new VC, as in step 3. In Figure 6.14, step 4 shows that the downstream node has made a flow classification decision, and also sends a redirect message upstream (in this case, to the IP switch controller under consideration) requesting that it use a different, specific VC for subsequent traffic belonging to this flow. Remember that in ATM, the VC identification is local to an individual node, so there is no relationship between the VCs used by different nodes, except as the ATM switch builds its mapping between input and output ports. Step 5 shows that subsequent traffic will be forwarded over the new VC. Finally, in Figure 6.15, step 6 shows that the ATM switch has constructed its mapping to relate the two VCs, and all traffic for this flow will subsequently be switched at Layer 2 with no further involvement of the IP switch controller.

IP switching thus provides high performance forwarding of IP traffic across an ATM infrastructure. Once a flow is established, the IP packets need not be reassembled from cells at each hop. Traffic that consists of long streams of packets will benefit most from flow switching, such as for file transfers (FTP), file sharing (NFS), web/browser interaction (HTTP), and multimedia streams of audio and video. Traffic that primarily occurs in short-lived flows, such as mail (SMTP, POP) and management (DNS, SNMP), are better handled with store-and-forward techniques. IP switching recognizes these at flow classification time and does not bother to set up flows for them.

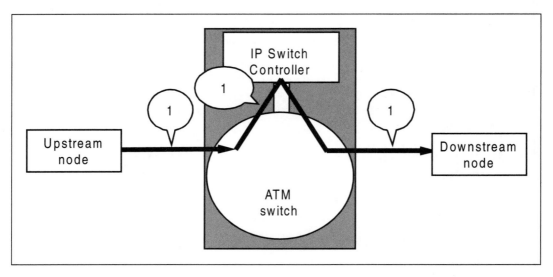

Figure 6.12   IP Switch Processing of Packets to be Routed

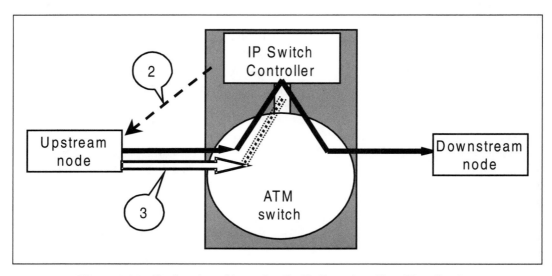

Figure 6.13   Redirection of Incoming Traffic Based on Flow Classification

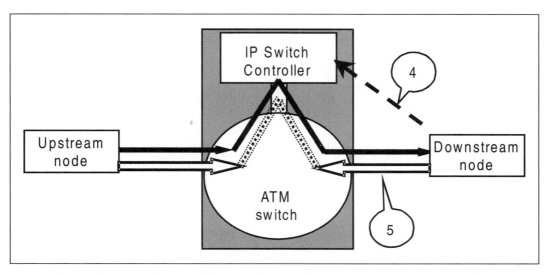

Figure 6.14   Redirection of Outbound Traffic Based on Downstream Information

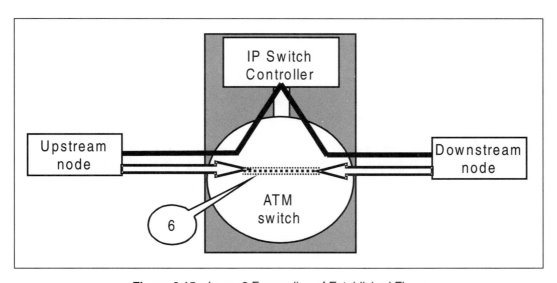

Figure 6.15   Layer 2 Forwarding of Established Flows

IP switching's inherent routing capability allows interconnection of subnets and VLANs across the intervening ATM infrastructure. In fact, IP switching supports all standard IP routing protocols, improving performance for unicast or multicast traffic flows. All standard SNMP MIBs and management tools are also supported. Ipsilon has even suggested that IP switching can be used over a WAN, creating high-performance wide-area IP networks that make efficient use of WAN link capacity. We believe that such performance claims need to be verified according to the types of traffic that characterizes your environment. Only then will it be clear whether your typical traffic flows are long enough to benefit.

One important shortcoming of IP switching is that only IP is supported across the ATM infrastructure; other protocols must be tunneled. Also, despite the fact that Ipsilon has published specifications for IFMP and GSMP, they are still non-standard, and the switch controller remains highly proprietary. In general, your authors wonder what the long-term viability and interest in IP Switching will be. First, MPOA has been ratified by the ATM Forum so there is now a standard for flow switching. Most customers tend to prefer a standards-based approach to proprietary ones. Secondly, Ipsilon's acquisition by Nokia raises some concern about future support and further development. Lastly, many of Ipsilon's partners may find it simpler to invest in their own packet-by-packet implementations, as standard hardware components become more available.

6.8 Summary

Many flow-switching techniques were originally developed on the premise that routing is slow and expensive. Packet-by-packet L3 switching products have demonstrated that this is no longer the case. With all the complexities and unknowns associated with flow switching, many people will prefer to implement L3 PxP in their LANs. Only if they choose ATM backbones for their LAN will they be forced into flow switching with MPOA. Flow switching is more likely to find its place in the WAN, becoming of more interest to service providers than to enterprise customers.

7 *Layer 3 Switching Case Study*

7.1 Introduction

The authors wanted to understand how the various vendors propose to solve production-networking problems with their new Layer 3 switching products. To address this, the authors asked a number of the leading vendors to respond to a case study involving the need for Layer 3 switching. The case study was one that was used by Strategic Networks in their fall seminar entitled Interop NetSwitch '97 Tour. *The authors have made no attempt to edit the content provided by the vendors.*

The authors intentionally used a case study that was not very detailed. Our motivation was to allow the vendors the flexibility to articulate what they believe are the key networking issues and how they can best be solved. The advantage of this approach is that it yields a range of solutions which correspond to the broad set of problems faced in production networks. The disadvantage of this approach is that it makes it difficult, if not impossible, to compare in a strict fashion one solution with the other.

In addition to using a case study that was not very detailed, the authors gave minimum direction to the vendors. We did, however, set a limit on how long their responses could be. In addition, we asked them to:

- Indicate the expected ship date for any product that was not currently shipping;
- Clearly state any design assumptions as well as decision criteria that they believe are important; and
- Describe pricing, if it is mentioned—indicate if it is list or if not, indicate the discount rate assumed.

One additional degree of flexibility that the authors gave to the vendors is that we did not restrict them to presenting a solution based on frame switching. We also allowed for solutions based on cell switching, a.k.a., ATM. The authors acknowledge that this further exacerbates the difficulty of comparing solutions in an unduly strict fashion. However, it does provide more input to the reader in terms of alternative solutions.

7.2 The Case Study

A pharmaceutical company has recently implemented a new set of networked applications to improve its time to market new products. These networked applications are a combination of SAP, WEB, and custom developed. Along with these new applications came a significant increase in traffic flow (both intra and inter-subnet), and an investment in switching technology for their wiring centers. The investment in switching increased bandwidth and network performance for a little while. However, now the inter-subnet traffic flows continue to increase week after week. As a result, the routers that the company purchased in 1994 are a bottleneck.

As shown in Figure 7.1, while the wiring center has been upgrading to switching, workgroups have just started to receive switched connections. The FDDI campus network that connects the 3 buildings has been in place since 1994 and is working fine. The network in total consists of 5,000 desktops, 50 subnets and 10 routers. In addition to Ethernet connections, there are 10 Token Ring segments that terminate into these routers. In essence this firm has made network investments all around their routers, but not in them. The routers each have a capacity of 100Kpps throughput, not enough to keep up with the FDDI backbone.

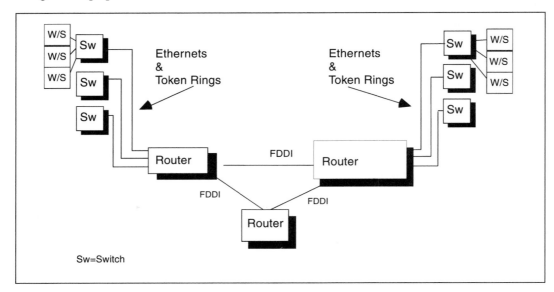

Figure 7.1   The Pharmaceutical Company's Existing Network

The current situation is stressing the existing network. Network executives within the pharmaceutical company are now exploring ways to remove the routing bottleneck while preserving the existing subnet structure. In addition, more WEB-based applications are being developed, including IP multicast-based applications to facilitate concurrent engineering. These new applications will further aggravate an already strained network.

7.3 The Cisco Response

The Cisco approach to this case study is to preserve the existing logical address structure while introducing high-performance Layer-Two (L2) switching and Layer-Three (L3) switching. The hierarchical design approach allows campus intranets to scale in a very deterministic and manageable way. Preserving the existing networks and subnets allows existing administrative policy to remain in effect. The hierarchical design also allows flexible technology choices to be made at each layer of the design. In formulating our response to this case study, Cisco has assumed that this customer requires a high degree of resiliency.

The overall approach is summarized in Figure 7.2. The design has three layers, designated access layer, distribution layer, and core layer. The access layer is the wiring closet. It has traditionally been Ethernet and Token Ring hubs. In this design, L2 switches are introduced into the access layer. Since hubs and L2 switches are both L2 devices, the network addressing is preserved when switching is introduced. The icons represent Cisco Catalyst family switches.

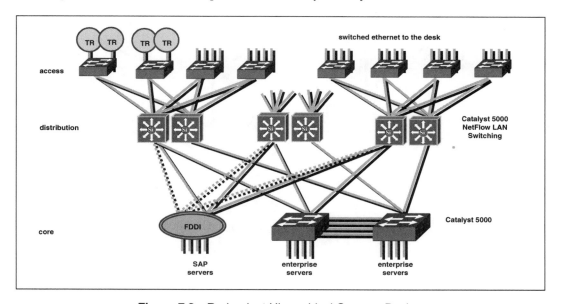

Figure 7.2   Redundant Hierarchical Campus Design

In the distribution layer, the existing routers are upgraded to Catalyst family switches with NetFlow LAN Switching (NFLS). NFLS has all the features of the Cisco Internetwork Operating System (IOS) with the added performance of L3 switching in hardware for IP. The icons represent a Catalyst 5000 family switch with the Cisco Route Switch Module (RSM) and the NetFlow Feature Card (NFFC). The RSM is a Cisco 7500 class router on a card, and provides multi-protocol routing. The NFFC provides hardware-based L3 switching of IP packets with ASICs. NFLS is characterized as packet-by-packet L3 switching because it supports header rewrite for all routed packets, in accordance with routing standards.

In the distribution layer, redundancy is provided with a pair of NFLS switches in each building. Each access-layer switch or hub is dual homed to the pair. Fast failover and load balancing over the redundant trunks is achieved in different ways. If the access-layer device is a Cisco switch, load balancing can be achieved using VLAN trunking. Figure 7.3 illustrates this feature. For switch A, the left trunk is the forwarding path for VLAN 1 and the blocking path for VLAN 2. The right trunk is the forwarding path for VLAN 2 and the blocking path for VLAN 1. If either trunk fails, all the traffic is directed to the remaining trunk.

In Figure 7.3, each VLAN maps to an IP subnet. The topology of each VLAN is a triangle between the access switch and the two distribution switches. Because the VLAN is constrained to a simple triangle, the scaling limits of spanning tree protocol (STP) do not apply. Cisco takes advantage of this with a feature called Uplink Fast. With Uplink Fast enabled at the access switch, a link failure is recovered to the redundant path in about three seconds. TCP sessions will easily recover from a network disconnect of three seconds.

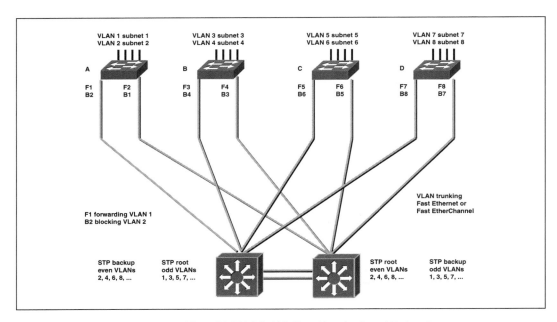

Figure 7.3   Virtual LAN (VLAN) Trunking for Load Balancing

Figure 7.4 illustrates IP gateway redundancy with Cisco's Hot Standby Router Protocol (HSRP). Client A is on VLAN 1, which is subnet 131.108.1.0. The gateway router is 131.108.1.200. NFLS switch X is the HSRP primary gateway for odd subnets 1.0, 3.0, 5.0, and 7.0. So switch X acts as 131.108.1.200, 131.108.3.200, 131.108.5.200 and 131.108.7.200. If power to switch X is disconnected, switch Y will take over as the HSRP gateway for both odd and even subnets. When this transition happens, switch Y will assume the HSRP IP address as well as the HSRP MAC address, so client workstations will not notice a change. The HSRP transition takes about two seconds with default settings.

Figure 7.5 shows a simpler way to achieve redundancy between access layer and distribution layer. Spanning tree is eliminated completely by reducing each VLAN just two links. Redundancy is reduced somewhat compared to Figure 7.3, but configuration is somewhat simpler. Load balancing is achieved by assigning hosts on different VLANs to different HSRP gateways. We take advantage of Cisco's ISL VLAN trunking protocol to overlay two (or more) VLANs on the trunks.

In Figure 7.2, the core layer consists of the existing dual-homed FDDI backbone with the addition of a switched Fast Ethernet backbone. Enterprise servers with Fast Ethernet NICs can attach directly to a Catalyst switch. Servers with existing FDDI NICs can remain FDDI attached.

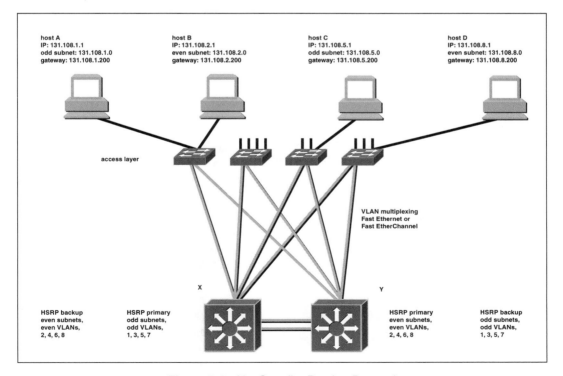

Figure 7.4   Hot Standby Routing Protocol

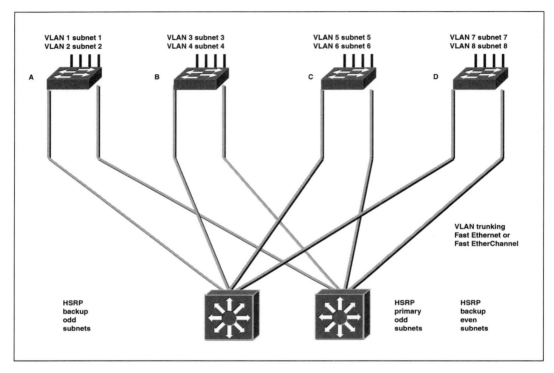

Figure 7.5   Simple Redundancy with No Spanning Trees

The existing logical structure can be preserved by using translational bridging (TLB) between the FDDI backbone and the Fast Ethernet backbone making them a single IP subnet. One reason for keeping the FDDI backbone in place is for trunking bridged Token Ring applications that use frames longer than the 1500 Bytes supported by Ethernet.

Scaling bandwidth can be achieved with Cisco's Fast EtherChannel (FEC). As illustrated in Figure 7.6, a FEC trunk is a bundle of two or four FDX Fast Ethernet trunks. If one link in a FEC bundle fails traffic is directed over the remaining links. FEC can be used to connect Cisco switches, Cisco routers, and high-speed servers. An enterprise server could be attached directly to the core network with a FDX 400Mbps FEC bundle. Gigabit Ethernet interfaces and switching cards will be available for Cisco products in 1998.

There is a rapid rise of IP multicast applications such as IPTV and Microsoft NetMeeting and NetShow. Multicast traffic can have a significant effect on an Intranet, and should be considered in this design. Figure 7.7 illustrates the protocol components of IP multicast. The IP multicast routing protocol is Protocol Independent Multicast (PIM). Multicast servers advertise sessions with Internet Group Multicast Protocol (IGMP). Multicast clients join sessions with IGMP as well. Cisco routers or NFLS switches keep track of the servers and clients and route the traffic efficiently. Cisco

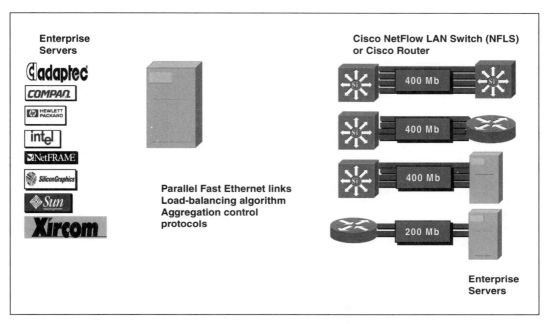

Figure 7.6   Scaling Bandwidth with Fast EtherChannel

routers or NFLS switches use Cisco Group Multicast Protocol (CGMP) to tell Cisco L2 switches which multicasts to distribute to which clients, which prevents flooding of multicast traffic to all ports. The Cisco IOS supports rate limiting for multicast sessions.

Figure 7.8 represents the option of providing an ATM backbone. The access layer and the distribution layer are the same as Figure 7.2, but ATM LAN Emulation replaces switched Ethernet in the core. The reason for provisioning an ATM backbone network could be support for high-speed real-time video applications. The green links represent ATM OC3 or OC12 trunks. Access into the core is by the LAN Emulation card for the Catalyst 5000 switch. The dotted green lines represent hot standby ATM trunks from the LANE card. Redundant LANE support services are supported by the Cisco IOS. In particular redundant LANE Server/Broadcast and Unknown Servers (LES/BUS) are provided on the two Catalyst 5500 switches in the core. Robust ATM routing and load balancing is provided by the PNNI protocol. The Catalyst 5500 is chosen because it incorporates both ATM and Ethernet switching.

Cisco recommends using Open Shortest Path First (OSPF) or Cisco's Enhanced Internet Gateway Routing Protocol (EIGRP) as the unicast routing protocol. The choice between OSPF and EIGRP will depend on several factors. Both OSPF and EIGRP support fast convergence and Variable Length Subnet Masks (VLSM) as well as summarized routing. OSPF is a standard protocol, and interoperates with other vendors with standard OSPF implementations. With EIGRP access lists can be applied between any two adjacent routers, whereas with OSPF access lists are not

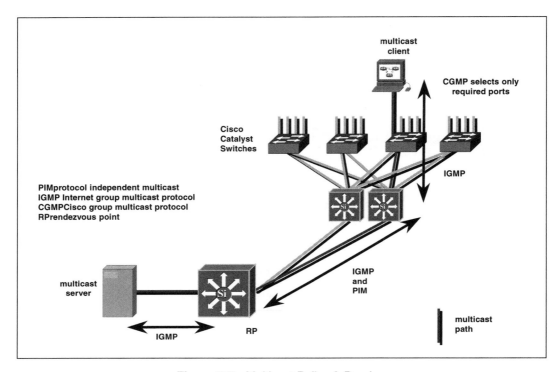

Figure 7.7   Multicast Policy & Pruning

allowed within an area. Upgrading from RIP to OSPF typically requires re-addressing, while upgrading from RIP to EIGRP does not.

Some designs try to maximize the use of L2 performance by putting all the hosts in a single subnet. Cisco advises you to consider the risks of putting more than a couple hundred hosts in a subnet. A single faulty NIC card can cause problems for the whole subnet. In addition, the more hosts in the subnet the harder it is to troubleshoot these problems. This is even truer for other proto-cols such as Novell IPX and AppleTalk than it is for IP. It is of limited benefit to have a structured, routed IP design if all your AppleTalk and IPX traffic is bridged everywhere!

The reader should be wary of designs that eliminate routing or focus all the routing into a sin-gle router on a stick. With the 20/80 traffic model the router on a stick is a bottleneck. The limita-tions of spanning tree protocol affect a campus-wide VLAN as they do an extended bridged network. STP convergence takes up to 50 seconds, compared to just a few seconds for OSPF or EIGRP. STP does not support load balancing over multiple redundant links, and blocks all loops in the topology. The Cisco IOS implementation of OSPF, EIGRP, and other routing protocols support load balancing over up to six paths.

Support for network-wide features are more important than the performance characteristics of any particular box within the design. For example, uniform administration and configuration will

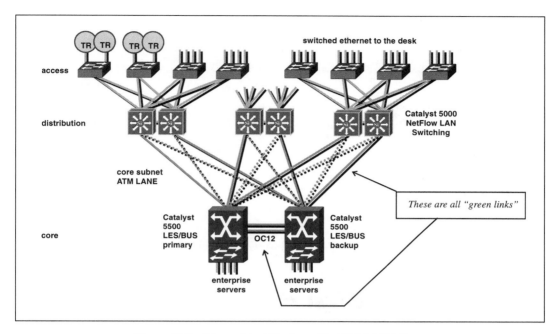

Figure 7.8 Hierarchical Design with ATM LANE Core

save time. Availability of extensive debugging and troubleshooting features will improve availability. Interoperability of protocols and features are an important consideration. Many features are required to handle all the protocols and policy requirements of the typical complex intranet.

And finally, a lot of thought should be taken to choose the appropriate design model for a large corporate intranet. Choose the best design before considering which specific products to use to implement the design. If you start with a particular product in mind, you may end up designing your network around the limitations of that product. In most cases raw performance is less important than application support and support from your vendor.

7.4 The Newbridge Response

The environment depicted in this case study is similar to many other network infrastructures. There is an increase in demand for new types of applications, yet the existing router-based backbone is ill-equipped to handle the new traffic load. Specifically, the following issues must be addressed:

Routing performance needs to be improved. More bandwidth is required. The introduction of new applications means that traffic volumes are increasing significantly. In the past, it was more than adequate for routers to process one or two hundred thousand packets per second. Now this rate of throughput is becoming a limitation. In addition, network latency (the time it takes for a packet to leave its source and arrive at its destination) and jitter (i.e., variation in latency) need to be reduced. Whereas these issues were of little importance when the network was only used for workgroup traffic and e-mail, they become intrinsic with the introduction of new, time sensitive applications.

New applications must be supported. In addition to mere routing performance, the network infrastructure needs to have the intelligence to adequately handle special applications, such as IP multicast and videoconferencing. For example, the network must guarantee bandwidth between communicating nodes, and allocate various levels of quality of service to different traffic flows.

Network management must be enhanced. The network infrastructure is growing dramatically in size. Furthermore, new applications are being introduced. These changes can easily complicate network management. The network infrastructure, therefore, must increase routing capacity without increasing the overall complexity.

A migration plan is required. A smooth transition is required to migrate from the existing solution to the next generation infrastructure. In an effort to minimize transition pains, the new solution must leverage existing hardware investments (e.g., NICs, cabling, hubs, switches, and routers), support existing applications and protocols, and preserve existing subnet structures.

In order to address all of these issues, Newbridge recommends its MultiProtocol over ATM (MPOA) solution, "Switched Routing." Based upon the ATM Forum's standard for doing bridging and routing over an ATM infrastructure, switched routing enables network administrators to provide high speed, scaleable LAN backbones that are easy to manage and cost effective.

Designing the Network

In the proposed network design (Figure 7.9), a CS 3000 ATM switch will be placed in each building. This will provide the campus with an OC-3 (155 Mbps) backbone. By using PNNI, a routing protocol developed by the ATM Forum, this backbone will be fully redundant, with load sharing, traffic management, and QoS capabilities between buildings. With an ATM backbone, this environment is both robust and scaleable. Furthermore, bandwidth is guaranteed between communicating devices, thus enabling all application types.

A set of Newbridge-supplied switches called Ridges will be used in each building to provide frame interfaces into the switched routing backbone. In this instance, Orange Ridges would be used to provide wire-speed routed 10/100 Ethernet ports. In addition, a Red Ridge will be used to provide FDDI connectivity, which would enable this environment to maintain its existing investment in router equipment.

By using Ridges, this design preserves the existing desktop and workgroup environment, while providing access to a higher speed routing backbone. Existing Ethernet and/or Fast Ethernet hubs and switches, for example, can be plugged directly into Ridge ports, as can individual high-end users equipped with 10/100 NICs. Furthermore, by mapping IP, IPX, and other conventional LAN protocols onto ATM VCs, this network environment supports all existing applications.

The final component associated with this network design is a route server. The route server is the "brains" of the network. It is responsible for discovering where each end user is located, and providing Ridges with the information required to reach each of these individual users. The Route Server is a central repository for enterprise-wide policies, such as access control lists, filtering information, and routing rules. Furthermore, it is a central access point for network troubleshooting.

The route server can be placed in any of the buildings associated with this case study. A redundant route server can also be deployed (either in the same building or in another building) to provide fault tolerance in the unlikely event of a hardware failure.

Integrated tightly with the route server is NetDirector, Newbridge's platform for management of the switched routing products. NetDirector provides a single set of tools to manage both the frame and ATM physical interfaces in this network environment. In addition, the PRISM suite of tools can be deployed to manage the applications and systems that reside in the network as well. These applications, coupled with extensive Java-enabled WEB management tools, make NetDirector an ideal management platform for this network.

Solving the Problems

By distributing routing functionality between optimized devices, switched routing alleviates many of the issues associated with routers.

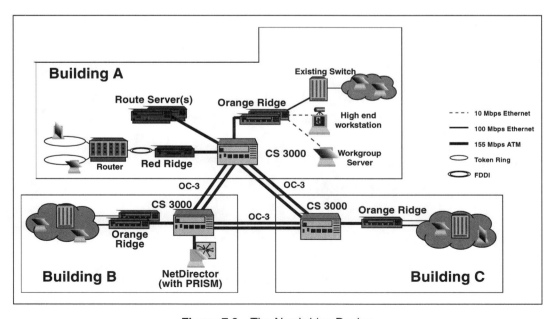

Figure 7.9   The Newbridge Design

Scaleable Wire Speed Routing Throughput

Switched routing vastly improves routing performance. In fact, as proven in the Harvard Network Device Test Lab (Figure 7.10), each Ridge provides wire speed bridging and routing throughput. That is because all forwarding is done in ATM hardware (as opposed to software, which is inherently slower). Furthermore, Ridges are able to detect flows of network traffic and map them onto ATM shortcut paths. This means that routing table lookups do not have to be performed on every single packet of data.

The switched routing environment is unique in that it can maintain wire speed routing performance across several hundred ports. Since it leverages ATM switches as a distributed routing backplane, adding new ports does not degrade overall routing capacity, as is often the case with a single router. In fact, the Newbridge environment tested in Figure 7.10 consisted of 50 routed ports. This test could have easily been scaled to support 600 wire speed ports. This level of scalability is intrinsic to environments that are experiencing an increase in users, as well as an increase in traffic volume. Consequently, it is vital to the network infrastructure portrayed in this case study.

Reduced Latency/No Jitter

In a conventional router-based infrastructure, every packet of data must be processed by every router that separates the source host from the destination. This takes time (i.e., latency). Furthermore, since some routers can be more congested than others, there is no way to predict exactly how much time this process takes (i.e., jitter). This makes routers ill-equipped to handle time-sensitive applications.

Switched routing, on the other hand, eliminates these issues. That is because routing table lookups are only performed on the first packet of an unrecognized traffic flow. After this lookup has

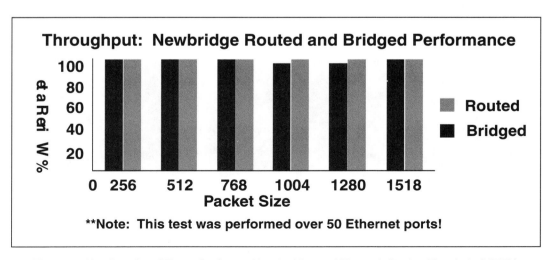

Figure 7.10   Results of Tests Performed by the Harvard Network Device Test Lab (NDTL)

been performed, the rest of the packets are mapped onto an ATM shortcut path that connects the originating Ridge to the destination Ridge, and the appropriate address information is cached on these Ridges for future usage. By using shortcut paths, router hops are eliminated. In fact, in the worst case scenario (i.e., when an unrecognized packet has been discovered and a Ridge must query the route server), there is only one router hop that has to be traversed. By minimizing router hops, switched routing minimizes network latency and jitter. As mentioned previously, this is vital when deploying isochronous (i.e., time sensitive) applications, such as the concurrent engineering tool.

As Figure 7.11 shows, testing performed by the Strategic Networks group indicates that switched routing minimizes latency and jitter to the point where it can adequately support all of the applications required in this network environment.

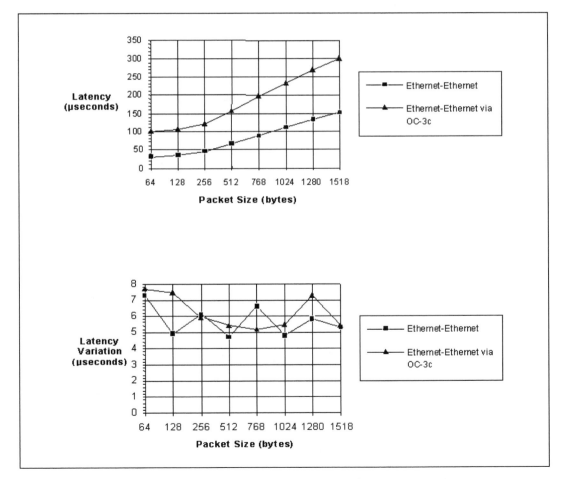

Figure 7.11　Results of Tests Performed by Strategic Networks

Support for Emerging Applications

By using short cut ATM paths between communicating nodes, switched routing offers other advantages over traditional routers. For one, the network infrastructure guarantees that there is adequate bandwidth allocated to each traffic flow for the entire duration of the communications process. By performing various levels of quality of service and flow control, bandwidth across the entire network can be utilized most efficiently. This will enable the company in this case study to deploy any application—from electronic mail to videoconferencing—over a single infrastructure. Furthermore, since these short cut paths can be point-to-multipoint as well as simply point-to-point, multicast applications are supported in this network infrastructure as efficiently as unicast ones.

Centralized Network Management

The switched routing architecture also facilitates the configuration, management, and troubleshooting associated with routing infrastructures. Specifically, switched routing assists network administrators by dramatically reducing the time and resources spent on reactive management tasks (e.g., responding to SNMP alerts, analyzing existing traffic patterns, detecting duplicate network addresses, and resolving network storms). That is because all access control lists, routing rules, filtering information, and other policies can be configured on a single, centralized device—the route server. This information is then disseminated to all Ridges, where it is implemented locally (Figure 7.12). With this architecture, network administrators need only configure a single device when making changes to existing routing policies. Similarly, when troubleshooting network problems, all information can be attained via this device. This is dramatically different from a traditional router-based infrastructure, where routing information is configured on a port-by-port, box-by-box basis.

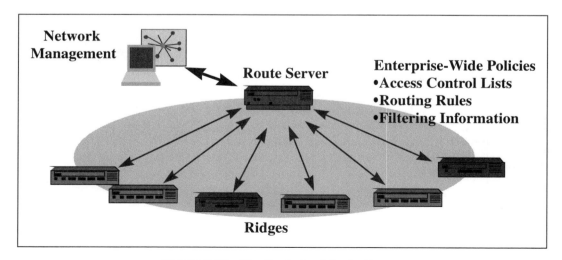

Figure 7.12   The Centralized Route Server

By having to configure each router individually, more time and resources are spent on network configuration, there is a greater risk of making configuration errors, and it is more difficult to detect and resolve network problems.

In fact, a recent study conducted by The Registry, Inc. concluded that transitioning from a router-based infrastructure to an MPOA-based solution can decrease time spent on reactive tasks by as much as 46%. This reduction in reactive tasks also spurred a 40% increase in proactive tasks, such as network design, capacity planning, application development, and network upgrades. Much of these gains were derived from the fact that administrators in MPOA environments spent 14% less time on network configuration and 25% less time supporting moves, adds, and changes, than they did when supporting a traditional router-based infrastructure.

Migration Path

As mentioned previously, with switched routing there is little or no change to the desktop and workgroups in this case study. By using Ridges, investments in existing Ethernet, Fast Ethernet, and FDDI equipment can be preserved. Furthermore, since IP, IPX, AppleTalk and other conventional protocols are mapped onto the ATM fabric, existing applications remain untouched.

By using switched routing, network administrators can also preserve their existing subnet structures. That is because Newbridge offers industry leading virtual networking services. In a switched routing environment, individual Ridge ports can be assigned membership into any IP subnet. Consequently, each port can assume the same subnet identity as an existing router port. This eliminates the need to reconfigure individual hosts, thus making the Newbridge solution truly plug-n-play.

In fact, with switched routing, individual subnets can be applied to many (or all) Ridge ports. This lets users move anywhere in their network environment and maintain access to their IP resources. Furthermore, with this feature, called VNETtracker, users can attain access to NetWare, AppleTalk, and other protocol-based resources, regardless of their physical location. This is very useful in network environments where end-users are constantly being added or are changing locations.

Cost

The benefits and issues listed above, although important to network administrators, become moot if the cost of the proposed solution is too exorbitant. Although the Newbridge solution leverages ATM, it is actually more cost effective than conventional router-based approaches.

For example, this network design would require three CS 3000s (one per building), five Orange Ridges, one Red Ridge, a Route Server, and NetDirector. This is a total hardware investment of approximately $156,000 (using ASP). This solution provides 60 wire speed routed 10/100 Ethernet ports, 36 ATM ports, and 1 FDDI port. As a result, the cost/routed port (fully managed) of this new network infrastructure is $1,608.

The cost savings become even more significant when one examines ongoing operation costs. According to The Registry, the 46% less time that was spent on reactive tasks resulted in an opportunity cost saving (per annum) of over $300,000. Furthermore, the 40% increase in proactive tasks found by The Registry resulted in a financial benefit of $600,000/year at the studied sites. These are substantial figures when one examines the scarcity of IT resources and the downsizing of IT budgets in recent years.

What To Look Out For

The term "Layer 3 Switching" is fairly broad. It is easy to get lost in all of the marketing hype surrounding this field. As a result, when choosing a backbone routing solution, there are a couple of key areas to consider:

- Reality vs. Hype—Are the products actually shipping? Is there a significant number of customer installations?

- Forklift Upgrades—Will implementing the solution require the replacement of existing equipment? Is the solution plug-n-play?

- Application Support—Will the network infrastructure support today's video, voice, and data needs? Will it grow with emerging requirements?

- Facilitated Management—Can enterprise-wide policies be centrally administered? Is access to network resources strictly governed by physical location? Is troubleshooting done on a box-by-box basis?

- Standards—Will the solution interoperate with other vendors' equipment?

Switched routing is a proven LAN internetworking solution that is installed in over 300 production networks. Based upon the only Layer 3 switching standard available today, MPOA, it is an open solution that will interoperate with other vendors' frame and cell-based technologies. Finally, switched routing is an ideal way of supporting a variety of traffic types, from e-mail to videoconferencing, over a single, cost effective LAN infrastructure. As a result, the Newbridge solution is a perfect fit for the network environment portrayed in this case study.

7.5 The Torrent Solution

The network presented in this case, even before addressing the backbone migration challenge, is already quite advanced. Layer 2 LAN switching is already deployed throughout the network to address workgroup bandwidth demands, and servers have been centralized into a high-availability data center. The router backbone, however, is a serious bottleneck, and must be upgraded.

Much has been said and written in recent years about the limitations of traditional routing technology. Networking vendors have offered a variety of switching technologies as alternatives to routing: Virtual LAN (VLAN) switching, ATM switching, IP switching, and most recently Layer 3 switching. Each of these approaches tries to replace the router backbone with a switched backbone incorporating routing intelligence, but delivering more bandwidth and some other capabilities.

The approach offered by Torrent Networking Technologies is different. Our IP9000 Gigabit Router scales full Internet-class routing to gigabit speeds, without the constraints of a Layer 3 switch. And the unique service provisioning features of the IP9000 Router deliver on the promise of ATM without the technology transition required. In the following paragraphs, we'll illustrate how the IP9000 Router can be used for backbone migration in this network.

Implementation Considerations

Before presenting the detailed implementation, it's important to identify key characteristics that any solution for this network should exhibit. Some of the factors driving our proposed solution are:

Minimize the overall impact of the migration. The existing router backbone is serving a logical network topology that's been defined and is working. It's essential that the new solution deploys incrementally into this backbone, and that the existing subnet structure be maintained. It's also vital that the new technology not carry a steep learning curve—it should be easy to understand and use by the existing staff trained in design and configuration of router backbones.

Build in support for new types of traffic. There's probably minimal IP multicast and multimedia traffic in this network today, and most existing applications are certainly fairly insensitive to bandwidth and delay variation. But within the next few years, this is very likely to change, as new webcasting and IP voice applications are rolled out. The new backbone infrastructure must have built-in support for full multicast routing and service provisioning to application flows.

Implement mainstream technologies for maximum cost benefit. This network uses both FDDI and Token Ring technology today, and has probably reaped the full benefit of the initial investment in these technologies. But it's become very clear that switched Ethernet/Fast Ethernet will offer dramatically better price/performance and will dominate LAN infrastructures. The backbone solution for this network needs to optimize around this, and should propose an effective migration away from other technologies.

Plan on tight coupling with the Internet. Today this network's Internet connection is probably a single T1-speed (or slower) frame relay connection to a local service provider, and a very small fraction of the LAN traffic is heading to/from the Internet. But in the future, expect to see much faster Internet connections—even as high as OC3 speeds—and much more data exchanged between local hosts and the Internet. E-commerce, Extranets, VPNs—all of these spell much tighter integration of public and private networks, and demands that backbone routing solutions be full Internet-class machines with large tables and a complete suite of routing protocols.

All these considerations demand a Gigabit router solution in the backbone. In the following section we'll examine the details of such a solution.

Implementation Details

Figure 7.13 illustrates the overall solution. A pair of IP9000 Gigabit Routers is used as a backbone, interconnected with a pair of Gigabit Ethernet links offering 4 GBps of total backbone

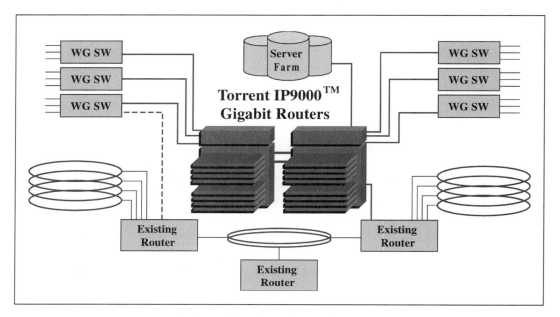

Figure 7.13 The Torrent Solution

bandwidth between the routers. Depending on the distance between the data centers, the Gigabit links may be either multimode or single mode fiber optic cable.

Each IP9000 Router is outfitted with redundant power supplies, redundant Gigabit Ethernet backbone connections (forming the mesh described above), and 48 ports of Fast Ethernet. For pricing purposes, we assumed that 1/3 of these ports were on multimode fiber (for long-distance wiring closets) and 2/3 on Category 5 twisted pair (for short-distance closets and local server connections). One full-duplex Fast Ethernet connection goes out to every wiring closet switch, and one is used for every server in the server farm.

The existing router backbone continues to be used as a backbone for Token Ring-attached hosts, and one Fast Ethernet connection is used between the two backbones. Over time, Token Ring hubs should be phased out in favor of workgroup 10/100 Ethernet switches.

At least initially, the two IP9000 Routers above form the complete solution. Over time, we'd expect to see migration from hubs to 10/100 switches in all the wiring closets, and expansion of the backbone router mesh to offer more Fast Ethernet ports. The following section outlines some of the key benefits of the IP9000 backbone solution.

Performance and Benefits

The network design just presented offers up to 20 Gigabits of capacity for backbone internetworking, and full routing performance for both unicast and multicast traffic. Each server and workgroup can drive and receive nearly 150,000 packets per second on its full-duplex Fast Ethernet link.

The backbone bottleneck that prompted investment in next-generation solutions has been completely eliminated.

The full routing performance of the IP9000 allows tight coupling of this network's backbone with the Internet. While Layer 3 switching solutions rely on bounded address spaces and "caching" for fast routing, the IP9000 Router is able to perform a full routing table search at wire speed and can support multiple ISP connections and heavy volumes of outbound traffic. Networks managers who saw the "80/20 Rule" of subnet traffic inverted by intranets recognize that the next "80/20 Rule" to invert is the percentage of traffic staying local to one enterprise, and will plan for Internet-class backbone solutions.

Conventional wisdom says that ATM technology is the only solution that can truly provision service (bandwidth and latency) to individual traffic flows, and that customers must choose between service guarantees or price/performance. But with the IP9000 Router, individual flows can be identified and allocated a slice of network bandwidth, along with minimum latency assurances. Simple over-provisioning of bandwidth may suffice for today's applications, but future voice and video traffic will demand absolution guarantees that can be enforced under any loading condition—the kind of guarantees offered in the IP9000 Router backbone.

Many new technologies carry a significant hidden cost of retraining the staff to be able to configure and manage them. The IP9000 Router is designed for drop-in deployment into existing router backbones without retraining—its management interface is designed to be instantly familiar to anyone managing a router network today. And because it supports a complete suite of standard protocols tested for interoperation with leading router vendors, it can be easily integrated with the router backbone in place.

Solution Cost

Internet-class routing, as it turns out, doesn't have to come at a carrier-class price tag. The full IP9000 configuration illustrated and described above comes at a North American list price of approximately $118,000, including all necessary software licenses and hardware components.

In addition to this investment in the new routers, there may need to be some incremental spending on network interface cards for servers, which should be minimal. In almost every case, existing wiring should be adequate; it may, however, be necessary to upgrade the inter-building wiring for the Gigabit Ethernet backbone links. Hidden costs, such as retraining of staff, are avoided.

Implementation Alternatives

A few possible variations on this design are worth noting.

While the design used Gigabit Ethernet as a mesh between the two backbone routers, it might be preferred to use parallel Fast Ethernet fiber connections. The "dollars per megabit" might be a little higher, but this could avoid a requirement to upgrade backbone links to single mode fiber. The IP9000 Router allows any number of parallel Fast Ethernet connections to be operated as a "virtual trunk" between two routers.

The case doesn't include any mention of how the WAN connections are provided out of this network; probably one of the existing routers is supporting a frame relay connection at T1 or fractional T3 speed. In the near future, service providers may offer cost-effective VPN services across a region at OC3 speeds, along with Internet access. The IP9000 Router will allow direct attachment to OC3 WAN or MAN backbones with various flavors of standards-based ATM/IP mapping, enabling full integration with next-generation WAN solutions.

The design used two 8-slot IP9000 Routers. Torrent Networking Technologies also offers a 16-slot system with double the bandwidth and density of a single 8-slot product. Depending on the distances involved and the cabling available between the buildings, it might be possible for this entire network to be served by a single 16-Slot IP9000 Router. This would reduce the cost by about $20,000 based on North American list prices.

Conclusion

This network design has illustrated how the IP9000 Gigabit Router can be used as an Internet-class router backbone for an enterprise network. This solution provides unique value-added capabilities as compared to a simpler Layer 3 switching solution, yet can be delivered at a similar price point, and at a fraction of what the current router backbone or an ATM alternative would cost. With the IP9000 Router, network managers don't have to bet against the Internet or opt for performance over service provisioning—they can get the full benefit of Internet-class routing and ATM-like service provisioning at an affordable price.

Note that the IP9000 Gigabit Router elements used in this case will all be generally available in the second calendar quarter of 1998.

7.6 The 3Com Response

3Com recommends the network upgrade be divided into two pieces—solutions for the router core and solutions for the workgroup edge connections. 3Com offers Layer 3 switches that can remove the router bottleneck at the core while preserving the existing subnet structure. 3Com's Layer 3 switches offer wire-speed routing of IP, IPX, and AppleTalk protocols that scale in performance from 4 to 56 million packets per second.

3Com's Layer 3 switches are the CoreBuilder™ 3500 and the CoreBuilder™ 9000. Note that the CoreBuilder 9000 was not shipping when this book went to press.

The 3Com CoreBuilder 3500 Layer 3 High-Function Switch (Figure 7.14) provides high-end switching and routing. Built around sophisticated third-generation ASIC technology, the Core-Builder 3500 switch provides wire-speed Layer 2 and Layer 3 traffic forwarding and supports real-time, multimedia network traffic using advanced policy-based services. Combined with flexible virtual LAN (VLAN) support, multicast services, multiprotocol routing, and network management

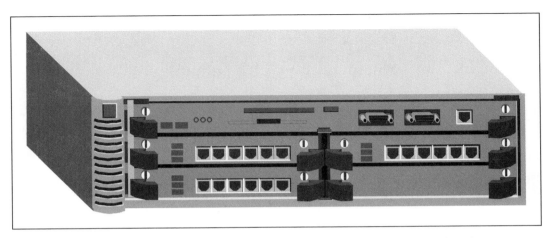

Figure 7.14   The 3Com CoreBuilder™ 3500 Layer 3 High Function Switch

with RMON and Roving Analysis Port, the CoreBuilder 3500 Layer 3 switch provides a robust and resilient networking infrastructure. It is designed to act as a backbone LAN router, replacing legacy LAN routers for Layer 3 forwarding functionality.

The CoreBuilder 9000 switch (Figure 7.15) combines support for multi-layer switching services Gigabit Ethernet and ATM into a common platform. A unique combination of Layer 2 and Layer 3 control features in the CoreBuilder 9000 switch removes the performance bottlenecks and topological constraints of today's router-based backbones.

Designed for deployment in the campus backbone, the CoreBuilder 9000 switch offers very high core switching capacity. Its scaleable architecture provides support for up to 112 OC-12c (622 Mbps) ATM ports or 126 Gigabit Ethernet (1000 Mbps) ports. Layer 2 forwarding rates on the CoreBuilder 9000 switch exceed 100 million packets per second, and Layer 3 switching rates scale to 56 million packets per second. These performance metrics make the CoreBuilder 9000 switch suitable for the entire range of campus and enterprise backbone applications: high-performance server connections and high-density aggregation for departmental edge switches.

The CoreBuilder 9000 switch provides extensive Quality-of-Service/Class-of-Service facilities for distinguishing between mission-critical data streams and data of lesser priority. A distributed management architecture, using embedded agents and RMON to collect and present data, it provides managers with the information they need to define a performance framework and establish policy controls for ensuring the smooth operation of an intelligent, application-aware network.

At the edge of the network, 3Com offers a choice of stackable and chassis products (both shipping now) for switched and shared connections that includes Ethernet and Token Ring. The CoreBuilder 5000 (Figure 7.16.) is a chassis-based product that provides up to 408 switched Ethernet and 119 switched Fast Ethernet and 306 Token Ring connections.

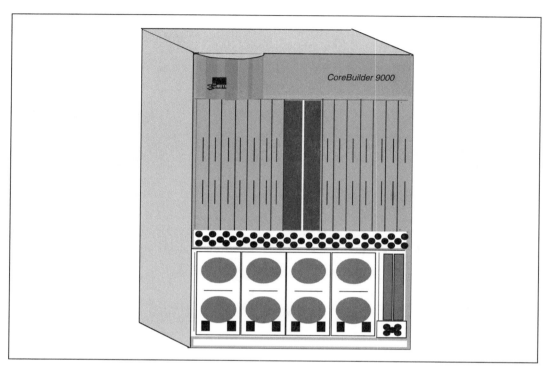

Figure 7.15   The 3Com CoreBuilder™ 9000 Switch

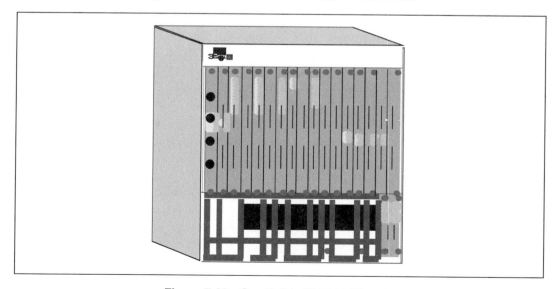

Figure 7.16   CoreBuilder™ 5000 Chassis

3Com has a complete line of SuperStack II (Figure 7.17) products that provide stackable connections for shared/switch Ethernet and Fast Ethernet and shared/switched Token Ring. The Super-Stack products can be stacked using Ethernet, FDDI, and ATM uplink connections.

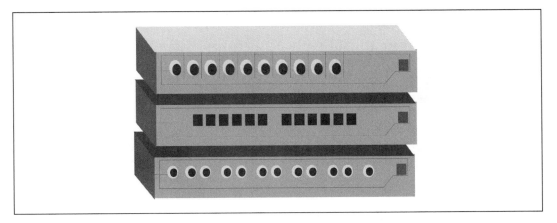

Figure 7.17   SuperStack II stackables

Problem summary and assumptions

- 3 buildings;
- routers on an FDDI backbone. Assumes three routers in each of two buildings and four routers in the third building;
- 50 subnets with Ethernet plus 10 Token Ring segments. Assumes 5 subnets per router with a subnet on each router port;
- 5000 desktops.

Proposed solution

The first step is to replace the legacy routers with CoreBuilder 3500 switches (Figure 7.18). For the two buildings that each have three routers there are 15 Ethernet ports and three Token Ring segments. Each CoreBuilder 3500 provides 18 10/100 Ethernet and 6 FDDI connections that can all route at wire speed. For the Token Ring ports we have installed the SuperStack II Switch 2000 TR that supports up to 12 switched Token Ring ports. The SuperStack II is connected to the Core-Builder 3500 through FDDI.

Initially we are keeping the FDDI backbone in place. Each CoreBuilder 3500 is interconnected via switched FDDI. Once the routers are replaced the FDDI bandwidth can more effectively be used. In the future the backbone can be upgraded to Gigabit Ethernet. The overall network design looks like the following (Figure 7.19):

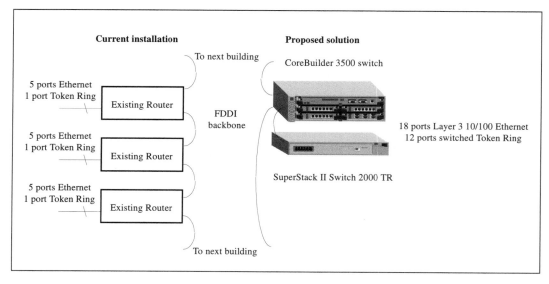

Figure 7.18   Building Solution

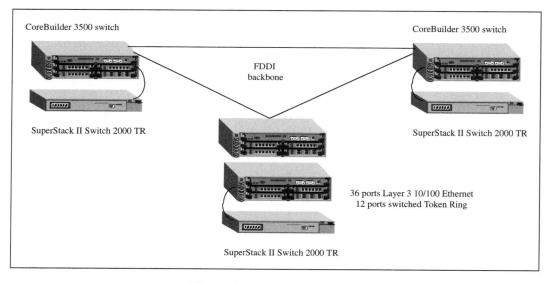

Figure 7.19   Network Solution

The CoreBuilder 3500 switches increase the bandwidth on each port to wire speed that will solve the bandwidth problem. The CoreBuilder 3500 switch also provides quality and class of service (QoS/CoS) support to allow prioritization and bandwidth reservation of traffic flows. For example, traffic from SAP applications can be given the highest priority and bandwidth limits can be established for web traffic. Furthermore, the CoreBuilder 3500 supports IP multicast so that users can automatically be added or removed from multicast groups.

Follow-on solutions

Replacing the routers with CoreBuilder 3500 switches solved the initial performance problem. With the increase in desktop traffic we propose upgrading the edge of the network using a combination of CoreBuilder 5000/9000 and SuperStack II 1000/3000 for switched Ethernet and Fast Ethernet connections. Currently the network is using three different technologies: Ethernet, Token Ring, and FDDI. As the network is upgraded it would beneficial to migrate toward a common technology using 10/100/1000 Mbps Ethernet. Scaling performance with Ethernet keeps the network simple, easy to manage, and more affordable. Over time we recommend replacing the Token Ring desktops with 10/100 NICs attached to 10/100 Ethernet switches. Most desktops can be configured using switched Ethernet connections using Fast Ethernet uplinks. When needed, the desktop performance can be increased to Fast Ethernet with Gigabit Ethernet as the uplink.

As the network backbone grows, we suggest moving to Gigabit Ethernet. The CoreBuilder CB3500 switches can be interconnected with Gigabit Ethernet. The network core can be upgraded to the CoreBuilder 9000 that can provide up to 168 Fast Ethernet Layer 3 or 28-Gigabit Ethernet Layer 2 switched connections.

7.7 The Extreme Networks Solution

Router Backbone Upgrade Needed

The most significant issue in the case network is that the existing routers are too slow. Capable of forwarding only 100,000 packets per second (pps), they are not taking advantage of the 100 Mbps bandwidth of FDDI. Even if the routers did take full advantage of FDDI's bandwidth, FDDI would immediately become the bottleneck because of its lack of speed and bandwidth scalability.

However, if the existing routers and FDDI backbone are upgraded to Summit LAN switches, the end users will realize improved performance as well as added benefits from the workgroup switches. FDDI is typically associated with the second wave of LAN switching, where 100 Mbps uplinks were added to first wave 10 Mbps Ethernet switches to alleviate client/server bottlenecks. FDDI simply cannot scale to meet current and future network needs.

With the rise in popularity of intranet and Internet communications, that legacy client/server network architecture has quickly given way to a more random any-to-any traffic pattern that requires greater scalability throughout the network.

Scalability means many things, but in today's local area networks, true scalability is achieved only with third wave LAN switches that scale in four dimensions: network size, bandwidth, speed, and quality of service. Extreme Networks is leading the third wave of LAN switching with Summit switches that embody these new scalability requirements.

Scale Performance with Third Wave LAN Switches

Network Size

The importance of scaling network size is to control the size of broadcast domains. Creating broadcast domains and routing between them avoids broadcast storms, which occur in large, flat, bridged networks and drove the shift to routers. However legacy routers were slow. Third Wave LAN switches provide all the benefits of IP routing at wire speed, eliminating the performance penalty and permitting deployment of layer three IP switching at any point in the network.

Bandwidth

Bandwidth is important in third wave LAN switching. A Third Wave LAN switch must have enough non-blocking bandwidth built into the switch itself to permit all ports to run simultaneously at wire speed in full duplex mode with out incurring performance penalties or slow down due to congestion.

Speed

Scalability in speed is important because it allows the network manager to build a "balanced" network with network speed matching the application, 10Mbs or 100Mbps at the desktop, 100Mbps in the riser, and Gigabit per second speed in the backbone and server farm where needed.

Application Sensitive Policy-Based Quality of Service

At the same time, the network manager needs to guarantee response times and bandwidth levels to specific users and applications. Many of them have rapidly transitioned to Fast Ethernet and are now considering implementing technologies like Gigabit Ethernet (GbE). These same network managers have growing concerns that providing infinite bandwidth won't always be a choice that they can make to solve networking problems.

As a result, they are looking at implementing bandwidth management techniques that allow them to provide service level guarantees for specific users and traffic groups. The solution to this problem is Application Sensitive Policy-Based Quality of Service, which allows the network manager to identify traffic groups based on switch port number, MAC address, VLAN, IP subnet, or application and apply specific quality of service profiles to those traffic groups.

This customer, in particular, has legacy applications and new applications that are critical to business operations. As a result, they will have to guarantee service for those applications to maintain business operations.

Key Technology Components

Because the first critical step is to upgrade the router backbone, wire-speed IP routing is imperative. In addition, the LAN backbone speed can be boosted with Gigabit Ethernet.

Scaling Backbone Speed

Gigabit Ethernet is the first logical step to scaling backbone speed. There is a natural convergence in the market to use Ethernet as the performance LAN technology of choice for end-stations, server farms, and backbones. With implementations at 10 Mbps, 100 Mbps, and 1000 Mbps, Ethernet delivers performance migration without any learning curve or roadblocks.

By using Ethernet as a common technology from the desktop through the backbone of the local area network, the cost of network ownership is greatly reduced. The network manager needs to be an expert for only one frame type and he can use a single set of tools to manage and debug the network.

Scaling Router Performance—Wire-Speed IP Routing

The routers must then be upgraded to wire-speed performance. Traffic patterns are less determinate now than ever before, so packets will likely traverse a router at least once. In legacy client/ server networks, most traffic stayed local to a single router port, allowing compromise on router performance. Today, the LAN router's performance is paramount to every traffic flow and must be wire speed, all the time, with no compromises!

Managing Bandwidth—Controlling the flow of IP Multicast Packets

Like many network users that have information that must be disseminated to many users, this customer is implementing IP multicast applications. IP multicast frames map into standard broadcast Ethernet packets. This means that IP multicast frames will permeate the network like any other broadcast packet.

The Internet Group Multicast Protocol (IGMP) is used in all IP multicast applications by servers to advertise multicast services and by clients that subscribe to them. Bandwidth management can be achieved by snooping IGMP frames and only forwarding IP multicasts to ports with subscribers rather than flooding them to all ports. Summit switches perform IGMP snooping on all ports without any performance impact.

In addition, ExtremeWare, which is integral to each Summit switch, can route IP multicast frames using the standard Distance Vector Multicast Routing Protocol (DVMRP). DVMRP is used by Internet routers to form the MBONE, which is an overlay network that runs on top of the Internet. ExtremeWare will support routing multicast packets based on the Protocol Independent Multicast (PIM) routing protocol. PIM is discussed in an information RFC and is expected to become part of a standards track in the Internet Engineering Task Force.

Step One: Add Summit Switches with Wire-Speed IP Routing and Gigabit Ethernet

Upgrade the Router Backbone without Changing the Subnetwork Structure

The first step is to create a backbone with a combination of Summit1 and Summit2 switches to accommodate the existing number of subnetworks. Accommodating the existing subnet structure is critical to scale the size of the network without changes to end-stations.

Implementing Summit1 and Summit2 Switches

The new backbone will use four Summit2 switches that will support the existing 50 routed subnetworks with a total of 64 routed ports. Each Summit2 switch provides sixteen autosensing 10/100 switch/router ports and two Gigabit Ethernet switch/router ports. The Summit2 switch also offers a redundant Gigabit port to provide physical layer redundancy and fault tolerance for one of the two Gigabit Ethernet ports.

Two Summit1 switches will aggregate the four Summit2 switches. Both of the Gigabit switch ports from each Summit2 switch can be load-balanced and connected to one of the Summit1 switches to provide non-blocking bandwidth to all ports on the Summit2. Load-balanced connections between the two Summit1 switches may be configured to increase bandwidth between them and also allow for enhanced fault tolerance. In the event that one of the load-balanced links fails, the other(s) will carry all traffic with no interruption of service.

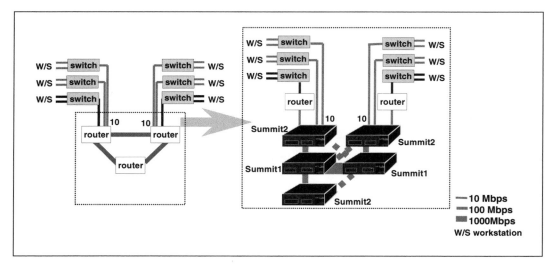

Figure 7.20   Step 1: Add Summit Switches & Dedicate router to Token Ring

The net result is the creation of a Gigabit backbone that offers wire-speed IP routing to each existing Ethernet (10 Mbps) subnetwork. These subnetworks may be transitioned slowly from the existing backbone to the new backbone to control the upgrade process and guarantee success. For the small number of Token Ring switches, we can dedicate the existing routers to those users and either leave the routers attached to FDDI or connect them to switched ports on the Summit2 switches.

Proving Performance

While it may be obvious that wire-speed routing performance is imperative for the router backbone upgrade, many vendors make wire-speed performance claims. It is important to take advantage of objective third party organizations that test products to verify vendor claims.

The Summit2 switch has been tested by Strategic Networks to be performance proven for Layer 2 switching at 2.38 million packets per second for half duplex operation. The Harvard Network Device Test Lab (NDTL) has tested Summit switches and verified wire-speed IP routing performance. Performance data may be found at http://www.snci.com and http://ndtl.harvard.edu, respectively.

In addition to testing Summit switches for throughput and packet loss, both Strategic Networks and Harvard NDTL tested unicast and broadcast latency. Unicast and broadcast latency were found to be identical—a testament to the fact that both capabilities are designed into the Summit. This is important for this customer case and for any other customers planning IP multicast applications. Summit switches will permit the implementation of the multicast applications without degradation of switch performance.

Step Two: Implement ExtremeWare Policy-Based Quality of Service

Moore's Law: Bandwidth Offered = Bandwidth Consumed

Once the backbone upgrade has been completed, there will be ample bandwidth for existing traffic. But network traffic always grows and, as such, consumes the available bandwidth. This specific customer has critical legacy business applications as well as new applications that require guaranteed amounts of bandwidth for normal operation. To guarantee service for these applications, Policy-Based Quality of Service, part of ExtremeWare software that ships with each Summit switch, provides the ideal solution.

Bandwidth Management: A Requirement for Scalability

Policy-Based Quality of Service allows the network manager to identify traffic groups based on several different identifiers: port number, MAC address, VLAN, IP subnet, IP address, TCP/UDP port number. For each traffic group, the network manager can assign a quality of service profile including minimum bandwidth, maximum bandwidth, and relative priority. For more information on ExtremeWare Policy-Based Quality of Service, see the white paper at http://extremenetworks.com.

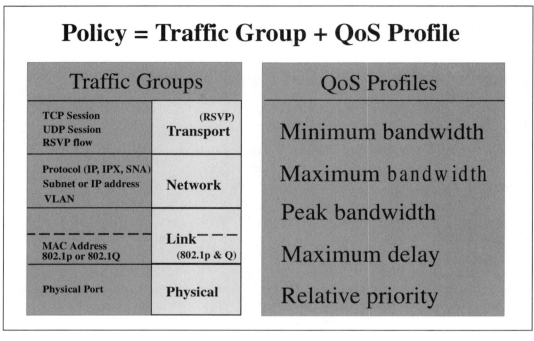

Figure 7.21   Policy-based QoS

Policy-Based Quality of Service will allow a minimum amount of bandwidth to be allotted for a specific traffic group to guarantee service. If bandwidth on a port is oversubscribed, the priority assigned to that traffic group will determine whether any of its frames will be dropped.

Managing Policy-Based Quality of Service and Summit Switches

All elements of a Summit switch can be managed from either the command line interface (CLI), a standard web browser, or SNMP. Both the command line interface and ExtremeWare Vista web-based manager are integral to every Summit switch at no additional cost. Each Summit switch has an integrated http, or web, server and reaching it is as simple as typing the IP address of the switch into your browser address field. ExtremeWare Enterprise Manager is an SNMP application that runs on top of WindowsNT, Solstice for Solaris, and HP OpenView for WindowsNT. Extreme-Ware Enterprise Manager is available as an option for the Summit switches.

The graphical tools in ExtremeWare Vista and ExtremeWare Enterprise Manager allow the simple configuration of untagged or tagged (IEEE 802.1Q) VLANs, configuration of IP routing, the configuration of quality of service profiles, and the association of those profiles with traffic groups. Each Summit switch supports up to 32 quality of service profiles and an unlimited number of traffic groups. Both ExtremeWare Vista and ExtremeWare Enterprise Manager allow the management of individual or multiple switches simultaneously. The network manager can easily create a consistent set of network policies and administer them on a network-wide basis rather than switch-by-switch.

Step Three: Upgrade Workgroup Switch Downlinks to 100 Mbps Fast Ethernet

Because the case did not clearly indicate the speed of the workgroup switch interfaces, the conservative assumption was that the switches only supported 10 Mbps Ethernet and a high-speed Fast Ethernet port was available, but not in use.

In the first step, the router backbone was upgraded in a manner that required minimal change to the network configuration and existing switches. At this point, it makes sense to upgrade the connection from the Summit2 switches to the workgroup switches from 10 Mbps Ethernet to Fast Ethernet.

Getting Something for Nothing

Since the Summit2 switch has sixteen 10/100 autosensing switched ports, no changes will be required to upgrade from 10 Mbps Ethernet connections to 100 Mbps Fast Ethernet connections. The same Category 5 UTP cable can be moved from a 10 Mbps Ethernet port on the workgroup switch to that Fast Ethernet uplink port on the same switch.

Reduced Cost of Ownership—The Natural Convergence Toward 10/100/1000 Mbps Ethernet

These three steps have created a hierarchical network of 10 Mbps switched Ethernet connections to the desktop, switched Fast Ethernet connections from the workgroup switches to the backbone, and switched Gigabit Ethernet connections between the backbone switches.

	Speed	Cost per NIC	Cost per switch port	Cost per Mbit
Ethernet	10 Mb/s	$45	$90	$13.50
Fast Ethernet	100 Mb/s	$85	$500	$5.85
Gigabit Ethernet	1000 Mb/s	$1,000	$2,800	$3.80
ATM 25	25 Mb/s	$250	$300	$22.00
ATM 155	155 Mb/s	$800	$1,000	$11.60
ATM 622	622 Mb/s	$5,000	$3,000	$12.86
FDDI	100 Mb/s	$1,500	$3,500	$50.00

Figure 7.22   Cost Comparisons

In addition to the network being ideally constructed for scalability, it is more cost effective than other solutions. Acquisition costs for 10/100/1000 Mbps Ethernet products are lower when compared at face value to other technologies. However, the convergence toward Ethernet as a single LAN technology simplifies the training, tools, and troubleshooting capabilities needed by the network manager, reducing overall cost of network ownership.

Best Return on Investment

	Incremental Cost	Total Cost/Mpbs	Total Cost/Users
Implement Summit Switches	$109,970	$219	$22
Implement Policy-based Quality of Service	$0	$219	$22
Upgrade Downlinks to Fast Ethernet	$0	$48	$22

The initial investment required for Step One, the router backbone update, is $109,970 for the purchase of four Summit2 switches at a list price of $14,995 each and the purchase of two Summit1 switches at a list price of $24,995 each. The cost per port of this solution starts at $219, with a cost per user of $22.

At Step Two where Policy-Based Quality of Service is implemented, no additional investment is required. Policy-Based Quality of Service is an integral part of ExtremeWare, which is shipped with every Summit switch.

Similarly, at Step Three, there is no additional investment needed for the upgrade of the downlinks from the workgroup switches to the Summit2 switches from 10 Mbps Ethernet to 100 Mbps Fast Ethernet. Step three reduces the cost per megabit to $48 with no change in the cost per user of $22.

7.8 The Bay Networks Solution

Bay Networks is pleased to provide a solution to the pharmaceutical concern's RFP. The RFP makes clear that the driving force behind the increasing bandwidth requirements are new SAP and Web applications. Access to these applications across the campus will be through the Ethernet/IP network. For this reason we propose the deployment of high performance routing switches to support the future Ethernet/IP growth of the network. Accelar routing switches will be deployed in each building to eliminate the router bottleneck and enable the deployed wiring closet switches to reach their full potential. Routing switches free up the existing routers to support the legacy requirements of the Token Ring applications.

This solution provides a massive improvement in campus wide performance, while retaining the ease of use and low cost characteristics of the existing network architecture. It is a manageable, flexible, and adaptable foundation for future migration to higher bandwidth services and real-time applications.

A New Solution Is Needed!

Backbones based on routers and FDDI had sufficient capacity when only 20% of traffic crossed to the backbone. Today Web and SAP applications cause at least half of all traffic to cross the router onto the backbone. The current FDDI backbone is limited to 100 Mbps (Megabits per second) and is showing the signs of strain. Needed: Scalability to gigabit speeds.

Dedicated Ethernet connections for end stations require 100 Mbps risers to connect to the backbone. 100 Mbps risers require the backbone to have even greater capacity. The best choice for Ethernet networks is Gigabit Ethernet. Initially gigabit connections will be used for interswitch links and for dedicated server connections. Needed: Routing capacity of at least 5 Mpps.

As networks scale to gigabit backbone capacity we must scale routing performance to match. A centralized SAP server connected via Gigabit Ethernet can generate 1.3 Mpps (Million packets per second). For users to cross a subnet boundary to this server, the router must process at least 1.3 Mpps. In reality, most backbone devices would need more than one gigabit connection. If there are 2 gigabit interswitch links and 3 gigabit connected servers, routing capacity must scale to 6.5 Mpps. The current router is limited to 100Kpps (Kilo packets per second), and therefore not capable of scaling to gigabit speeds. High-end routers are limited to 1Mpps, so a new router platform is not a viable solution either.

Needed: Low Cost Routing

Traffic levels will continue to increase dramatically, as much as 50–100% per year. We have made the point that routers are not an option for gigabit routing. If such a solution becomes available it would be prohibitively expensive. Yet IS budgets increase only slightly, if at all. The challenge is to increase routing capacity, but at significantly lower price points.

Routing Switches Are the Answer!

We have come to the conclusion that this network needs a device capable of three things: scalability to Gigabit Ethernet, high capacity routing, and low cost. Routing switches are the solution to all three needs.

Accelar routing switches use routing engines distributed onto the line cards for maximum scalability. As line cards are added to a routing switch, more routing engines are added, thereby scaling performance. Each routing engine can support ports at 10 Mbps, 100 Mbps, or gigabit speeds. Distributed routing and a passive 15 Gbps backplane allow Accelar routing switches to scale to support future need. Accelar routing switches support up to 96 10/100 ports, 12 gigabit ports, or a combination of the two. Accelar switches provide scalable connectivity to wiring closet risers, servers, and the gigabit backbone.

Accelar routing switches have an ASIC-based architecture that integrates IP routing into hardware. Routing switches bring the high performance of Ethernet switches to bear on the problem of IP routing. Accelar routing switches, capable of routing 7 Mpps, are the only solution providing routing that scales to gigabit speeds.

Another advantage of ASIC-based routing switches is low cost. ASICs allow routing switches to be priced low like Ethernet switches, not high like routers. Accelar Fast Ethernet ports cost about $700, compared to slower Fast Ethernet router ports at $5000–$10,000. Accelar routing switches set a new standard for low cost routing.

The installed base of routers loses on all counts. They lack sufficient backplane capacity for multiple Gigabit connections. They have limited routing capacity—and router ports are expensive.

Migration to a Routing Switch Backbone

The goal is to take a network based on a distributed router backbone and migrate it to a backbone made up of routing switches, Gigabit interswitch links, and Gigabit server connections. (Refer to Figure 7.23.)

This migration begins in one building and continues in increments across the campus. This allows the benefits of routing switches to be realized and network managers to become comfortable with the technology. The migration starts by replacing the L2 switch in one building with a routing switch. Initially the routing switch is a higher capacity Ethernet switch. The next step is to turn on IP routing within the routing switch. When building 1 is converted and stable, every other building is converted in the same manner.

Stage 1: Improving Building Performance

The goal of Stage 1 is to move routing within the building from the router into the routing switch. The end result is inter subnet routing within the building being performed by the routing switch while routing onto the backbone remains in the router.

Step 1: Install routing switch and connect to risers, backbone router, and servers. The first step is to replace the existing Ethernet switch with the routing switch. The routing switch aggregates all wiring closet risers, connects directly to the backbone router, and connects to all distributed servers. The routing switch has greater internal capacity and Fast Ethernet port density, allowing migration of risers and departmental servers. Where appropriate, increase riser connectivity to 100 Mbps. Thus far the installation is simple and straightforward because Accelar routing switches are configured initially as L2 switches only.

Step 2: Turn on IP forwarding. This step will configure the routing switch to route IP. This is done through the graphical device manager and Bay Networks Optivity. When this is accomplished, all IP communication within the building is performed by the routing switch, not the router.

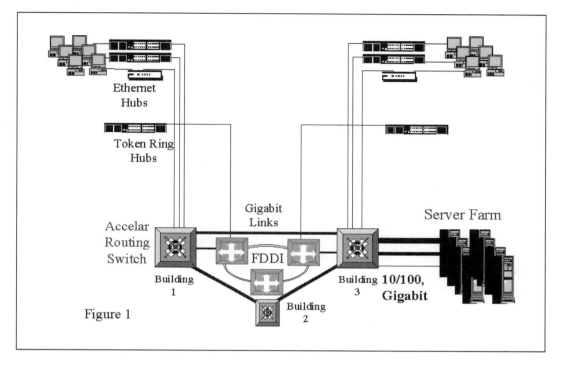

Figure 7.23   Routing Switch Backbone

Step 3: Repeat Steps 1 and 2 in other campus buildings. When building 1 is converted and stable, install routing switches in each building and configure IP forwarding.

Benefits realized in stage 1:

- Offload intrabuilding IP routing from backbone router
- Wire speed IP performance within the building
- Increased network capacity within the building

Stage 2: Wire Speed across the Campus

The goal of Stage 2 is to form a routing switch backbone and move campus-wide IP routing from the routers to the routing switches. The end result is that the routing of all the IP traffic is performed by the Accelar routing switches while the routing of all the legacy protocols is performed by the router.

Step 1: Connect routing switches with Gigabit fiber interswitch links. Use existing fiber cable to interconnect building routing switches. This forms a second backbone consisting of routing switches and gigabit links. All IP traffic travels over this new backbone at wire speed. Legacy protocols and Token Ring continue to travel over the router/FDDI backbone. The FDDI backbone can be decommissioned as soon as legacy applications are migrated from FDDI to Gigabit or Fast Ethernet attached servers.

Benefits realized in stage 2:

- Offload campus-wide IP routing from routers
- Eliminate router performance penalty campus-wide
- Wire speed IP communication across the campus

Stage 3: Server Centralization without Router Penalty

Migration to a routing switch backbone provides great performance improvements and enables server centralization without the normal router performance penalty. The goal of Stage 3 is to centralize distributed servers for tighter security and reduced administration costs.

Step 1: Centralize distributed servers. Move appropriate servers into the centralized data center. Connect these servers directly to the routing switch backbone or create a server farm that connects to the backbone. The routing switch backbone provides the increased backbone capacity and high packet processing capability needed for server centralization.

The new backbone also provides scalable network access for servers. Server access to the network can be at 10, 100, or 1000 Mbps, as the server and application require. Routing switches provide high density 100 Mbps ports and sufficient Gigabit connections for servers. Place high performance servers running business critical applications on gigabit connections. Place non-critical applications and low to medium performance servers on 100 Mbps connections.

Benefits realized in Stage 3:

- Improved security and lower administrative costs for centralized servers
- Scalable network access for centralized servers
- Wire speed IP communications to all servers on the network
- Wire speed IP communications regardless of end user location

Product Description - Accelar 1200
- 8 slot chassis, 2 reserved for switch fabric, 6 I/O slots
- 96 10/100 ports, 12 Gigabit ports or combination
- Redundant Gigabit links—LinkSafe Option
- Redundant switch fabric for fail safe operation

High Performance
- Remove router performance penalty with wirespeed IP routing
- 15 Gbps switch fabric
- 7 Million packets per second IP routing
- Latency less than 10 microseconds

Figure 7.24   Accelar 1200

Ease of Installation
- Standards-based IP routing
- No proprietary protocols
- No subnet changes
- No end station reconfiguration

Low Cost Routing
- $775 per port (list price for 96 10/100 ports in Accelar 1200)
- $2,750 per port (list price based on 1000BASE-SX module)

Solution	Qty	Description	Price
Accelar 1200 Switch	3	Chassis,100BASE-FX, 1000BASE-SX	$155,160
Network Mgt	1	Optivity Enterprise for Windows	$17,995
Phone Plus Service	1	7/24 maintenance	$9,000
Installation Service	1	Accelar installation services	$3,350
Total			**$185,505**

7.9 The Xylan Solution

This pharmaceutical company is experiencing one of the most common set of problems in the enterprise marketplace today.

The Challenges

New Enterprise Requirements Planning (ERP) applications implemented: Many new corporations are streamlining their IT processes by installing such applications as SAP, Oracle, or AAP. These applications typically require centralized application servers, and increased access by all individuals across the network. This dramatically changes both the traffic types and patterns from traditional departmental LAN models. (See Figure 7.25).

Switching in the wiring closet adding pressure to the backbone: The "outside-in" approach to implementing switching is very common. As routers form the strategic backbone for many networks, replacing the shared hubs in the wiring closet is a natural place to start implementing switching. The goal is generally to provide more bandwidth per user. Many times, however, the impact on the backbone in terms of total number of Mbps now pouring onto it is not fully

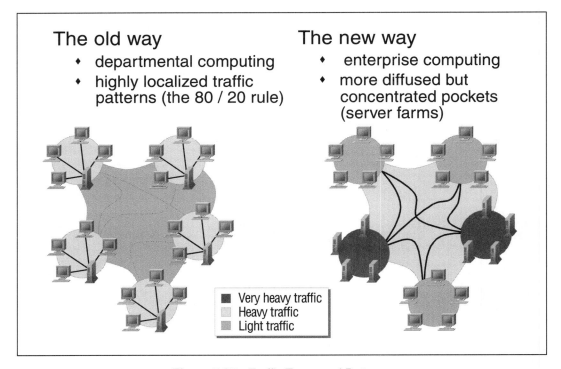

Figure 7.25 Traffic Types and Patterns

accounted for. If this is coupled with new applications, the increased capacity placed on the backbone can be enormous.

100,000 pps of routing performance no longer adequate: As new, network-dependent applications are installed using centralized servers, 100% of traffic now flows from the workstations over the network. Traditional routers were not engineered to handle this much traffic, and thus the pps limitations and slower, software-based routing becomes a critical bottleneck.

Maintaining existing subnets and planning for more IP applications, including multicast: Segmentation in large networks is required. In traditional networks, this was accomplished with physical segmentation into departmental LANs. Ideally, to minimize administration, any change to switching should not impact existing subnets. Any change to switching should also account for scaling of traffic and applications, as well as IP multicast capabilities.

Converging on a strategic infrastructure: Any IT manager will tell you that the most pressing matter in networking is managing and reducing long-term cost of ownership. This is accomplished primarily by reducing network diversity, reducing protocols, software applications and versions, and network equipment. This is the attraction of switching to many corporations. The concept of "one network, one switch" allows corporations to reduce the sheer number and types of "boxes" in their network, while reducing training, spares, network management, etc, and provide themselves with a very clean, well-managed infrastructure with which to roll out new applications efficiently.

The Xylan Solution

The Xylan switching solution (Figure 7.26) is ideal for corporations making these transitions. The Xylan OmniSwitch family provides for:

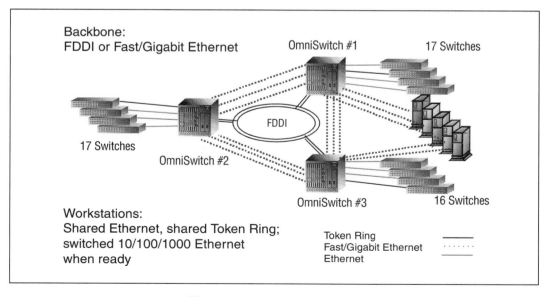

Figure 7.26   The Xylan Design

Investment protection, smooth migration: While the industry seems to be converging on IP as a protocol, and Ethernet as the frame-based technology of choice, the question often asked by customers is, "What about my Token Ring users?" or "How do I route IPX?" These questions are commonly asked because many of the Layer-three switching vendors only support IP and Ethernet. Xylan's philosophy of supporting and switching between all media and routing both IP and IPX has allowed us to provide the infrastructure of thousands of corporations worldwide. In the case of this pharmaceutical company, their Token Ring traffic can now be switched, providing cost savings, less disruption, and improved performance. When these users are ready to migrate to Ethernet, it's a simple card change in the same switch.

Parallel support of FDDI and Ethernet technologies: As in this instance, many corporations have installed FDDI backbones. Some protocols, such as NetBios, are not well suited for Ethernet's smaller MTU size. The capability to install Fast Ethernet or Gigabit Ethernet alongside FDDI, and move the applicable traffic over to Ethernet makes a smooth transition. This frees up congestion on the FDDI links for the NetBios traffic, and allows smooth transition to full Ethernet, as business requirements dictate.

Faster and cheaper routing: Critical to this customer, as with most clients, is layer-three performance and cost (Figure 7.27, Figure 7.28). Xylan's HRE-II provides ten times the routing performance of the router in the case study (1M pps routing of IP and IPX), and because its done in silicon, it's much cheaper than traditional routing.

Standards-based support for traffic management and QoS: With more IP applications coming, specifically IP multicast, the Xylan solution is a good match. With support for IGMP and DVMRP for multicast, VLANs for policy-based security and broadcast management, 802.1p, 802.1Q, RSVP, and guaranteed QoS, Xylan provides all the software and hardware tools required to maximize application performance and quality of service.

Frame and cell migration path: Most customers are convinced there will be both frame and cell based technologies present in their networks. WAN interfaces and certain QoS applications are better suited for ATM, while non-delay sensitive data and server connections are clearly well suited to frame-based technologies. The point is that the switch you deploy should give you both cell and frame technologies for maximum flexibility and manageability at minimum cost. At Xylan, we have tightly integrated ATM and LAN interfaces in one switch. We offer 10/100/1000 Ethernet, ATM interfaces, and well as Token Ring, FDDI, and many others.

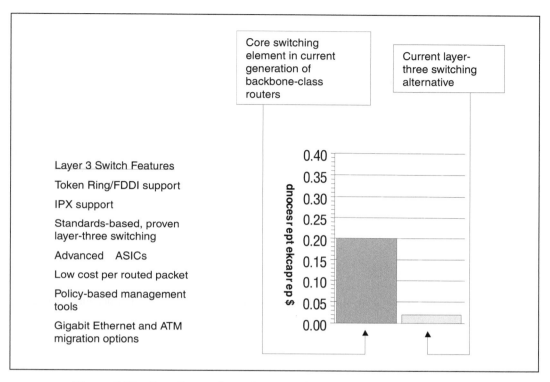

Figure 7.27   Cost Comparison of Layer 3 Switches vs. Traditional Routers

Items	Qty	Price
OmniSwitches	3	43,200
Ethernet ports	96	17,850
F Ethernet ports	36	16,350
Token Ring ports	18	26,550
FDDI ports	3	23,850
Routing engines	3	14,985
Total		$142,785

Figure 7.28   Cost of the Xylan Design

8 *The Current LAN Marketplace*

8.1 Introduction

Approximately every three or four years, there is a fundamental shift in the networking industry based on the introduction of a new Internetworking technology. In the late 1980s that shift was driven by the development of routers. In the early to mid 1990s the shift was driven by the introduction of Layer 2 switching. It is critical to both IT organizations and Internetworking vendors that they understand these shifts. IT organizations need to ensure that they do not waste their capital budgets by investing in network equipment that will soon be antiquated. Internetworking vendors need to ensure that their product strategy is synchronized to the emerging requirements of the marketplace.

Your authors believe we are approaching another fundamental shift in the network industry, driven by the development of Layer 3 switching. As part of our work at Strategic Networks, we have conducted extensive research into the current LAN marketplace, focusing primarily on the emerging market for Layer 3 switching technology. Our goal was to create a LAN marketplace assessment with four primary components (notice the parallel with our evaluation criteria in Chapter 2):

- What is currently in place;
- What is driving and/or inhibiting change;
- What alternatives are being considered; and
- What decision processes and criteria are being used by IT organizations.

We believe that this assessment will help corporate IT organizations put plans into motion to upgrade their LANs in the broader context of what hundreds of other IT organizations are planning. We also believe that this assessment will help the marketing organizations within the Internetworking vendor community better position their products to be successful in this embryonic marketplace.

Three data collection models were used to gather information for this assessment:

- A paper handout survey of over 200 attendees to the Interop NetSwitch '97 Tour during June, 1997. More than 100 responses provide general background data about familiarity with Layer 3 switching technology and about short-term purchase plans.

- Telephone interviews of over 300 network professionals in the United States, Canada, and Europe. Interview candidates were selected from people who had attended an Interop NetSwitch Tour in 1996 or 1997, or who had registered on the Strategic Networks web site. In addition to general background data, these interviews explored network growth expectations, current environments, budgets/plans, and decision authority for network purchases.

- On-site interviews with ten enterprise organizations, including individuals with decision-making, network planning, and network operations responsibilities. More detailed information was collected from these interviews, such as network topology, performance concerns, and specific organizational issues.

In addition, your authors begrudgingly admit to collectively having more than fifty years of industry experience in a variety or roles, including CIO, Consulting Engineer, Product Manager, Network Manager, Engineering Manager, Director of Market Research, and Consultant.

We would like to offer three notes of caution to the reader. First, all survey respondents had either attended a seminar on deploying LAN switching or registered their visit to the Strategic Networks web site. Thus, they are probably not representative of the broader network population. However, you will see that the survey respondents are representative of early adopters of high speed LAN technology

The second note of caution is that network organizations are extremely heterogeneous. Some of the dimensions along which end-user organizations vary include the degree to which they:

- Work in an environment in which IT is recognized as being strategic to the business;
- Make centralized vs. decentralized decisions on technology and/or vendors;
- Are early adopters of technology;
- Buy the best of breed vs. an integrated system;
- Are network savvy;
- Are well tied into the business issues their company is trying to solve; or
- Have reached the limits of their current architecture and are actively looking for alternatives.

Because of these variances, there are often significant differences among organizations that can get lost in the data aggregation process. These variances can be in terms of both the technologies the organizations deploy and the processes they use to evaluate technology. For example, three of the ten on-site interviews were with enterprises that had firm plans to implement Layer 3 switching in the very near term. This was in distinct contrast to the one that had not yet deployed any Layer 2 switching and had a difficult time even conceptualizing what they would do with Layer 3 switching.

The third note of caution is that your authors believe that surveys about future actions require skilled interpretation. It is often impossible for a network professional to know exactly what technology he or she will be deploying 18 to 24 months in advance. Most have little influence over, or even insight into, the major factors that will affect the decisions they make in that timeframe, including such factors as the development of alternative technologies, the pace of standardization, the "street" prices for products, as well as business requirements to support new functions or capabilities.

For example, in the late 1980s, every survey taken of network professionals indicated that they fully intended to deploy the OSI protocol suite when it was available. In fact, very few actually did. Because of this inherent weakness of using survey data to forecast the future, we provide both survey results and our interpretation of the data. Instances in which the survey respondents give consistent answers to a topic asked in various ways in multiple questions are highlighted, as well as instances for which we question the validity of the responses.

8.2 What is Currently in Place

To characterize the current LAN environment, we analyzed the number of networked desktops, the existing LAN technologies, the relative penetration of hubs and switches, the existing protocols, as well as the existing Layer 3 routing functions in use. Figure 8.1 shows the number of networked desktops within survey respondents' networks. As you can see, approximately 40% of the respondents came from small companies (100 to 999 networked desktops), while roughly 33% come from mid-sized companies (1,000 to 5,000 desktops).

We asked survey respondents to indicate which LAN technologies are currently being used within their networks. Their responses are contained in Figure 8.2, from which we can draw a number of conclusions:

- The dominant LAN technology is some variant of Ethernet;

- Almost the same number of companies that are using shared Ethernet are using switched Ethernet;

- The use of Layer 2 switching is not reserved for only medium- and large-sized companies;

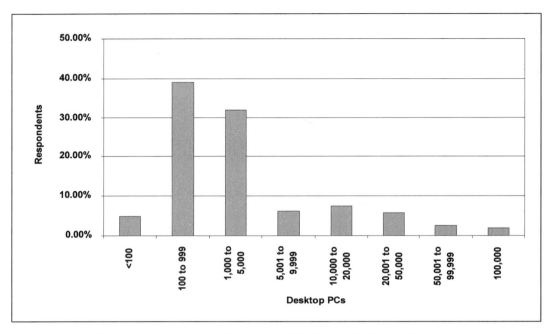

Figure 8.1   Number of Enterprise PCs Connected to the Network

- There has been a tremendous acceptance of both switched Fast Ethernet (over 50% of the respondents) as well as shared Fast Ethernet (over 30% of the respondents); and

- Roughly one out of every four respondents has deployed ATM.

It is interesting to combine the insights gained from Figures 8-1 and 8-2. In particular, while the survey base is primarily small- to mid-sized companies, given the LAN technologies they currently have in place, your authors are comfortable suggesting that these survey respondents tend to be early adopters of new LAN technology.

Layer 2 switching was first introduced to the marketplace in 1993. Since that time, the market has grown to a point where it is expected to be worth roughly $7 billion in 1998. Given this meteoric growth, another key component of the characterization of the current LAN marketplace is the relative penetration of hubs and Layer 2 switches. As shown in Figure 8.3, while virtually 100% of the survey respondents had a hub at the site at which they worked, only 78% of the respondents had any Layer 2 switching within that site. This matches your authors' experience with leading-edge IT organizations in the U.S. In particular, most, but not all, U.S.-based IT organizations have deployed Layer 2 switching. However, it is rare to find a company that has deployed it ubiquitously, i.e., to every desktop. It is important to note that this does not generalize internationally. For example,

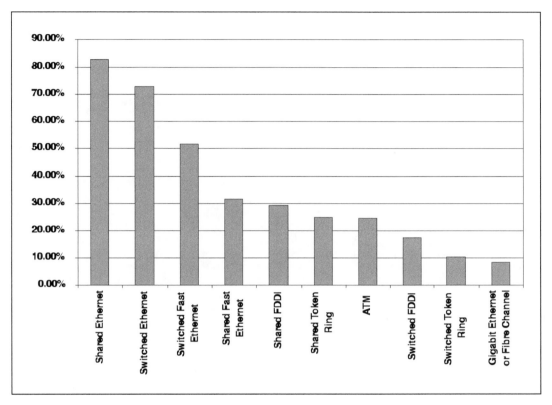

Figure 8.2   LAN Technologies in Current Use

based on our work in Canada, we would expect that only about 40% or 50% percent of Canadian companies have already deployed Layer 2 switching. From the survey data, it appears that U.S. respondents have four to six times as many switches installed as European respondents.

Principle: *There is considerable potential for network professionals to expand their utilization of Layer 2 switching, primarily to the desktop.*

As recently as a few years ago, it was common for network professionals to boast that they supported every possible protocol in their networks. This is changing rapidly. An increasing number of our clients have set a strategic direction to have TCP/IP be the protocol stack for all future applications. In order to quantify if the establishment of TCP/IP as the strategic protocol stack has had an impact in production networks, we asked the survey respondents to indicate which protocols were present somewhere in their networks. As shown in Figure 8.4, IP has a higher penetration than any other protocol.

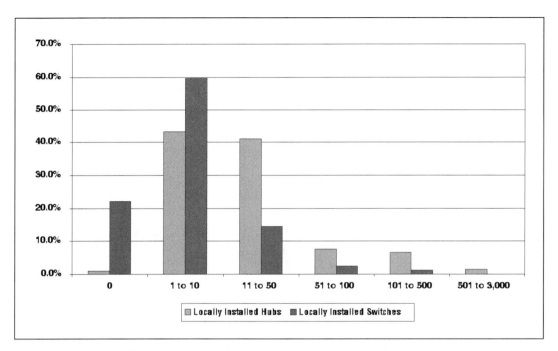

Figure 8.3   Relative Penetration of Hubs and Switches

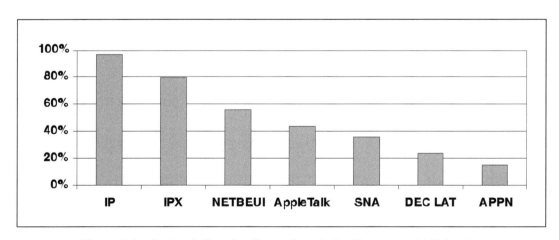

Figure 8.4   Protocols Running Somewhere in the Respondents' Networks

Combining the insights gained from Figures 8-2 and 8-4 with other work we've done leads us to conclude that in the year 2000 the predominant desktop LAN technology will be some variant of Ethernet and the dominant protocol stack will indeed be TCP/IP.

Principle: *The networking industry tends to gravitate to a small number of standards-based, long-lived technologies.*

Because of this convergence within enterprise networks on Ethernet and TCP/IP, most vendors have focused their Layer 3 switching solutions on these key technologies. Due to the resultant competition between vendors, as well as to the economy of scale that results when a large segment of the Internetworking industry focuses on a few key technologies, we believe that the price/performance ratio of products focused on Ethernet and TCP/IP will improve much more than the price/performance of other products.

Principle: *In order to realize significant price/performance improvements, network professionals should focus on Ethernet (broadly defined) as their desktop LAN technology and TCP/IP as their protocol stack.*

As was discussed in Chapter 3, routers perform switching, routing, and Layer 3 special services. By definition, Layer 3 switches perform some routing (at least traffic forwarding based on the L3 address, and may perform route processing). However, in order for Layer 3 switches to be considered as a viable alternative to a router, your authors believe these devices also need to perform at least the same Layer 3 special services that people are currently using routers to perform. This belief follows from our work with organizations who told us that if they deployed a router service such as security close to their users, they did so for a reason. If they are to use Layer 3 switches to upgrade their LAN infrastructures, in general they want to deploy the same functions at the same places in their networks.

The Layer 3 services that the highest number of survey respondents are using routers to perform include:

- Security (47%);
- Encapsulation (35%); and
- VLAN interconnection (18%).

8.3 What is Driving and/or Inhibiting Change

Troublesome Issues

As was discussed in Chapter 2, many technologies fail in the marketplace, largely because they fail to fulfill any real market need. To determine if Layer 3 switching meets a real market need, we asked the survey respondents to rate the importance of a number of ongoing, day-to-day, networking issues. In particular, we asked the respondents to rate the issue a 1 if it was of minor concern, 2 if it was important, and 3 if it kept them up at night. Table 8.1 lists the percentage of respondents who rated the issue a 3, i.e., it kept them up at night.

Table 8.1   Issues That Keep Survey Respondents Awake at Night

Concerns	% of Respondents
Problem Detection/Location/Resolution	57.1
Minimizing Unplanned Downtime	50.2
Security	47.1
More Bandwidth in the Backbone	38.7
Staffing Resources	32.3
Capital Costs of Upgrades	27.3
Cost of Operation	27.0
Maximizing the Useful Life of Capital Investments	25.3
Keeping Up with Unplanned Growth	25.3
Understanding/Measuring Network Traffic and Patterns	24.9
Ensuring Timely Changes (moves, adds, deletes)	24.2
Planning for Growth	22.0
More Bandwidth to the Desktop	16.2
Migration Planning	14.3

The fact that fault isolation and resolution is the number one issue keeping the respondents up at night is not a surprise. This has been a well-known fact within the networking industry for years. What is interesting here, is that in spite of the efforts of the entire industry (i.e., vendors, customers, consultants), insufficient progress seems to have been made in this area.

Principle: Network professionals will be limited in their ability to leverage their investments in network technology as long as they are preoccupied with fault isolation and resolution.

We believe that the importance of minimizing unplanned downtime is driven by two factors. First, the cause of unplanned downtime is yet another fault to be isolated and resolved. Perceived in this way, there is no new information gained from the rating for minimizing unplanned downtime, once we have agreed that fault isolation and resolution is the most important issue keeping network professionals up at night.

The second factor is that over the last few years most companies have come to rely increasingly on their networks. By that we mean the company's ability to do business is severely hampered if the network is down. Although some Layer 3 switching will certainly be deployed in wiring closets, your authors believe that the primary location where Layer 3 switches will be deployed is at central aggregation points, such as collapsed backbones, server farms, and campus network ingress/ egress. At these aggregation points, minimizing downtime (planned or not) is key to the success of responsible network professionals.

Principle: It is mandatory that Layer 3 switches offer the highest possible level of reliability.

Accurately measuring the importance of security in the marketplace is difficult. Survey results in this area are highly varied and often contradictory. For example, it is easy to point to surveys that show security is one of the industry's top issues, and equally easy to find surveys that show it is of relatively little importance. Your authors interpret this apparent contradiction to mean that network professionals are confused about security. Our clients struggle with issues such as: How do I deploy stringent security without overly affecting the business? How much security is enough? What processes and procedures do I need to enact? We do believe, however, that security is important to this particular set of respondents. In addition to so indicating on this question, they also told us that security was the number one Layer 3 special service that they were running on their routers (47%).

Principle: To be successful at replacing routers in the marketplace, Layer 3 switches must provide the same level of security that traditional routers provide.

With few exceptions, all of the remaining items listed in Table 8.1 as keeping network professionals up at night revolve around providing higher performance with a limited budget and limited staff resources. When comparing Layer 3 switches to traditional routers, all vendors of Layer 3 switches are promising an order of magnitude increase in performance with a corresponding order of magnitude decrease in cost. If vendors can indeed deliver on these promises, Layer 3 switches will be very successful in the marketplace because they address real market needs.

Impact of Applications

In order to understand the types of applications that are having the biggest impact on enterprise networks, we gave the survey respondents a set of eight types of applications. We then asked them to indicate the three application types that are having the biggest impact on their networks. We also gave the respondents the ability to indicate "other" as one of their top three. Figure 8.5 contains a summary of their responses.

It's no surprise that electronic mail leads this pack: usage continues to grow, people are becoming more dependent upon it, and more large files (reports, spreadsheet models, and presentations) are being mailed across enterprises. Client-server applications also stand out from the rest, as a relatively close second to e-mail. We interpret this as a growing awareness of the potential, not only for increased traffic volume, but also for changing traffic patterns, according to which servers are located where. Many of our consulting clients are centralizing servers for more cost-effective management and support, pulling them out of their former workgroup locations.

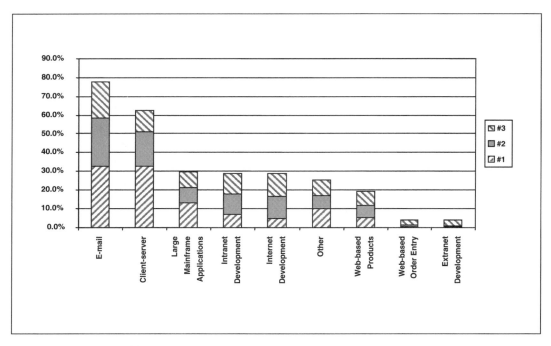

Figure 8.5   Top Applications Most Affecting Networks

Figure 8.5 also suggests that the network impact of developing intranet and Internet-based applications has grown in importance to be nearly equivalent to mainframe applications. Or is it the opposite, that the importance of mainframe applications has slipped relative to other categories? Perhaps people are just more familiar with mainframe communication requirements and more comfortable predicting their effects. On the other hand, your authors expect concern over the impact of all types of web/browser-based applications to continue growing, as browsers cost less or are free, and become the user interface of choice for access to all kinds of information. While we cannot simply aggregate the five categories based on web/browser technology (respondents may have checked more than one), they may well outgrow the significance of other categories in the very near future. The number of tools available to make web presentation easy, the number of firms developing applications, and the popularity of the browser interface at the desktop will all push growth. Adding these to other types of client-server applications, the likelihood for more and more traffic leaving the workgroup practically explodes onto the backbone. Layer 3 vendors should be challenged to *demonstrate* the improvements their products will make in any given network under these conditions.

As discussed in Chapter 2, we used to have an 80/20 rule for networking, i.e., only 20% of network traffic went out of the local subnet. Your authors believe that increased use of web/browser-based applications is one of the major drivers that will permanently revoke this old law.

Even if the users of a web/browser-based application and the application server itself are on the same subnet, the application is still likely to generate inter-subnet traffic. This follows from the propensity for this type of application to provide hypertext links to other systems. Hence, a user clicking on one of these links is immediately off merrily surfing the web, crossing subnet boundaries, and consuming routing capacity. While it is technically possible to facilitate this style of computing using traditional routers, it will be prohibitively expensive to do so.

Principle: The more web/browser-based applications a corporation deploys, the more viable Layer 3 switching is for them.

Figure 8.5 spoke to the multitude of computing styles, including web/browser-based, client-server, and mainframe, that typically exist concurrently within enterprises. To understand how network professionals cope with the demands placed on them by both the increasing number of networked applications as well as this increasing number of styles of computing, we asked them to indicate the techniques they use in this volatile application environment.

The survey responses to this question are summarized in Figure 8.6 and are entirely consistent with our experience. For example, we would expect that the option of providing more training would rate relatively high and that the option of providing more staff would rate relatively low. This follows because the great majority of our clients tell us that adding staff is not an alternative in their organizations for one of two reasons. Either they are under a virtual hiring freeze that is not likely to be lifted anytime soon, or they struggle to find qualified candidates for jobs they are allowed to fill. Given such constraints on adding staff, most of our clients are putting more emphasis on training their existing staff to support new technologies.

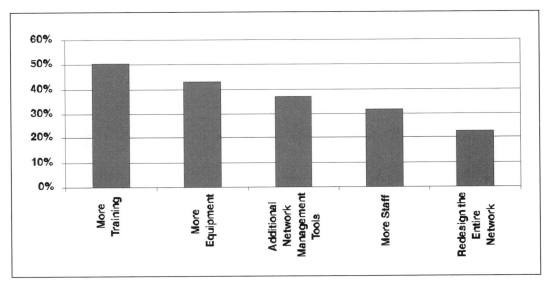

Figure 8.6   Respondent Techniques for Coping with Application Effects

Principle: A vendor's probability of competitive advantage in presenting a Layer 3 switching solution is directly proportional to the ease of use of their products.

While somewhat obvious, it is still interesting to observe that in spite of tightly constrained budgets, the survey respondents are roughly twice as likely to add more equipment to the network as they are to redesign the entire network. We believe that there is a simple, but powerful lesson here relative to the deployment of Layer 3 switching.

Principle: The probability of successful deployment of Layer 3 switching technology is inversely proportional to the amount of network redesign required by the vendor's products.

Figure 8.6 also shows that IT organizations feel they are almost as likely to need new network management tools as they are to need more equipment in response to application requirements. This matches our experience—we find that many organizations believe network management can help with the major problems listed in Table 8.1. The first three (fault isolation and resolution, minimizing unplanned downtime, and security) are classic network management issues. However, we meet many network professionals who also believe that network management tools can help with their other issues, such as providing more bandwidth, when budget and staff resources are tightly constrained.

Network Management

To test our hypothesis that network management is a key issue for network professionals, we asked the survey respondents to indicate the importance of network management to their operational activities. As can be seen in Figure 8.7, 64% of the respondents rated network management as either very or extremely important. From our work with clients we believe this is a significant shift from how network professionals viewed network management as recently as 12 to 18 months ago. We also see this interest in network management being in both operational and strategic areas, where strategic includes such activities as baselining, capacity planning, network design, and applications management.

Principle: The probability for successful deployment of a Layer 3 switching solution is directly proportional to the quality of the network management capability that is provided by the vendor. By quality we mean both functions and ease of use.

Growth

Growth, broadly defined, is typically a factor that drives change in enterprise networks. As shown in Figure 8.8, the survey respondents do not expect much growth in either the number of buildings they support or the number of subnets in their network. In fact, approximately 80% of the respondents expect less than a 10% change in either of these. It is interesting to observe that the distribution of responses for the growth in the number of buildings and the number of subnets is virtu-

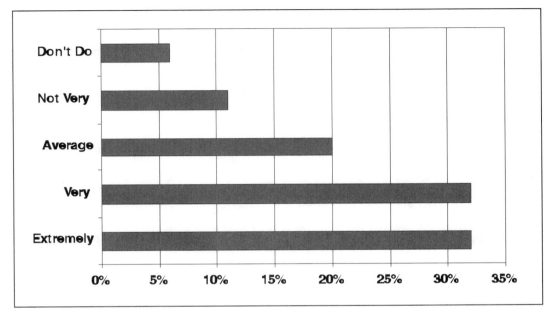

Figure 8.7   Importance of Network Management

ally identical. Combined with our experience, this suggests that organizations generally are not making changes to their subnet structure. The primary exception to this would be when they add new facilities.

Principle: *The probability for successful deployment of a Layer 3 switching solution is enhanced if the vendor's products allow the IT organization to maintain their existing subnet structure.*

It is interesting to see the reported increase in number of users—roughly 40% of the survey respondents are expecting a double-digit increase in the number of desktops attached to their networks. This resonates with what is happening for many of our clients. Most do not typically have some killer application that drives them to deploy new technology. Rather, they are driven by *more* of the *same*, i.e., more networked desktops, needing access to more applications, which have larger data sets, and residing on an increasing number of servers.

Please note that we are somewhat critical of the responses to the questions about expected growth in traffic volumes. It is our experience that most network professionals have a solid grasp on the growth of aspects of their network such as the number of buildings, subnets, and users. However, it is also our experience that very few network professionals have any solid quantification of how the traffic volume in their networks is changing. Consequently, we believe that the survey respondents gave a quick estimate without much thought in response to this question. In particular,

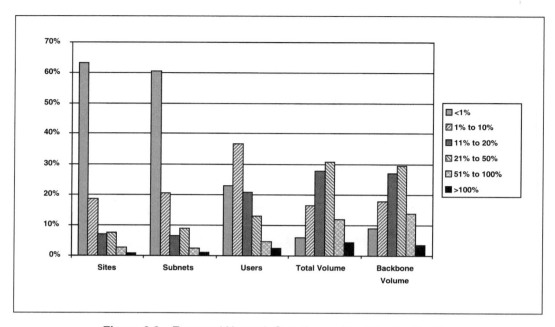

Figure 8.8   Expected Network Growth over Next Twelve Months

from our experience baselining enterprise networks, we have yet to find a network that was growing at less than 20% per year. We have, in a few cases, come across networks that were growing at more than 100% per year.

To put these growth figures into perspective, if a network is growing at 27% per year, the volume of network traffic doubles in three years. If a network is growing at 41% per year, the volume of network traffic doubles in only two years.

Principle: *Vendors of Layer 3 switching products are more likely to be successful if they can help potential customers quantify the need for increased routing capacity. This need is driven primarily by the combination of increasing traffic and shifting traffic patterns.*

Benefits and Features

To investigate what features are of interest to IT organizations, respondents were asked to identify which ones they would consider to be benefits of Layer 3 switching, relative either to traditional routing or to Layer 2 switching. The numbers of people identifying each feature as a benefit are shown in Table 8.2. Entries of "NA" indicate that we did not ask about the feature in that category.

Table 8.2   Features Identified as Benefits of Layer 3 Switching

Feature	Benefit vs. Traditional Routing	Benefit vs. Layer 2 Switching
Greater throughput	87%	NA
Scalability	84%	83%
Firewalling/security	NA	79%
Easier management	77%	NA
Lower latency	76%	NA
Lower cost per port	76%	NA
Filtering	NA	73%
VLAN interconnection	62%	60%

A very interesting aspect of Table 8.2 is that this is *not* one of those times when survey respondents rated everything of equal importance. More detail to appreciate this aspect is presented below.

One observation that can be made from Table 8.2 is that, with the possible exception of VLAN interconnection, a significant number of respondents perceived Layer 3 switches to be better than routers for each feature. A second observation has to do with cost. Given that Layer 3 switches do cost roughly one tenth the cost of a traditional router, we were very surprised that nearly one-quarter of the survey base did not see "lower cost per port" as a benefit of Layer 3 switching vs. traditional routers.

Principle: *Vendors of Layer 3 switches must educate their potential customers on the* economic *benefits of Layer 3 switches vs. traditional routers.*

To qualify further their views of benefits, we asked respondents to indicate the relative importance of features they considered to be benefits of Layer 3 switching. We provided a 5-point rating scale, where 1 meant the feature was not at all important and 5 meant the feature was very important to their organizations. Table 8.3 depicts the features that respondents thought were benefits of Layer 3 switching relative to Layer 2 switching, and Table 8.4 shows their ratings of Layer 3 switching versus traditional routing. In both cases, "highly important" is the combined percentage of "4" and "5" ratings, and "neutral" represents the "3" rating.

Table 8.3   Importance of Benefits: Layer 3 Switching versus Layer 2 Switching

Benefit	Highly Important	Neutral	Average Score
Firewall/Security	65.9%	26.1%	3.92
Scalability	65.0%	26.5%	3.85
Filtering	46.0%	41.9%	3.49
VLAN Interconnection	44.8%	36.6%	3.30

Given both the newness of Layer 3 switching and the fact that the majority of the survey base has only recently deployed Layer 2 switching, there is potential for survey respondents to be confused over the benefits of Layer 3 vs. Layer 2 switching. However, Table 8.2 shows this does not tend to be the case. As a general rule, the respondents understand that Layer 3 switches will offer them much more scalability as well as added functions, i.e., filtering and security. However, Table 8.3 shows that respondents are notably less convinced of the relative importance of L3 vs. L2 switching for interconnecting VLANs. One possible explanation is that the respondents do not know what added functions they would get in a Layer 3 switch that would help with interconnecting VLANs. However, we believe that the low response rate to the use of L3 switching to interconnect VLANs is due to the fact that so few of the respondents have actually deployed VLANs.

The results in Table 8.3 are consistent with findings from other questions. In particular, they emphasize again respondents' interest in the security capabilities of Layer 3 switching.

The first observation from Table 8.4 is that the most important feature (greater throughput) is rated so by twice as many respondents as the least important one (VLAN interconnection). It is equally interesting that "lower cost per port" is only highly important to about half the respondents. There is a possible connection between this and the fact that in Table 8.2, nearly one-quarter of the survey respondents did not identify lower cost per port as a benefit of Layer 3 switching relative to traditional routing.

Table 8.4   Importance of Benefits: Layer 3 Switching versus Traditional Routing

Benefit	Highly Important	Neutral	Average Score
Greater throughput	78.2%	18.1%	4.06
Scalability	68.9%	21.8%	3.91
Easier management	58.9%	35.3%	3.73
Lower latency	61.2%	30.6%	3.69
Lower cost per port	51.7%	39.1%	3.62
VLAN interconnection	39.3%	44.0%	3.26

Principle: *IT organizations respond notably more quickly to a network being functionally broken than to one that is economically broken.*

Migration to New Technologies

Having analyzed factors such as the issues that keep network professionals up at night, the changing styles of applications, as well as network growth, the authors wanted both to identify and prioritize any other factors that either drive or inhibit organizations in deploying network technology in general. To this end, we asked survey respondents to indicate which factors influence their migration to new networking technologies. We again used a 5-point scale, where 1 meant the factor was very insignificant and 5 meant the factor was very significant. Figure 8.9 shows which factors were ranked as important to the respondent base, giving the combined ratings of either a 4 or a 5.

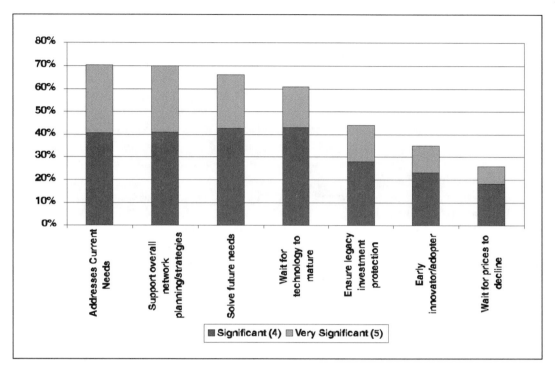

Figure 8.9 Importance of Factors Influencing Migration to New Technologies

The top three factors can be summarized as network professionals are motivated to deploy new technology if it both meets current needs and simultaneously supports future requirements. In addition, where one exists, the deployment of new technology needs to be in concert with the company's networking strategy. Notice that only about one-third of the survey respondents stated that maintaining a strategy of early adoption was important in their decisions to migrate to new technologies. Even without such a strategy, remember we found earlier that significant numbers of sites had installed L2 switching, Gigabit Ethernet, and ATM. Thus we maintain our assessment that the survey base tends to be early adopters of networking technology, for strategic reasons or not.

While not quite as significant as the top three factors shown in Figure 8.9, an inhibitor to the deployment of networking technology is the immaturity of "version one" of any product. What makes this observation all the more dramatic is that the survey base represents early adopters of networking technology. If 60% of this group are inhibited by technologically immature products, your authors believe that this will be an even greater inhibitor for the broader population base.

More than 40% of the survey base indicated that it was very important to them to ensure that any new technology also provided investment protection for legacy network products. We interpret this relatively low percentage by suggesting that this is not really a decision criterion for most companies—it is a requirement. Finally, only 26% of the survey base find it important to wait for the price of new technology to drop prior to deploying it. This is totally consistent with the group being early adopters of networking technology.

Budget Factors

In general, your authors have found that accurate budget information is notoriously difficult to collect. An indication of the budget sizes for survey respondents is shown in Figure 8.10, but it is important to note that 31% of respondents either declined to answer or did not have budget information available during the survey.

Anecdotal information we obtained from questioning seminar attendees around the U.S. suggests that budgets are mostly increasing at very modest rates, usually less than 10%. Compared with annual traffic growth of 40% and more, lack of corresponding budget growth is a significant concern for most network professionals. Results from this particular survey were somewhat different. Although nearly 40% of all respondents did not provide budget growth information, of those who did, nearly 25% expected more than 25% increases in the next year.

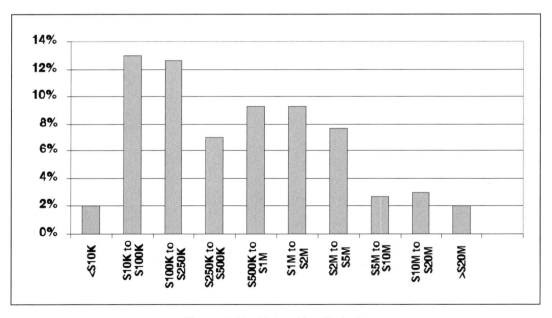

Figure 8.10   Networking Budgets

Other Inhibitors

To round out the analysis of forces with impact on networks, we sought to identify any factors that would specifically inhibit deployment of Layer 3 switching technology. To this end, survey respondents were asked to indicate any and all barriers to deploying Layer 3 switching. As shown in Figure 8.11, the top barrier is the lack of standards/lack of proven technologies. This further validates the data in Figure 8.9 that indicated even our early adopters are concerned about the lack of technological maturity of the products. Your authors believe that this inhibitor will be more of an issue for some types of Layer 3 switching products (those based on flow switching) than others (packet-by-packet products).

The second inhibitor, no proof of performance benefits in a real-world network, will disappear rapidly. There are currently volumes of test data from multiple independent laboratories that quantify the performance of this technology. In addition, many IT organizations are in the process of deploying Layer 3 switches; we believe these will provide both performance data and reference accounts.

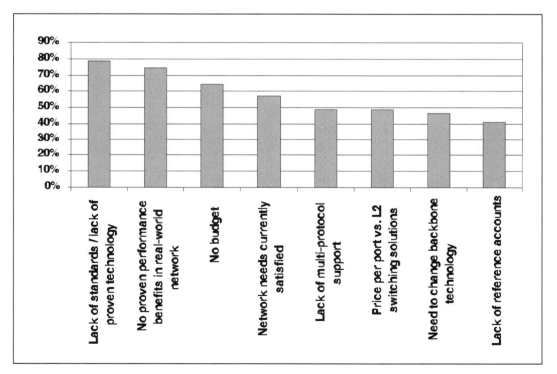

Figure 8.11   Barriers to Implementing Layer 3 Technology

The third most common inhibitor, no budget, is perplexing. We found that only a small percentage of survey respondents expect their networking budgets to decrease. Most network organizations will experience modest budget increases, so there appears to be money available for network equipment. Hence, we believe that the issue of "no budget" actually means no budget has been specifically allocated for Layer 3 switches.

Principle: *One way that vendors of Layer 3 switches can be successful is to convince prospective customers that their Layer 3 switch is really a router, only notably less expensive and with notably higher performance.*

It is insightful to look at the next most important inhibitor, network needs currently satisfied, in conjunction with both the no-budget inhibitor and our previous discussion of the price premium relative to a Layer 2 switch. We believe that many survey respondents have only recently deployed Layer 2 switching because the number of switches installed at most sites is rather low. The switches that were installed, however, removed some, if not all, of the major bottlenecks in those networks. Many of these same respondents thus do not yet understand why they now need to introduce one more new technology into their networks.

Principle: *Most enterprise networks are not functionally broken. They are, however, economically broken.*

What we mean here is that, with a few exceptions such as the need to support applications demanding extremely low and predictable latency, today's mix of LAN technologies will support existing and emerging business requirements. However, as network traffic doubles and traffic patterns shift, the need for routing capacity increases noticeably and today's technology mix will not scale economically.

Just over one-half of the respondents thought that having a switch only support IP would be a significant impediment to their deployment of Layer 3 switching. When your authors talked to IT organizations about using a Layer 3 switch for IP and leaving the existing router to handle all other protocols, the reaction was mixed. Those who liked the idea seemed to appreciate the performance improvements that Layer 3 switching would bring to their IP traffic. Those who did not like the idea were concerned with trouble-shooting a network that might have as many as four types of equipment (hubs, Layer 2 switches, Layer 3 switches, classical routers) coming from multiple vendors.

Principle: *To be successful, vendors of Layer 3 switching equipment must assist their customers to develop LAN architectures that incorporate Layer 3 switching effectively and appropriately.*

In fact, we believe that these architectures should address the use of Layer 3 switching as a replacement for either Layer 2 switching and/or classical routers. The architectures should also address network management in general, and troubleshooting in particular.

8.4 Alternatives Being Considered

Purchase Plans

To gain an understanding of which technologies the survey respondents intended to be deploying in their networks over the next 18 months, we asked two questions. The first requested a response of Yes or No on their intention to deploy various types of network technologies some time in the next 18 months. Figures 8-12a and 8-12b summarize the percentage of respondents who intend to deploy the indicated technologies.

There are a number of conclusions that can be drawn from Figures 8.12a and 8.12b:

- Hubs will remain a dominant piece of network equipment.

- Approximately 25% of the IT organizations who currently use hubs will not be increasing their investment in hubs.

- Ethernet Layer 2 switches of some variety, whether to support primarily Ethernet or Fast Ethernet, will continue to be dominant elements of network technology.

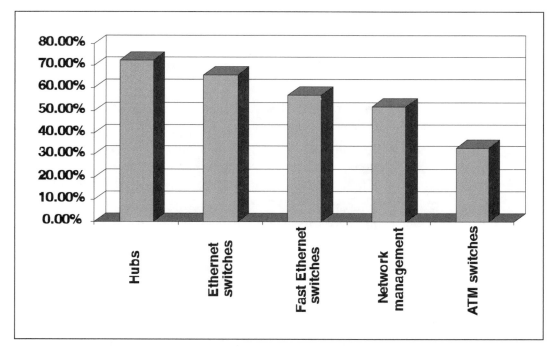

Figure 8.12a　Intentions to Purchase Network Equipment (a)

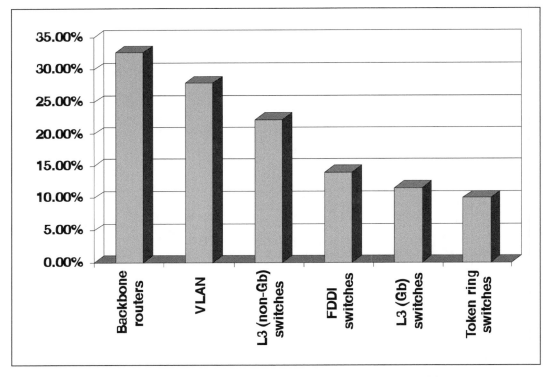

Figure 8.12b   Intentions to Purchase Network Equipment (b)

- Unlike Ethernet Layer 2 switches, Token Ring Layer 2 switches are the technology people are least likely to acquire.

- The respondents are more likely to increase their investment in network management than they are to increase their investments in a myriad of connectivity options, including ATM, backbone routers, and Layer 3 switches. Note that this is consistent with the data depicted in Figure 8.2.

- The respondents are as likely to increase their investment in backbone routers as they are to acquire a Layer 3 switch.

The second question built on the first. For each technology that they intended to deploy, we asked the survey respondents to indicate *when* they intended to deploy it: within six months, between six and twelve months, between twelve and eighteen months, or didn't know.

The answers are summarized in Table 8.5. Note that allowing for round-off errors, each row sums to 100%. This 100% is not the entire survey group, but 100% of the respondents who indicated that they were going to deploy the relevant technology.

Table 8.5   Network Purchasing Plans for 1998-1999

Product	% Planning to buy	% within 6 months	% within 1 year	% within 18 months	% "No Time frame"	% stated "Major Purchase"
Hubs	72.4	68.9	24.1	2.4	4.7	18.5
Switches (L2)	65.8	64.4	23.9	5.3	6.4	45.5
Fast Ethernet Switches (L2)	56.8	53.8	31.0	7.0	8.2	53.9
Network Management	51.8	50.3	30.1	6.3	13.3	38.6
ATM Switches	32.9	30.4	47.8	14.1	7.6	72.5
Backbone Routers	32.6	41.4	37.9	9.2	11.5	67.2
VLANs	27.9	39.2	36.5	9.5	14.9	56.3
L3 Switches (with Gigabit)	22.3	41.5	35.4	13.8	9.2	60.4
FDDI Switches	14.0	50.0	30.6	8.3	11.1	67.9
L3 Switches (without Gigabit)	11.6	15.6	28.1	25.0	31.3	71.4
Token Ring Switches	10.0	42.9	53.6	--	3.6	40.9
Other[1]	14.0	48.0	32.0	8.0	12.0	45.0

1.   "Other" products cited ranged from sniffers to audio and video distribution systems. No single mention could be ranked from this open-ended question.

Your authors place far more creditability in what people say they are going to deploy sooner (i.e., within six months) rather than later (i.e., 12 to 18 months, or "don't know"). With that guideline in mind, there are several observations that can be made from Figures 8-12a and b and Table 8.5:

- Hubs are the technology most people intend to buy. In addition, "hubs" had the highest percentage of people who intended to buy in the next six months.

- Ethernet switches, whether 10 Mbps or 100 Mbps, are the second most popular technology (after hubs) that the survey respondents intend to buy. They also have the second highest (after hubs) percentage of respondents who intend to acquire them in the next six months.

- Backbone routers were in the middle of the pack in terms of which technologies people intended to buy (32.6%). However, they had a moderate percentage of people who intended to buy soon and a fairly high percentage of people who did not know when they would buy.

- Layer 3 switches, with or without Gigabit Ethernet, are among the least likely technologies for the survey respondents to acquire. However, the percentage intending to buy Layer 3 switches without Gigabit Ethernet within six months is nearly the same as those intending to buy backbone routers within six months. Those intending to buy Layer 3 switches with Gigabit Ethernet had the highest proportion of those who did not know when they would purchase.

- Network management was in the top tier of technologies that companies intend to purchase. However, it had the second lowest percentage of respondents who intended to buy within six months. It also had the highest percentage of respondents who didn't know when they would buy.

Principle: *IT organizations have concrete plans to make sizable investments in both hubs and Layer 2 switches.*

Principle: *The backbone router market is vulnerable. IT organizations who delay their purchases for 6 to 12 months are likely to decide not to acquire a backbone router.*

Principle: *The Layer 3 switching market has solid short-term potential given the newness of the technology.*

Principle: *While network professionals uniformly state the importance to themselves of network management, they are confused about how to realize its potential.*

Backbone Upgrade Strategy

Your authors also wanted to gain an understanding of how the survey respondents intended to upgrade their backbone LANs. Approximately 30% currently use a router to implement a collapsed backbone LAN. About one-third of this group (11% of the total pool of respondents) have no intention of modifying their existing router-centric, collapsed backbone LAN. We found approximately one-third (36.8%) of all respondents claiming firm commitment to a strategy of using LAN switches to replace routers in their backbone LANs, with about one-third of these (13.6% of all respondents) firmly committed to the use of ATM switches. This is consistent with what we saw in Figure 8.2, where 26% already are using ATM somewhere in their networks. Fewer than half (44.5%) say they are evaluating L3 options for upgrading. Given the overlap in these categories and the early adoption history of these respondents, we believe that far more than half of IT organizations are still evaluating their options to upgrade LAN backbones.

Principle: *There is currently no clear technology of choice as seen by IT organizations for upgrading backbone LANs.*

Quality of Service Strategy

In the last year, your authors have noticed a distinct increase in interest from IT organizations on the topic of quality of service (QoS). To quantify this, we asked the survey respondents to indicate their QoS strategies, with top responses shown in Table 8.6. Perhaps the most interesting observation is that virtually no one (5.2%) stated that QoS was unimportant to them. However, while implying that QoS is important, almost half the respondents (45.3%) have not yet developed a strategy for implementing QoS. As was the case with upgrading backbone LANs, we believe that a higher percentage of all IT organizations have yet to develop a strategy for implementing QoS than indicated by the survey respondents.

Table 8.6   Quality of Service Strategy Options

Statement of Strategy	% of Respondents
Quality Of Service Is Important To Us, But We Have Not Determined What Our Strategy Will Be To Deliver It In Our Network	45.3%
Our Strategy For Quality Of Service Is To Use LAN Switches With Packet Prioritization Capabilities	24.7%
Our Strategy For Quality Of Service Is To Use ATM Switches With Bandwidth Reservation Capabilities	11.8%
Our Strategy For Quality Of Service Is To Use Enhanced Routers And New IP Protocols Such As RSVP	8.0%
Quality Of Service Is Not Important To Us	5.2%

Principle: *There is currently no clear agreement among IT organizations about how to implement QoS.*

The most common strategy for implementing QoS (24.7%) was to do so via LAN switches using packet prioritization capabilities. The fact that 11.8% of the respondents intend to implement QoS via ATM switches is again consistent with respondents' previous responses relative to their use of ATM technology, as well as with ATM's inherent QoS capabilities.

Plans for Gigabit Ethernet

We specifically asked respondents about their intent to incorporate Gigabit Ethernet into their LANs. We believe that the 31% stating intention to use Gigabit Ethernet in their networks is consistent with the technology base respondents currently have in place. In particular, recall from Figure 8.2, roughly 50% already have switched Fast Ethernet deployed, while roughly 30% already have shared Fast Ethernet deployed in their networks. For these IT organizations, Gigabit Ethernet is a logical next step.

It is also interesting to note that only about half of the respondents who intend to use Gigabit Ethernet currently intend to couple that usage with the deployment of Layer 3 switching. Your authors believe this could be a mistake for two reasons. The first reason is that many Layer 2 switches have limited ability to control broadcast storms. As we mentioned in Chapter 2, broadcast storms consume resources: people, network, and servers. At gigabit per second speeds, a broadcast storm has the potential to consume all of the computing power in the network just processing bogus packets. It seems to us that a large number of IT organizations may not yet have considered this possibility.

A second concern we have with using Gigabit Ethernet in conjunction only with Layer 2 switches is the inherent limitations of the spanning tree protocol. We discussed one of these in Chapter 2, the inability to have simultaneous, active links between devices such as Layer 2 switches, which has the potential to limit the scalability of a network. We believe this will be a serious short-term issue for those trying to use Gigabit Ethernet in either a collapsed backbone or campus backbone network. The second limitation of spanning tree is the time required for a network to re-converge after a link failure, which can vary from thirty seconds to several minutes. Such a time period would equate to packet losses that could be as small as a million packets or as large as several millions of packets for Gigabit speeds.

8.5 Decision Processes and Criteria

Value and Authority

To establish some context for understanding the decision making process that IT organizations use for major networking purchases, we first needed to understand what the survey base considered to be a "major" network purchase. Figure 8.13 depicts the dollar amounts that the survey respondents associate with a major network purchase.

Having quantified what constitutes a major network purchase, we asked the survey respondents to identify who makes the final decision about a major network purchase. Their responses are detailed in Figure 8.14. Our interpretation is that depending upon the company you are in, just about anyone can and does make the final decision on major networking purchases. More specifically, in over one-third of respondent companies, the final decision on major network purchases is made by either a committee or "other." After that, the most common final decision maker is the CEO/President—but only 13% of the time.

It is useful to combine the insights provided by Figures 8-13 and 8-14. Not only can just about anyone make the final decision relative to major network purchases, but there is no consensus among the survey respondents as to what even constitutes a major network purchase.

Principle: *Network organizations are notably heterogeneous in terms of how they make decisions for major network purchases.*

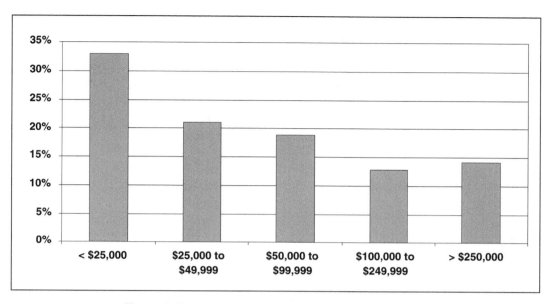

Figure 8.13   How Much Constitutes a "Major" Purchase

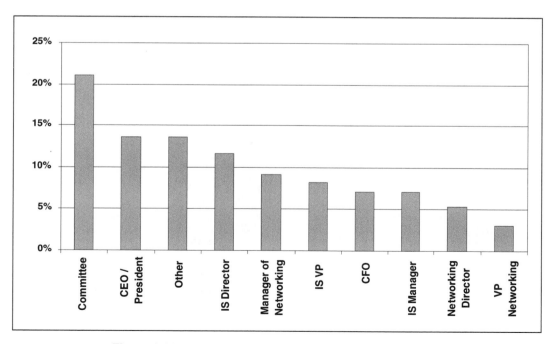

Figure 8.14   Final Decision Authority for Network Purchases

Pricing Implications

As we stated previously, your authors believe that most enterprise networks are not functionally broken, but they are economically broken. Given this premise, we wanted to quantify how much network professionals would have to save in order for them to buy a Layer 3 switch instead of a router. Figure 8.15 details those answers. Interestingly enough, 30% of the respondents would not need any financial incentive to encourage them to buy a Layer 3 switch versus a traditional router. Roughly 10% of the respondents would require a reduction of 50% or more.

We see three viable explanations for why the survey base expects and/or demands such a small saving in order for them to buy a Layer 3 switch instead of a traditional router. One explanation, as detailed in Table 8.4, is that some of the survey respondents are really driven to purchase Layer 3 switches based on their perceived advantages over traditional routers, i.e., throughput, scalability. The second explanation also has its roots in Table 8.4, which shows that roughly 20% of the survey base do not regard lower per-port cost as an advantage of Layer 3 switching versus routing. Hence, as we concluded previously, many IT organizations have not yet internalized the tremendous cost-saving potential of a Layer 3 switch versus a traditional router. The third explanation is that two-thirds of the respondents have no intention of acquiring Layer 3 switching in the next 18 months. Hence, it is highly likely that the majority of survey respondents have not spent much time analyzing the advantages of Layer 3 switching in general, and the cost benefits of Layer 3 switching in particular. This last comment is supported by the fact that 60% of survey respondents (Figure 8.11) stated that they are satisfied with their current network needs.

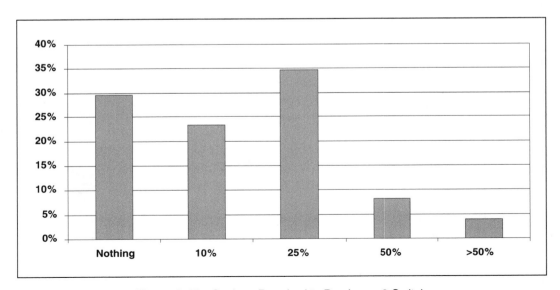

Figure 8.15 Savings Required to Buy Layer 3 Switch

Recall that survey respondents have already made a significant deployment of Layer 2 switches (Figure 8.2) and intend to increase that investment (Figure 8.12a). Because of the strong appeal of Layer 2 switching, we asked the survey respondents how much of a premium they would be willing to pay for a Layer 3 switch versus a Layer 2 switch. Their answers to that question are summarized in Figure 8.16, which shows that 35% of the population are not willing to pay more than what a Layer 2 switch costs to get a Layer 3 switch. Also notice that approximately 85% of all respondents were only willing to pay a premium of 10% or less for a Layer 3 switch as compared to a Layer 2 switch.

The authors draw two conclusions from the data shown in Figure 8.16. In our experience, it is very difficult to have IT organizations creditably discuss the extra price they would be willing to pay for a technology that they are not actively considering for deployment. Stereotypically, IT organizations at this stage of technology adoption "want it all." They want the extra capabilities of the new technology at no extra cost, either in dollars or in staffing.

The second conclusion, as we've noted multiple times previously, is that the survey base is somewhat naïve relative to the cost of a Layer 3 switch. This observation is supported by the fact that the distribution of responses shown in Figures 8-15 and 8-16 is strikingly similar, prompting us to conclude that the respondents answered both questions quickly, with minimum reflection.

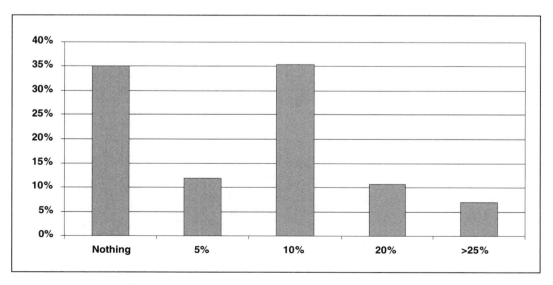

Figure 8.16   Acceptable Premium over Layer 2 Switch

Selection Criteria

To gain some insight into the decision criteria that respondents would use to choose among Layer 3 switching products, we asked them to rate a variety of factors relative to their importance in the decision to either purchase or recommend a Layer 3 switching product. We allowed for three possible answers: very important, important, or not important at all, scoring them 3, 2, 1 respectively. Figure 8.17 and Table 8.7 summarize the responses to this question.

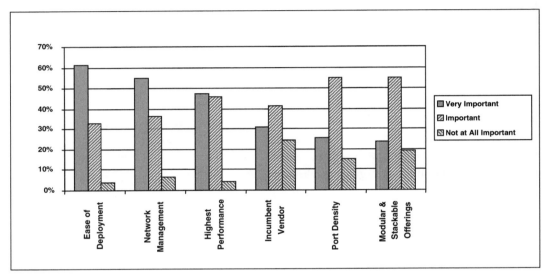

Figure 8.17   Importance of Factors in Layer 3 Switch Selection

Table 8.7   Importance of Factors Influencing Purchases

Factor	Very Important	Important	Average Score
Easy Deployment	62.2%	33.7%	2.58
Net Management	56.5%	36.7%	2.49
Highest Performance	48.3%	47.3%	2.43
Incumbent Vendor	32.5%	42.1%	2.07
Port Density	26.9%	57.3%	2.11
Form Factor/Package	24.5%	56.1%	2.05

The clearest conclusion to be drawn from these is that ease of deployment of a Layer 3 product is an extremely important decision criterion to the respondents. This is consistent with the fact that the great majority of respondents will not be making any significant additions to the staff in their organizations (Figure 8.2). As mentioned previously, we also believe that one class of L3 switch (Packet-by-Packet) will be easier to deploy than another (flow switching).

Respondents have clearly indicated that network management is the second most important issue to them when choosing a Layer 3 switch. It is insightful to combine the issues of ease of deployment and network management into a single category, serviceability and manageability. Having done this, the level of importance is quite consistent with the data we presented in Chapter 2, particularly where serviceability and manageability were typically more important decision criteria than were technology and architecture.

We suspect that choosing the highest performing switch may not actually be quite as important to the marketplace as it appears above. This is a difficult question to ask adequately in a paper survey. When the authors probed this issue during the on-site interviews, there were some IT organizations who subscribed to a philosophy of always buying the highest performing network hardware. However, this was relatively rare. More typically, IT organizations wanted enough capacity to meet what they perceived their needs to be over the next two or three years. There was little to no interest on the part of these IT organizations to pay for more capacity than they thought they would use in that time frame.

We can view the importance of high port density as a decision criterion somewhat analogous to the importance of highest throughput as a decision criterion. IT organizations certainly want high density. However, as a general rule, they will not pay a premium for a device that supports notably more ports than they foresee needing. At the same time, it is clear to us that Layer 3 switches with very low port density may have significant problems with scale as the network grows.

To exemplify this point, consider a somewhat hypothetical IT organization which has deployed a Layer 3 switch that only supports 6 Gigabit Ethernet ports. Further assume that this switch (Figure 8.18) is supporting three Layer 2 switches, each of which connects several hubs. In addition, the L3 switch also supports an L2 switch that connects to a number of servers. Notice that the Gigabit Ethernet link between these two (the L3 switch and the L2 connecting the servers) is a potential bottleneck.

As the number of Layer 2 switches exceeds six, the IT organization is forced to deploy a second L3 switch. However, because traffic needs to flow between the two L3 switches, they must be connected, as shown in Figure 8.19. Note that this connection between the L3 switches consumes one of the scarce ports on each switch and becomes another potential bottleneck.

As the requirement to connect additional L2 switches increases, the network is incapable of scaling (Table 8.8). One of the key assumptions in constructing Table 8.8 is that there is only a single Gigabit Ethernet link between each pair of L3 switches. The network would be somewhat more scalable if that assumption were relaxed. For example, the design would scale to connect more L2 switches if each L3 switch had two Gigabit Ethernet links for connection to other L3 switches. However, such a design would have other points of blockage and delay.

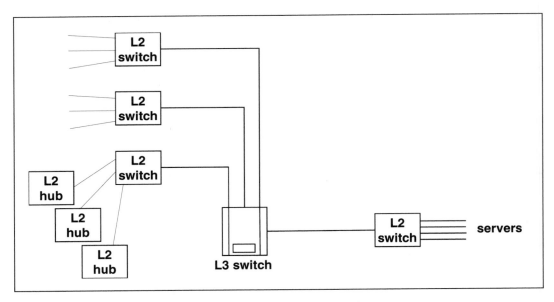

Figure 8.18   Low Port-Density L3 Switch

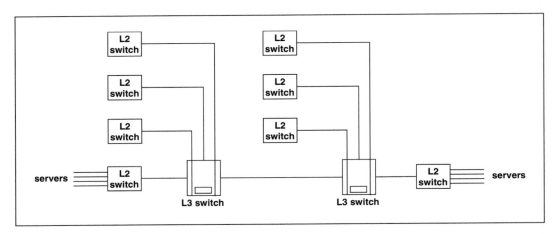

Figure 8.19   Two Low Port-Density L3 Switches Connected

Table 8.8   Scalability of a Six-Port Switch

Number of L3 Switches	Maximum Number of L2 Switches That Can Be Connected
1	6
2	10
3	12
4	12
5	10

To generalize the above situation, let NS stand for the Number of L3 Switches and let NP stand for the maximum Number of Ports on each switch. Then the maximum number of Layer 2 switches that can be connected is:

$$\text{Maximum Number} = \text{NS} * (\text{NP} - \text{NS} + 1)$$

Principle: *If an IT organization reaches the port limits of a small Layer 3 switch and begins to cascade the switches, things get very bad, very quickly.*

Returning to our discussion of Figure 8.19, the relatively low importance that respondents placed on a single vendor having both modular and stackable offerings is consistent with the market for Layer 2 switches. In particular, stackable Layer 2 switches have not been as successful in the marketplace as stackable hubs. However, there certainly are cases where the capability of a single vendor to offer both stackable and chassis-based products is important. For example, we've worked with one university that made a commitment to buy all its Layer 3 switches from a single vendor, in part to increase the likelihood of interoperability. The university would like to deploy chassis-based L3 switches in the campus backbone, as well as in some larger departmental networks. However, they definitely want the option of a stackable switch for the majority of the department and residence hall networks. This university used the criterion of having both stackable and chassis-based Layer 3 switch products to determine which vendors would receive their Request For Proposal (RFP).

From Figure 8.19, we also see that just under 30% of respondents thought incumbent vendor was not at all an important factor in the selection of Layer 3 technology. Interestingly enough, roughly the same percentage of respondents gave each of the other two responses, i.e., that the incumbent was an important factor (41%) and that the incumbent was a very important factor (31%).

Importance of Multiple Vendors

To provide some insight into the role of the incumbent vendor, the survey respondents were asked to indicate how important it was to have multiple vendors in their network solution. Their answers are summarized in Figure 8.20. Typical benefits that survey respondents saw from a multi-vendor solution were that they were less likely to be locked into a proprietary solution, that they could play one vendor against another to get better pricing, and that they would have a better selection of technologies and products.

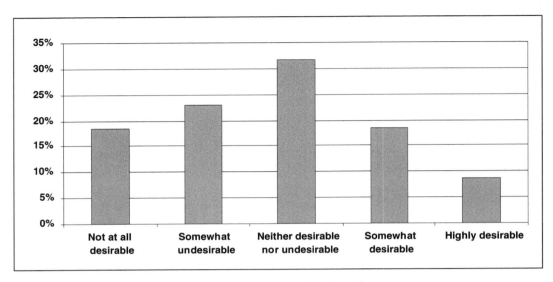

Figure 8.20   Importance of Multiple Vendors

The distribution of answers shown in Figure 8.20 is not quite symmetrical. The survey respondents have a moderate preference for a single vendor, and this is in line with our experience. In particular, over the last 12 to 18 months, we have had a growing number of our clients ask us to evaluate RFP responses and go back to them with the one vendor they should select. The most common reason motivating our clients to choose a single vendor seems to be that they are worried about interoperability issues among products from different vendors, particularly if the technology is relatively new.

Another trend we've seen recently is that many of our clients have chosen a single strategic vendor per technology. For example, they might have one vendor for Layer 2 switches and another for routers. Ideally, they do this in a way that avoids proprietary technology. This gives them the option to replace a vendor over time with a manageable amount of effort if a vendor is not meeting their requirements. When IT organizations who fit this preceding description evaluate Layer 3 switching technology, they typically look at their incumbent vendors and a maximum of one or two additional vendors as candidate suppliers.

We believe that over the next 12 to 18 months there will be clear winners and losers in the network equipment market. One possibility is that current Layer 2 switch vendors will become dominant in the Layer 3 switching market at the expense of current router vendors. A second possibility is just the reverse; i.e., current router vendors will dominate the Layer 3 switching marketplace at the expense of current Layer 2 vendors. A third possibility, which could be complementary to either of the other two, is that one of the Layer 3 start-up companies will rise to become a major player in the marketplace. We think the dynamics will be interesting to watch!

9 *Summary and Recommendations*

9.1 Background

These are the most demanding times in history to be a network professional. Business change is constant and has two key characteristics. The first of these characteristics is that businesses are increasingly relying on networks in order to function. The second of these characteristics is that the rate of growth of data traffic is typically an order of magnitude higher than the rate of growth of the network resources that are available to support the emerging requirements.

Given the gap between the growth rate of network requirements and resources (The Gap), network professionals must continually reinvent how they provide business critical network services. The authors believe that the deployment of Layer 3 switching is a key component of that reinvention. To assist the reader, the authors will both suggest criteria that can be used to evaluate Layer 3 switches as well as to identify ten steps that are key to the successful deployment of this new technology.

9.2 Characteristics of Layer 3 Switches

This section will list some of the criteria the author's recommend that network professionals use to evaluate alternative Layer 3 switches.

- Number and type of interfaces supported, i.e., Ethernet (10/100/1000 Mbps), FDDI, Token Ring, and ATM
- Throughput
- Distributed architecture

- Efficient route table search process
- Protocol support, i.e., IP, IPX
- Standards based routing protocols, i.e., RIP, RIP II, and OSPF
- Policy-based management capabilities
- Advanced IP multicast capabilities
- Standards based software and hardware QoS capabilities
- Integrated security
- Resiliency broadly defined
- Amount and type of buffering
- VLAN support
- Trunking
- Efficient support for multicast and broadcast traffic
- Enhanced ASIC capabilities such as programmable ASICs
- Accounting/metering
- Network Management tools

9.3 Ten Steps to Success

This section will summarize ten steps that enterprise users can take that the authors believe will lead them to the successful deployment of Layer 3 switching. Note that a number of these steps reflect the author's belief that network professionals continually reinvent themselves in order to manage the pressures induced by The Gap.

Deploy Standards Based Solutions

Proprietary solutions tend to do well in the marketplace only if they are available significantly before standards based solutions are available. This is not the case with Layer 3 switching. Standards based, Layer 3 switching products that run at wire speed are currently available. The authors do acknowledge that there could be some compelling reason, such as notably lower cost, to encourage network professionals to implement a proprietary solution. However, we believe that this should be the minority of instances.

Migrate Away from a Four- or a Five-Level LAN Architecture

The authors, like most equipment vendors, have slideware that depicts a four level LAN hierarchy. Our slides show shared hubs connecting desktops. These hubs connect to Layer 2 switches in the wiring closets and these Layer 2 switches connect to a Layer 3 switch in the basement. In most cases, this Layer 3 switch is connected to a traditional router. The router interfaces to the WAN and also routes all the protocols that the Layer 3 switch will not route. In the case of 3Com's Fast IP, added intelligence is required in the NIC.

The authors believe that this multi-tiered architecture is totally acceptable for today. We say this in part because this architecture optimizes the price/performance of multiple classes of network hardware. More importantly, this architecture leverages the existing investment in network equipment.

However, on a going forward basis, this architecture is notable sub-optimal. The cause of this sub-optimality is the support costs involved with operating four or five levels of functionality within a given LAN infrastructure. As described in chapter 2, support costs typically represent more than half the cost of LAN ownership.

Possible ways to reduce the number of levels include:

- Eliminate the NIC from having an active role in routing;
- Connect all future desktops with Layer 2 switches instead of hubs;
- Do not distinguish between Layer 2 and Layer 3 switches, i.e., deploy one class of device that you configure based on your needs; and
- Deploy Layer 3 switches that have the appropriate WAN interfaces.

Closely Analyze a Vendor's Product Line

The previous section of this chapter detailed specific functionality that you should look for in a Layer 3 switch. However, you should also examine the status of a vendor's entire LAN product line. In particular, you need to examine those portions of the vendor's product line that are relevant to the LAN architecture you intend to deploy, noted above.

The authors would like to point out that at any point in time, some vendors are selling leading edge products, while some are selling more mature products. Perhaps more importantly, most large vendors' product lines are an amalgamation of products that were internally developed, were the result of one or more acquisitions, or are being OEMed. Enterprise customers need to determine where a given product sits on the product life cycle. More specifically, is the vendor still making significant investments in the products, or is it at or near to end of life?

Closely Examine a Vendor's Service and Support Capabilities

This step involves a variety of tasks. At a simple level, it involves determining who services the products, the equipment vendor or a third party, and where the service centers are located. It also involves identifying the cost for each service option, i.e., support eight hours a day, five days a week (5 x 8) with a two hour response time versus support seven days a week, twenty four hours a day (7 x 24) with a four hour response time. At a more complex level, this step involves determining if your intended vendor will accept a contract that drives the right behavior. This could include bonuses for good performance as well as penalties for poor performance.

Avoid Deploying Small Devices at Network Concentration Points

In this context, the authors use the term small to refer to two parameters of a switch. The first is the switch's throughput capacity. The second is the number of interfaces the switch supports.

As previously discussed, when network professionals combine multiple small switches to make up a big switch, bad things happen. One design option is to move the small switch to the periphery of the network. While this is clearly doable, it increases the amount of labor required to support the network.

Obtain Independent Test Results that Indicate How the Layer 3 Switch Would Work in Your Network Environment

It is typical that version one of any product has some flaws in it. Realizing that, the authors recommend that you obtain test data that show how the switches you are interested in are likely to perform in an environment similar to yours. You should look to see that the switch can support wire speed routing on all ports simultaneously even with key Layer 3 special services enabled, i.e., QoS, accounting, filtering. In some cases, you might have to perform this testing yourselves.

Re-examine Your Vendor Management Strategy

One piece of this step is a continuation of the previous step, i.e., creating tests that define levels of acceptability for a new technology. Another piece of this step is to determine how many vendors you would ideally like to have in your network in general, and as a supplier of Layer 3 switching in particular. For example, one large financial firm that the authors are familiar with has the strategy to deploy Layer 3 switches from two vendors. One of these vendors will be the firm's incumbent router vendor. The other is intended to be a new vendor. The firm's intention is to introduce a new vendor in order to apply pressure to the incumbent router vendor.

Examine the Implication of Each Switch Relative to Tactical Network Management

The vast majority of network management resources is consumed doing tactical activities, i.e., installation, configuration, fault isolation, and resolution. The authors suggest that enterprise users determine the ease of performing these tasks for each Layer 3 switch under consideration. As a minimum, these tasks should not be any more difficult with the new equipment than they currently are. Ideally, these tasks will be notably easier using the new equipment.

Examine the Implication of Each Switch Relative to Proactive Network Management

By proactive network management, the authors mean functions such as service management, capacity planning, network design, budget planning, and chargeback. The standard refrain that the authors constantly hear from enterprise users is that they would like to do more proactive network management. However, these users face a variety of limitations. One of these limitations is that all of their time is typically consumed performing tactical management. It is this constant refrain that encouraged the authors to include the previous step in this list.

The second limitation is the difficulty that stressed enterprise users have in implementing a function such as capacity planning. In order to do this, they need to identify what entities they are planning for, establish acceptable levels of usage, determine what information they need to quantify the current usage, and identify what tools and processes they need to gather the relevant information. While every enterprise has its own unique issues, the majority of each of these processes are somewhat generic. Given that, enterprise users should be able to get assistance deploying proactive network management from their hardware vendors.

Refine Your Approach to Stakeholder Management

As previously mentioned, the authors have recently been involved with organizations who were evaluating Layer 3 switching in a somewhat fractured manner. By that we mean that the people who were evaluating the technology had a significant disconnect from both the business unit managers as well as the people who had to sign off on the funding request.

This type of disconnect is a prescription for project failure, independent of the technology. The authors recommend that enterprise users implement a service management function. A key component of service management is to document the services offered by the networking organization and to identify a few key performance and financial metrics. Another key component of service management is to market these services within the enterprise. While certainly not foolproof, this approach positions the enterprise user to justify the deployment of Layer 3 switching in the context of supporting the agreed-to service descriptions.

Appendix 1:
List of Vendors and Switches

As part of the Strategic Networks tests, six switches were tested. However, the vendors involved decided to publish results for only three of the six switches. Table 1 provides a brief overview of these three switches. For reference purposes, an indication of the availability of high-speed ports is included. However, this is a highly volatile area. For definitive information, the reader is encouraged to contact the vendors.

Table 1   Participant Vendors and Switches

Vendor	Switch Model	Test Date	Fast Ethernet Ports Tested	Fast Ethernet Ports Maximum	Ethernet Ports Included	Higher Speed Ports Available for Switch
Cabletron Systems	FN100-16TX	3/97	16	16	up to 16 (all 16 ports are 10/100 autosensing)	none
Cabletron Systems	MMAC-Plus SmartSwitch 9H423-28 V1.05.04	3/97	20	28	336	Gigabit Ethernet
NBase Communications	Megaswitch II NH2012R	3/97	10	12	None	Gigabit Ethernet

Comparative Test Results

Unidirectional Throughput/PLR

- Fast Ethernet-to-Fast Ethernet Unidirectional Throughput/PLR
- Interpreting Unidirectional Throughput/PLR Benchmarks

Congestion Test Results (Fast Ethernet-to-Fast Ethernet Unidirectional)

- Interpreting Congestion Tolerance/Control Benchmarks

Latency Test Results

- Unicast and Broadcast Latencies of Fast Ethernet-to-Fast Ethernet Switching
- Unicast and Broadcast Latencies Variation
- Interpreting Latency Benchmarks

Unidirectional Throughput/PLR

Fast Ethernet-to-Fast Ethernet Unidirectional Throughput/PLR

Throughput is defined as the maximum forwarding rate the switch can support without packet loss. Another way to think about throughput on the basis of a single unidirectional stream is as a measure of the maximum number of back-to-back packets that the switch can process without buffers overflowing and packets being lost. For example, a switch that achieves 99% of theoretical throughput for a stream of minimum-sized Fast Ethernet packets and has the capacity to buffer 150 packets per stream could accommodate a one second long burst of back to back packets before packets begin to be lost. If the buffer is increased to 1,500 packets per stream, this would mean that it is possible to burst for ten seconds before packets begin to be lost. Of course, a switch with throughput at 100% of the theoretical rate can accommodate arbitrarily long streams of back-to-back packets.

Chart 1 compares the unidirectional throughputs at minimum-sized packets for all the switches in the evaluation. The test setup was capable of a maximum of 10 streams. All of the switches in Chart 1 are capable of small packet throughput at or very near wire speed for all the stream counts tested. When the packet size is increased slightly, all the switches in the evaluation have full wire speed throughput.

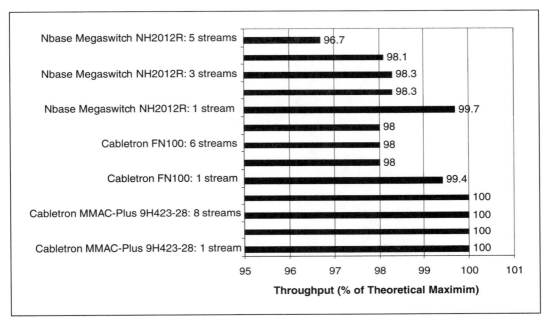

Chart 1   Fast Ethernet-to-Fast Ethernet Unidirectional Throughput (64-Byte Packets)

It should be borne in mind that Chart 1 presents data for switches with a range of port densities—a juxtaposition that tends to favor the switches with lower port counts, because it is easier to achieve 100% throughput for a smaller number of streams.

By definition, switches that achieve 100% of theoretical throughput do not lose packets. On the other hand, switches with less than theoretical throughput are generally losing an appreciable number of packets under the extreme conditions of these tests. For the latter switches it is worth verifying that that packet loss is introduced gracefully at only the highest levels of offered load and does not occur across a wide range of loads. The Packet Loss Rate (PLR) tests summarized in Chart 2 indicate the packet loss data for only the maximum stream count shown in Chart 1. These results are for 100% offered load at the stream counts indicated. In all cases PLR was very load-sensitive and restricted to the highest offered loads (as it should be). In all cases dropping the offered load to 90% reduced the packet loss to zero. It should be noted that PLR is not equal to simply the difference between theoretical throughput and measured throughput because of the different techniques used to measure throughput and PLR.

Interpreting Unidirectional Throughput/PLR Benchmarks

Thirty-second long unidirectional bursts of back-to-back minimum-sized packets occurring simultaneously for as many streams as the switch can support represents a very extreme test of

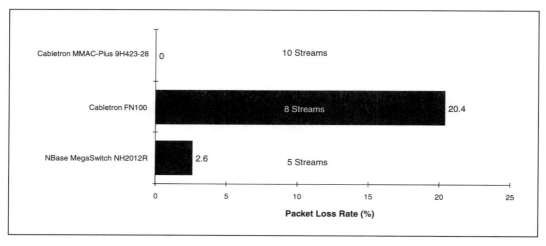

Chart 2 Fast Ethernet-to-Fast Ethernet Unidirectional PLR at 100% Offered Load (64-Byte Packets)

throughput performance. In the first place, real networks have a distribution of packet sizes that usually contain a large number of small packets, a significant number of large packets, and relatively few intermediate-sized packets. These real-world packet size distributions generally place lower demands on the switch than traffic consisting entirely of minimum-sized packets.

Real-world traffic is also bi-directional which, for half-duplex Fast Ethernet, results in collisions that reduce the maximum attainable throughput. In fact, tests of bi-directional Ethernet throughput (with 50% of the traffic flowing in each direction) indicate that for 64-byte packets, collisions will limit achievable throughput to something on the order of 60% of theoretical when averaging over 30-second intervals. These results are consistent with simulations and empirical observations that CSMA/CD Ethernet networks saturate at approximately 65% utilization with small packets.

In spite of these observations, even at low levels of average utilization, bursts of back-to-back packets can generate demand for wire speed throughput for a short period of time. However, these time periods tend to be very short, due in part to the limits imposed by sliding window transport protocols. Even for highly aggregated traffic, empirical studies of Ethernet traffic conducted at Bellcore indicate a maximum burst duration of less than 15 back-to-back packets for a Fast Ethernet with utilization in the range of 9% to 15%. The frequency of these maximum-sized bursts was on the order of two per second. From this data, it appears that the maximum burst duration of a fully loaded Fast Ethernet at 65% utilization would be less than 60 to 100 back-to-back packets. Another point worth noting is that most applications that generate long bursts of back-to-back packets are performing bulk transfer of data and taking advantage of larger packet sizes, which are less demanding of throughput from switches.

In view of these observations, unidirectional throughput at or very close to theoretical wire speed should be regarded as a measure of *reserve* performance of the switch's forwarding engine under extreme conditions involving long bursts of traffic. Throughput close to the theoretical limit, coupled with adequate buffering, can be sufficient to handle any bursts of back-to-back packets that one is likely to encounter in a practical network without packet loss. Therefore, 100% of theoretical unidirectional throughput should not be viewed as an absolutely necessary characteristic of a good switch.

From this discussion it is obvious that switches with the kind of throughput shown in Chart 1 will lose very few (if any) packets as the result of having insufficient processing power to keep up with multiple parallel Fast Ethernet streams. Packet loss is more likely to be observed during periods of congestion when multiple input ports are contending for a single output port. In the case of congestion, packet loss is attributed to insufficient buffer size or inefficient buffer management rather than to inadequate throughput performance.

Congestion Test Results (Fast Ethernet-to-Fast Ethernet Unidirectional)

Chart 3 shows congestion test results that are typical of most switches that employ passive approaches (i.e., buffering) to congestion tolerance. For switches in this category, the maximum number of back-to-back packets that can be forwarded over the port under contention may be limited by either the maximum number of packet locations in the buffer or by the buffer capacity in bytes. For small packets, the number of packet storage locations is often the limiting factor, while for larger packets, limited buffer capacity frequently causes the number of back-to-back packets that can be stored to decrease in proportion to packet size.

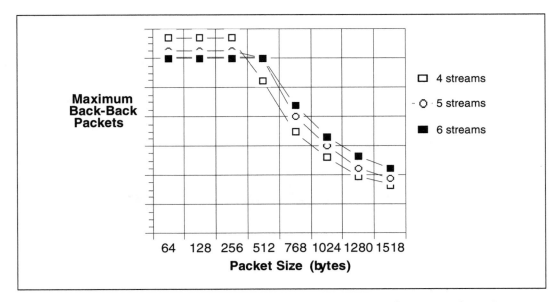

Chart 3   Typical Congestion Test Data for Switches without Congestion Control

While these generalizations explain some overall patterns in the data, there are obviously as many design approaches to buffer organization and allocation schemes as there are architectures for the switching fabric. One design variant is to dedicate sufficient fixed capacity to each buffer location to handle any size of packet. This approach results in the maximum number of back-to-back packets being relatively independent of packet size, which extends the flat part of the curve in Chart 6 out to 1,518 bytes. Another class of design might involve dynamic allocation of buffer capacity where the number of possible locations depends on the size of the packets being stored. For switch designs in this category, the "one over n" part of the curve in Chart 3 may extend back to 64 bytes.

Chart 4 summarizes the results of the congestion tests for switches that employ passive congestion tolerance schemes. Many Ethernet switches with passive congestion tolerance can handle bursts of more than 300 back-to-back packets across the range of packet sizes. The Cabletron switches in the evaluation employ comparatively small buffers, because this vendor believes that shared resources, such as servers and backbone connections, should be configured with higher speed ports (in this Gigabit Ethernet)—eliminating congestion through network design.

For switches that use active congestion control mechanisms based on back pressure, testing is performed to determine how effectively the switch can throttle back the traffic sources over a range of offered loads in order to prevent packet loss due to buffer overflow. Throttling effectiveness is determined by plotting the rate at which the switch allows the tester to forward packets versus the offered load that the tester is attempting to forward. A switch performing perfectly in this test would produce results as shown in Chart 5. Since this is a five-stream test, the maximum offered load on the x-axis is 500%. Comparison of the number of packets actually sent and received by the tester is used to compute PLR.

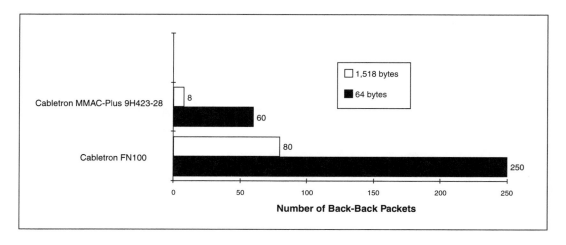

Chart 4   Congestion Tolerance Test Maximum Number of Back-to-Back Packets without Loss
(5 input streams to 1 output stream)

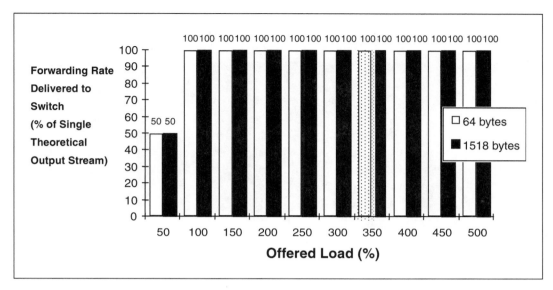

Chart 5   Ideal Forwarding under Congestion for Switches with Active Congestion Control
(5 input streams to 1 output stream)

Chart 6 shows the actual congestion test results for the switches with active congestion control. The NBase MegaSwitch II is effective in this test at throttling back an offered load of five wire speed input streams to slightly less than a single wire speed stream output stream. The traffic sources are "over-throttled" slightly to an aggregate forwarding rate of about 98% of the capacity of the output port, but no packets are lost over the range of offered loads and packet sizes. The NBase switch applies back pressure on a per packet basis, causing collisions only for those packets destined for a congested output port. Destination addresses are decoded by a fast table lookup that verifies availability of buffer space at the output port as the packet is still being received.

Interpreting Congestion Tolerance/Control Benchmarks

Congestion tolerance/control is an important issue because contention for output ports is a common cause of packet loss for Fast Ethernet switches. This is because a half-duplex or full-duplex Fast Ethernet output port can only empty the output buffers as fast as a single input port could fill it. Therefore, when systems on multiple Fast Ethernet input ports attempt simultaneous access to a shared resource over a single Fast Ethernet output port, this port can be temporarily oversubscribed by several times. In this way, a number of traffic bursts can aggregate to overflow the capacity of available buffers.

Congestion can also result from traffic being forwarded from a higher-speed port (Gigabit Ethernet or ATM OC-12c) to a Fast Ethernet port or when a higher speed port is oversubscribed with traffic from several Fast Ethernet input ports. Although all the congestion tests conducted in

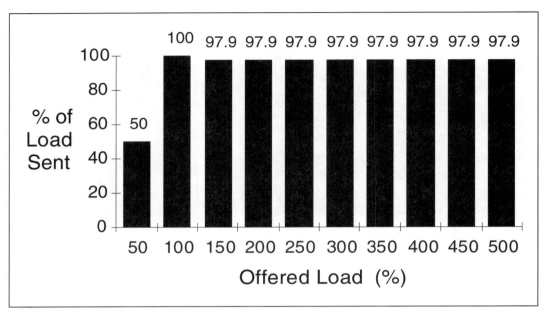

Chart 6   Congestion Control Test Fast Ethernet-to-Fast Ethernet Unidirectional Forwarding Rate
(5 input streams to 1 output stream)

this evaluation are for Fast Ethernet-to-Fast Ethernet switching, the results should provide a good indication of the performance that can be expected of each switch in the case of congestion stemming from a higher-speed port oversubscribing a single 100 Mbps Fast Ethernet port.

Packet loss requires recovery at the transport layer that consumes enough time to have a very noticeable effect on the application level response time experienced by an individual user. Retransmitted packets also have a tendency to exacerbate the congestion problem since retransmission adds to the traffic load on the network.

Recent studies have been published establishing that the burstiness of LAN traffic typically intensifies as the number of active traffic sources increases. In more traditional modeling of LAN traffic, researchers had assumed a Poisson distribution of packet interarrival times which lead to the expectation that aggregated traffic would become progressively less bursty as the number of active sources is increased. Additional work has shown that Variable Bit Rate (VBR) video traffic resulting from multimedia applications tends to have the same statistical characteristics as the more typical set of network applications. Therefore, deploying multimedia applications including VBR video will add significantly to the burstiness of LAN traffic.

This improved understanding of the statistical nature of LAN traffic has led to more refined simulation models predicting that PLRs are relatively insensitive to buffer sizes. In other words, holding switch architecture and other design parameters constant, increasing buffer size will result in a less than proportional reduction in the number of lost packets. However, because of the many differences in switch designs, buffer size alone is not a very reliable indicator of the ability of a switch with passive congestion tolerance to deal with port contention and hence the rationale for the congestion test as part of the Fast Ethernet switch evaluation.

Modern networking protocols use "windowing" mechanisms to allow multiple packets to be transmitted before an acknowledgment is required. For TCP, NFS, and Burst Mode NetWare VLM the network manager can configure the window size on a station-by-station. TCP and Burst Mode NetWare have the additional ability to dynamically adapt window size in response to traffic conditions—generally the window size is reduced in response to excessive PLRs. For example, the transport protocols in a Fast Ethernet-attached server would dynamically adapt the window size to the point where Fast Ethernet port buffering on the switch proved to be adequate to eliminate packet loss. However, the best performance at the application layer will be the result of setting the window to its maximum feasible size. At the maximum window size (64 packets for the NetWare VLM and 64 Kbytes for TCP and NFS), high performance systems are able to transmit as many as 50 to 64 packets in a single burst of back-to-back traffic.

For small workgroup applications where packet bursts are less likely to aggregate, a capacity of 50 to 75 back-to-back packets should be adequate for effective congestion tolerance. For a large workgroup switch or for collapsed backbone configurations, the higher levels of traffic aggregation possible over a single Fast Ethernet port mean that this number should be increased to 100 to 300 packets depending on the number of shared segments, the utilization levels, and whether servers or other shared resources are attached to Fast Ethernet ports. In general, network designers will try to take maximum advantage of the switch's high-speed ports to reduce the likelihood of congestion in accessing shared resources. In networks where this approach can be strictly implemented, the need for congestion tolerance on the Fast Ethernet ports is reduced, and the 50 to 75 packet range should prove adequate.

Another issue is whether passive congestion tolerance or active congestion control is preferable. One observation is that congestion control schemes that apply back pressure on a per port basis will delay *all* traffic on the throttled segment whether or not it is destined for the congested output port. Because traffic destined for other non-congested switch ports is blocked by a congested port, a phenomenon somewhat analogous to "head of line" blocking in cross-point matrix switches can occur. Eliminating these additional delays is the rationale behind the NBase MegaSwitch scheme of applying back pressure per packet rather than per segment.

Therefore, one might speculate that the choice between active congestion control and passive congestion tolerance may often come down to a tradeoff between avoiding packet loss altogether versus minimizing the average network response time. The former alternative provides a large reduction in response time for the few users who would be affected by packet loss, possibly at the expense of increasing response time for a larger subset of the network population. Therefore, back pressure congestion control may have the effect of taking the delay that could be caused by lost packets and spreading it out as a small increase in delay for a larger number of users.

Active congestion control applied per segment is best suited to those switch applications in which each low speed port is dedicated to an individual desktop system or to those client-server application environments where most of the traffic on the switch ports is directed to/from a server resource connected to the switch via a higher-speed port.

On the other hand, a switch with passive congestion tolerance and enough buffer capacity for large bursts of back-to-back packets can eliminate packet loss under all practical circumstances with the advantage that it can be deployed throughout the network with somewhat less regard for the traffic flows and client-server system configurations.

Latency Test Results

Unicast and Broadcast Latencies of Fast Ethernet-to-Fast Ethernet Switching

Chart 7 presents the Fast Ethernet-to-Fast Ethernet Unicast transit delay, or FIFO latency, for all of the switches in the evaluation. Looking at transit delay is the only way to be able to compare the network delay characteristics of store-and-forward switches with cut-through switches. However, it should be noted this chart is included primarily for consistency with other reports because the Fast Ethernet switches in this evaluation support only store-and-forward mode switching.

Please refer to the later section *Interpreting Latency Benchmarks* for a full discussion of cut-through versus store-and-forward latency if some clarification of these concepts is needed.

Chart 8 presents the same delay data as Chart 7. However, in Chart 8 the packet transmission times have been subtracted to yield the last bit in-to-first bit out (LIFO) delay that corresponds to the standard definition of store-and-forward latency as the time delay in processing the packet.

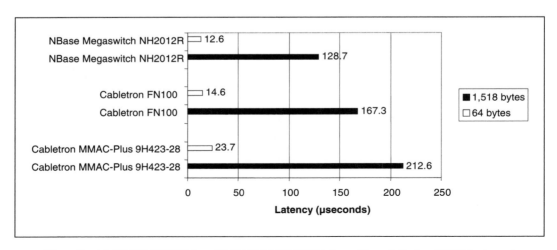

Chart 7   FAST ETHERNET-to-FAST ETHERNET Unicast Transit Delay (FIFO Latency)

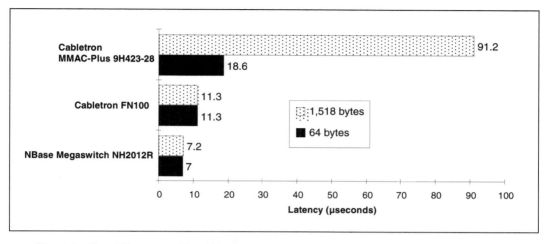

Chart 8   Fast Ethernet-to-Fast Ethernet Unicast Latency Within modules (LIFO Latency)

Chart measurements are for ports located on the same module or a part of the same fixed configuration switch.

Chart 9 presents the corresponding latency measurements when the ports are located on separate modules of the modular switches in the evaluation.

Chart 10 summarizes the comparative results from the Fast Ethernet-to-Fast Ethernet broadcast latency test. This test was designed to determine whether broadcast latency is sensitive to port number or port location. The results are summarized as the minimum and maximum broadcast

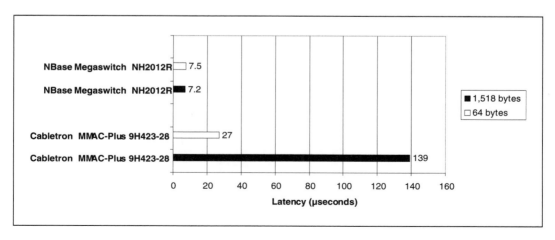

Chart 9   Fast Ethernet-to-Fast Ethernet Unicast Latency Between Modules for
Modular Switches (LIFO)

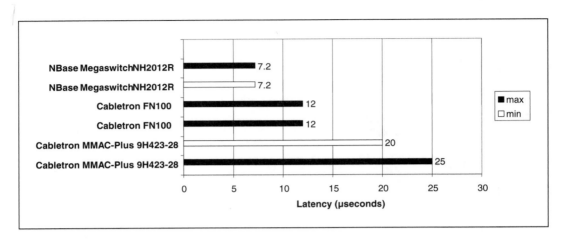

Chart 10   Ethernet-to-Fast Ethernet Broadcast Latency vs. Port Number for 64-Byte Packets (LIFO)

latencies measured for 64-byte packets over the output ports monitored (up to 18 in the test setup). This chart is useful in determining whether users on some ports might receive somewhat better service for applications or services that make use of broadcast/multicast packets.

Unicast and Broadcast Latencies Variation

Latency variation is defined as the difference between the maximum and minimum latencies recorded over 10 trials. Chart 11 summarizes the maximum latency variation recorded for switching Fast Ethernet Unicast and broadcast traffic over the range of legitimate Ethernet package sizes. The rationale for this chart is that it provides an overview of the worst case latency variation that could be expected for all possible traffic flows through the switches that were tested. Low latency variation is one of the strengths of switches that employ time division multiplexing or arbitrated shared medium architectures. In testing 10/100 switches based on these architectures and ASIC designs, latency variations of less .3 microseconds were recorded. In general, switches with shared memory architectures have tended to exhibit somewhat higher latency variation. However, in these results the FN100, a shared memory switch, has the lowest overall latency variation at less 2.5 microseconds. These results indicate that ASIC-based switch designs can yield very low latency variation regardless of the switch architecture. The importance of latency variation is discussed in the following section of the report devoted to the interpretation of latency benchmarks.

Interpreting Latency Benchmarks

For most applications, the latency (and end-to-end transit delay) of the LAN switches tested is low enough to have negligible impact on the response time and performance perceived by the user. This is because latency of less than 250 microseconds or so is typically very small compared

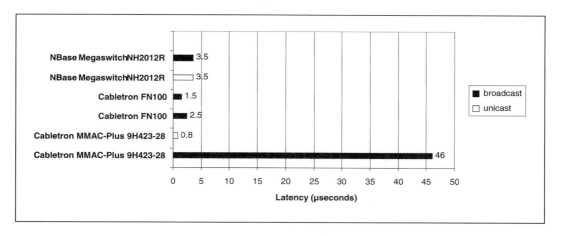

Chart 11   Maximum Latency Variation for Fast Ethernet-to-Fast Ethernet

to the overall end-to-end system latency, which can accumulate to many milliseconds when application queuing delays, receiver buffering/interrupt delays, and wire delays are all considered.

Exceptions can arise for simple LAN protocols, such as non-Burst Mode NetWare, which require that each transmitted packet be received and acknowledged before the next packet is sent. This property makes the end-to-end transit delay encountered by individual packets have an additive effect on user perceived response time for large file transfers and similar applications. This phenomena has led some network managers to insist that client and server systems using such "ping pong" protocols not be separated by even one router hop. More modern protocol suites, such as TCP/IP, DECnet, and Burst Mode NetWare circumvent this problem in large degree by using "windowing" schemes that allow a number of packets to be sent before an acknowledgment from the destination. Windowing enables the processing of multiple in-flight packets to overlap, masking much of the delay encountered by individual packets.

As shown in Figure 1, interposing a store-and-forward switch between source and destination increases total end-to-end transit time by an amount equal to the switch latency for a given packet size plus the time it takes to fully receive a packet of that size. For Fast Ethernet networks the time to receive a 64-byte packet is 5.12 microseconds versus 121.4 microseconds for a 1,518-byte packet. Therefore, the incremental end-to-end transit delay of store-and-forward switches is dependent on the packet size being forwarded.

On the other hand, a cut-through switch increases the end-to-end transit delay by an amount equal only to its latency as long as there is no contention for output ports. However, with cut-through operation limited packet processing is possible and packet filtering may be limited to the elimination of undersized packets resulting from collisions. When multiple input ports are contending for a single output port (or the output segment is congested), the cut-through switch must revert to what is essentially store-and-forward operation by buffering packets until the output port

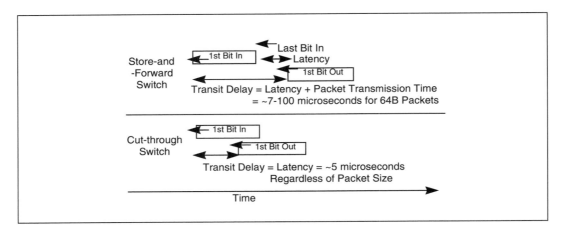

Figure 1 Incremental End-to-End Transit Delay of FAST ETHERNET Switches

becomes free. Under these heavy traffic conditions, cut-through and store-and-forward switches will exhibit more nearly equal end-to-end transit delays.

Another rather obvious point is that with the faster network transmission times of Fast Ethernet and Gigabit Ethernet, the differences in transit delay between cut-through and store-and-forward latencies become progressively less significant. Furthermore, Fast Ethernet and Gigabit Ethernet switches are primarily being deployed in some sort of backbone application where the requirement for advanced Layer 2 packet filtering and/or Layer 3 switching dictate a store-and-forward mode of switch operation.

When comparing the Unicast latency performance of modular switches it is important to consider both the "within" and "between" latencies to get a complete picture of switch capabilities. This is because a switch with very low "within" module latency may or may not have comparably low latency when module boundaries are crossed.

In today's application environments, broadcasts are mostly used for inter-system communications rather than by user applications. Therefore, latency for broadcast packets generally has less impact on user perceived response time than Unicast packet latency. In fact, most of the switches in this evaluation have Unicast latency that is somewhat lower than broadcast latency, reflecting the challenges that replicating packets poses for some switch architectures.

Today, most multimedia applications use Unicast packets. However, the situation may change if multimedia applications begin to take advantage of Fast Ethernet multicast packets as a means of efficient, simultaneous distribution of the identical information to a number of client systems on the LAN. Because most switches process multicast and broadcast packets in the same way, user response times for such applications would be somewhat sensitive to any significantly longer broadcast latencies. It is more important to note that multimedia applications are much more sensitive to latency *variation*, since this can have a major effect on the smoothness with which video and audio data is presented to the user. If multimedia applications are being planned for deployment over switched Fast Ethernet, it may prove beneficial to consider only switches that maintain both Unicast and broadcast latency variation to less than 200 microseconds or so. Latency variation on this order of magnitude has a negligible effect on user perceptions of continuity in multimedia applications.

Delays and variation in delay of much longer than 200 microseconds can result from buffer storage in the switch during periods of congestion or from collisions or lost packets. Therefore, if multimedia applications are an important requirement for the switched network, the network designer should try to eliminate collisions using full duplex Fast Ethernet and congestion within the switch through judicious use of high-speed ports. Alternatively, one could consider a Fast Ethernet switch with a proprietary scheme for real-time traffic prioritization that can eliminate these more significant causes of delay and delay variation.

Appendix 2:
Bay Networks
Accelar 1200 Routing Switch

Independent Test Evaluation by Strategic Networks Laboratories

Preface

At what point does a switch become a router or, a router become a switch?

What are the advantages of a routing switch?

Legacy routers are well known, tried and trusted; the ever present combination of hardware and software. They are monolithic routing decision programs directing packets through a maze of hardware gates and Phy interfaces. Routing intelligence was the sole property of the central processor and it's associated address tables. Speed was not the issue. The issue was flexibility. Flexibility provided by the ability to perform occasional functionality enhancements in the form of a software upgrade.

Then the client-server paradigm was born and the World Wide Web became its benefactor. Now speed has become an issue. The first reaction was to increase the processor speed and stay with the legacy software solution. A "stop-gap" effort at best. Addi-

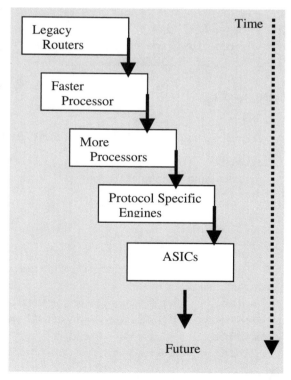

tional processors, protocol specific routing engines, look-ahead algorithms, all excellent approaches to an ever growing problem, falling short in the inflationary environment of the Internet.

In parallel, the microelectronics industry was continuing to make advancements in technology and manufacturing techniques. Processors were getting faster, cheaper and flexible. The ability to "spin" an ASIC customized for routing, or at least a portion of it, became reality. In the midst there was, a brief love affair with the cell, but only as a minor distraction from the real problem. Routing decisions and packet switching needed to pace the demands being created by new applications. The marriage of the switch and the router was an inevitable event.

The question then remains, *"How much of the routing intelligence can be placed in hardware?"* A question that Bay Networks Routing Switch is squarely aimed at answering.

Strategic Networks and Harvard Network Device Test Lab set about the task of answering this question by testing the Accelar 1200 for it's ability to provide wire speed Layer 3 switching and routing. The remainder of this report is detail about the Accelar's architecture and the results of the tests.

Methodologies

The methodologies applied in this test are derived from the Request For Comment papers, RFC 1242 and RFC 1944, published by the Benchmark Working Group. These documents clearly define the concepts of measurements with respect to packet Throughput, Latency and Frame Loss Rates. The definitions are as follows:

Throughput

Definition:
The maximum rate at which none of the offered frames are dropped by the device.

Measurement units:
N-octet input frames per second
input bits per second

Latency

Definition:
For store and forward devices: The time interval starting when the last bit of the input frame reaches the input port and ending when the first bit of the output frame is seen on the output port.

For bit forwarding devices: The time interval starting when the end of the first bit of the input frame reaches the input port and ending when the start of the first bit of the output frame is seen on the output port.

Measurement units:
Time with fine enough units to distinguish between 2 events.

Frame Loss Rate

Definition:

Percentage of frames that should have been forwarded by a network device under steady state (constant) load that were not forwarded due to lack of resources.

Measurement units:

Percentage of N-octet offered frames that are dropped. To be reported as a graph of offered load vs. frame loss.

The fourth test type, Latency Under Load, is defined and performed by Strategic Networks as a means of measuring latency variation. Many devices will show varying levels of latency through the course of a multi-trial test suite. This can be the result of blocking scenarios, buffer allocation errors and even processor interrupt delays. To expose these potential problems, Strategic Networks adds a level of complexity to the Latency test by inducing background load on an increasing basis. The "load" consists of a stream of 64-byte packets with the appropriate packet detail to allow for Layer 2 or Layer 3 functionality. The load streams are fed into the device under test (DUT) via packet injectors, each stream flowing from a single source port to a single destination port at full line rate. The number of streams injected into the device are determined by one of three factors:

- Limitation on total number of tester injection ports

- Significant detremental impact on the DUT

- Number of ports existing on the DUT

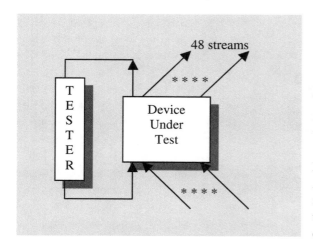

The latency measurement is made, not on the load streams, but on a single control test stream. Load is increased on the DUT in defined increments as measurements of latency are made on the control test stream. The control test stream format is also modified across a range of packet sizes. For this test suite, the packet sizes included 64, 128, 512, 768, 1024, 1280 and 1518 bytes. Due to the high port densities of the Accelar 1200 route switch, the load consisted of 39 streams of Layer 2 traffic. This translates to 78 ports of 100Mb/s half duplex traffic or 7,800,000 bytes per second. This is approximately 53% percent of the overall capacity of the route switch. This is a significant load considering it is steady state, not burst traffic, meaning that a significant number of egress buffers are in continuous use ,as well as central memory resources. This is discussed in more depth in the test results section.

It is also important to note that test results were taken both intramodule and intermodule so that the impact on the switch fabric could be taken into account. This is particularly pertinent data given recent implementations of switch components and the trend towards pushing routing functionality out towards the I/O interface.

The configuration of the Accelar 1200 route switch while under test was as follows:

- An Accelar 1200 chassis with dual 650 watt power supplies
- One Silicon Switch Fabric control module
- 8-16 port autosensing 10/100BASE-TX modules

The Accelar 1200 Architecture

In order to fully comprehend the test results, a comprehensive understanding of the DUT's architecture is required. The results of the Accelar 1200 tests were very good even at high density and load. The key to understanding why this level of performance was achievable lies in the manner in which the switch was architected.

To understand how Bay Networks arrived at this design it is also imperative to understand the advancements in switch technology which lead up to the existing design.
Consider the recent past 5 years and the number of switching architectures which have been applied to products.

Bus Architecture

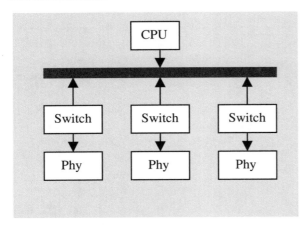

The Bus architecture employs are common bus on which all devices pass packets amongst each other and to the CPU. Additionally, there may also be other devices on the bus such as Address Resolution Logic (ARL) or interfaces to Uplinks. The key point to understand in this architecture is the bottleneck the main bus represents, since it is a simplex device. Only one switch and one flow of packets may use the bus at any given time. Another aspect also lost on many decision makers is the means by which priority messages get to the CPU.

In a content situation, it is critical that the CPU is able to get certain messages, such as Spanning Tree changes (Layer 2) and route updates (Layer 3). Heavy bus contention can easily impact this process. Switching is usually localized with a certain number of physical ports being "assigned" to a switching ASIC and associated buffers and ARL. Hybrids of this include providing links between each port switch and localized input and output buffers.

Full Mesh Architecture

An alternate method for switch development is the full mesh approach. Essentially the switch is broken down into many subswitches, each of which is allocated to a group of physical ports. This can be a very strong design but usually forces a multiple move scenario. An inbound packet destined for another port must be fully buffered at the inbound port, the routing decision made, and then, the packet fully buffered at the out bound port until delivery. This means each packet at certain times within the switch occupies buffer space in two queues and the movement

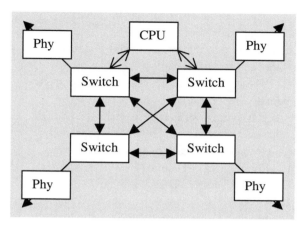

between queue can be a costly operation if the packets are large and associated with a stream of data as opposed to a burst. The one aspect which is almost eliminated is that of queuing packets to the CPU for processing.

Ring Architecture

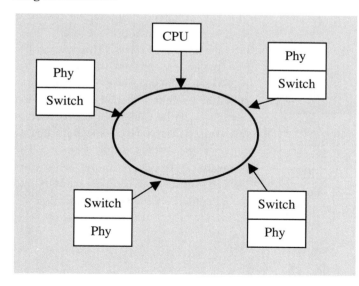

This is an architecture which was successfully deployed by BayNetworks in the 28000 series of Fast Ethernet switches. Typically, this device acts much like a Token or FDDI ring would, with a ring usage token being passed around to each local switch ASIC. Possesion of the token meant the local switch could move packets from inbound to outbound queues or the CPU. Unless most of the functionality is moved to the local switch ASICs, the ring becomes the bottleneck, especially in packet flow scenarios. BayNetworks overcame this problem by this very same technique. Depending upon manufacturing techniques, this can be a very expensive proposition.

Crossbar Architecture

The crossbar approach had been technically abandoned some years back due to expectations that the model would not scale to large and fast implementations.

The crossbar can be only one switch or potentally hundreds! Each crossbar acts like a rotational switch, similar to turnabouts one might see at an old train depot. The problem here is contention. Each individual crossbar can only connect two points at a time. This means that for large fabrics with many crossbar switches, if a packet must pass from one inbound queue to an outbound queue, an

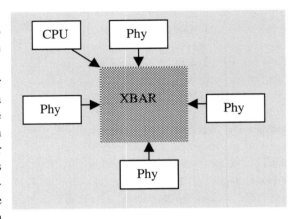

open "pathway" must exist between the two queues. If any of the crossbar switches between these two points is allocated, the other traffic must wait until it is clear. This requires very fast crossbar switches and a very intelligent processor to manage the fabric. In addition, large amounts of buffer space must exist for both inbound and outbound queues.

Centralized Memory Pooling Architecture

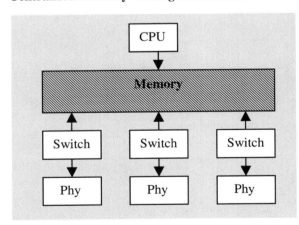

The last technique employs the use of a large centralized memory queue as a holding area for port queues. This means that movement of packets between ports becomes a pointer operation. The packet is stored in the central memory, the outbound queue is identified and a pointer is added to this queue so that the local switching engine can get the packet from memory. The downside to this architecture stems from the need for a lot of very fast memory and the potential for CPU access contention.

The Accelar Architecture

Where the Accelar switch departs (and learns) from past architectures can be found in two key approaches:

- Movement of route management from software to hardware
- Empowerment of the local switch processors to make forwarding decisions.

Clearly, if switches are to be able to route quickly and effectively, advances in routing software would have to be imprinted into switch hardware. Accelar has achieved this by designing custom ASICs which provide route management in a hardware function. This is accomplished by focusing on a key aspect of networking, the protocol. The ASIC embedded in the route switch have

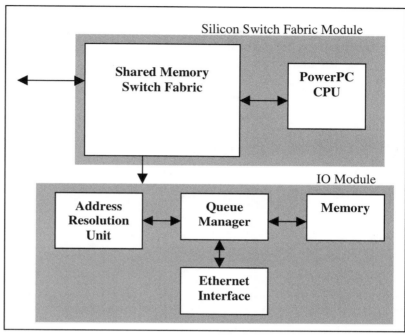

extended knowledge of IP. Concentrating on one protocol allows for a deterministic approach to ASIC design, since the number of nodes in the routing decision tree is greatly reduced. This allows hardware engineers to build a fairly finite state machine into hardware and implant this knowledge into a route switch at high speed.

The second approach uses a technique Strategic Networks calls "empowerment." This gives the necessary components the ability to make decisions without an overseeing functionary. In the Accelar, the central processor, a Motorola PowerPC CPU, provides horizon convergence but does not make the actual routing decisions. Knowledge of the routing landscape is pushed out to the I/O modules and their associated forwarding engines. This allows each I/O module to make routing decisions locally, whether the packet is bound for an intra- or intermodule port. This empowerment schema allows for parallelism within the switch increasing its capacity to switch and route, since no one component becomes the bottleneck.

This is further enhanced by the use of a centralized memory pool, allowing for write-once, read-many scenarios like IP multicast. In a simpler form, having a central memory queue also minimizes packet copies which are expensive both in terms of time and memory usage. The Accelar performs one other function which allows it to function at peak efficiency-- look-ahead address resolution. Immediately upon receiving a packet, a copy of a portion of the packet header is sent to the Address Resolution Unit (ARU) for forwarding determination. By the time the rest of the packet is resident in central memory, the ARU has already determined which port it is destined for and made the appropriate pointer allocations. Remember, of course, at no time was the central processor involved.

Other features worthy of note when reading through the next section:

- 7 million packets, per second, Layer 3 forwarding rate
- 15Gbps "backbone" capacity (i.e., shared memory)
- 2 MB of very fast dynamically allocated memory for egress queuing
- High and low priority queue for unicast and multicast traffic

Test Results

This section describes the results of each methodology, pointing out the implications of the results and highlighting noteable aspects of the test data.

For all of these tests, the DUT was configured as was detailed in the Methodologies section.

Throughput

Throughput was measured for both Layer 2 and Layer 3 packet types. Each of the charts on the right compare the total packet throughput for 48 streams (96 ports) of 100Mb/s Fast Ethernet traffic to the calculated theoretical maximum, taking into account the minimum packet gap.

Not only was the measured throughput identical to the potential maximum allowable throughput, but both the Layer 2 and Layer 3 throughput values were identical. For all intents and purposes, there was no depreciable difference when using either Layer 2 switching or Layer 3 route switching with IP traffic.

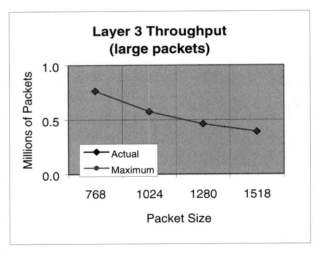

It is also important to note that these values are for intermodule traffic. No economies of scale were achieveable with respect to switching within one particular blade of the Accelar switch. All traffic was required to go into the central memory pool, a pointer was operation completed for the addition of the packet to the output queue, and the forwarding of the packet was accomplished.

The implications are three fold:

- The central memory pool does note present a bottleneck, with respect to writing and reading packets from memory queues.

- Egress packet queues on each I/O module are sufficient for this level of traffic
- Processing of Layer 3 packets took place on the I/O module, offloading the routing decision process from the central CPU.

Packet Loss

The inverse to Throughput measurements is that of Packet (or Frame) Loss. While throughput describes the maximum capability of a device to forward data, Packet Loss quantifies the amount, and in some cases, the rate at which packets are lost across the switch. The impact of lost packets is usually realized in two ways; heavier traffic due to retransmission of packets and a high collision rate due to the heavier traffic.

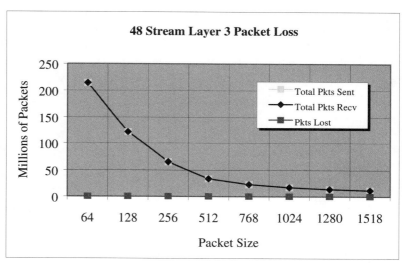

In the case of the Accelar 1200, at the highest test density, there was no detectable packet loss. This is worthy of note considering there are 7,142,880 Layer 3,64-byte packets in transit across the switching fabric during any given second. This is a total of 214,286,400 packets for the duration of a 30-second test.

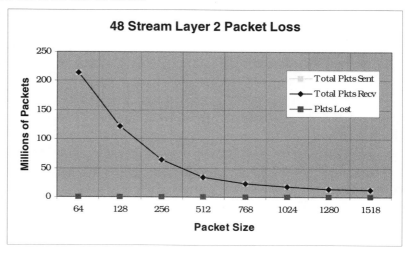

With respect to the Accelar's ability to make this possible, it is most probable that the localized and distributed nature of the switch allows the total traffic stream to be partitioned into smaller, more manageable collections of streams.

Layer 2 Latency

Knowing that the throughput and packet loss rates were equivalent to the mathematical maximums, the other factor which can greatly impact a device's ability to perform is the concept of latency. Latency is a large factor in the "life" of a packet considering that most packets will be required to cross a number of store and forward devices before reaching their destination. This means that a packet must suffer through the collective latency of the devices, the latency over each segment of the infrastructure, and those induced at the endpoints as a result of buffering.

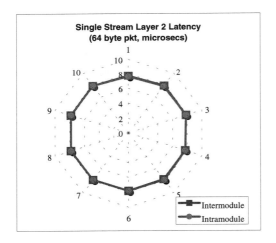

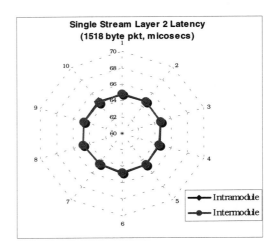

Latency is not a static number. Latency has a tendency to drift due to changes in traffic flows and packet sizes. By looking at the Layer 3 latency graphs above note that, for 10 trials, latency drifted only a few hundred nanonseconds from trial to trial, both for intra and intermodule traffic. Changes in latency per trial are most likely a result of buffer allocation and reallocation. There are also millisecond differences in the way in which the traffic injector acts. This creates slight changes in data flow and timing from trial to trial. These latency differences are so low, they can be practically ignored. The key conclusion to draw from these results is the nearly invisible difference between intra and intermodule latencies.

It is also important to note that the figures shown in the graphs above are FIFO latencies and can be adjusted for LIFO by applying a 6-nanosecond deviation per bit per packet size. For example, the latency of trial 1 of the 1518-byte test would be adjusted by (6 nano-seconds*1518-bytes*8-bits/byte) 72864 nanoseconds. The reason we provide LIFO numbers is due to the fact that most testers provide only FIFO data. The reader must make adjustments to allow for LIFO data on a per component basis.

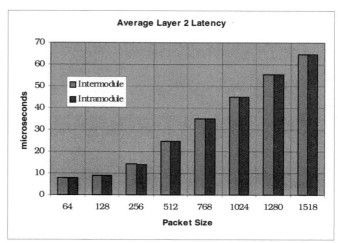

Layer 3 Latency

Latency with respect to Layer 3 traffic normally has a big impact on a switch. The overhead associated with processing the packet header and performing the address resolution task can add many microseconds to a packets stay within the switch fabric.

Looking at the graphs below (LIFO in this case) not only are the low latencies very apparent but even more intriquing is the lack of variance between packet size and between mod-ule.

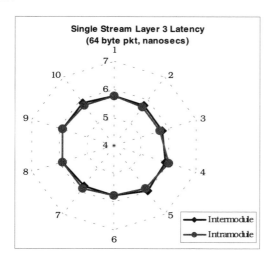

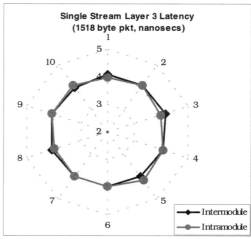

This implies that no additional processing was needed to handle the same flow volumes which were injected at Layer 2, when now using Layer 3 packets. The graphs show (in order of trial, clockwise) very little deviation, the only difference being a slightly smaller latency for larger packets. This is likely due to the decreased number of packets flowing across the switch due to the larger packet size. The operation of placing a packet in central memory should have very little

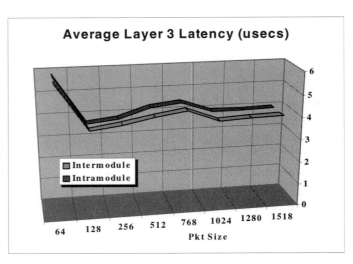

additional latency involved whether the packet is small or large. The larger packets actually reduce the load on the I/O modules because there are fewer packets to actually process and determine forwarding paths for. The key to this is remembering that the Accelar is a write-once, read-many device. Meaning that the packet is placed in memory only once. All that is moved are queue pointers in the queue lists of the egress port. Smaller packets (64bytes) would generate additional processing due to the large number of pointers and sheer number of packets being written and read from memory. Larger packets (1518 bytes) mean fewer pointers, in some cases translating into lower latencies.

For the sake of completeness the graph to the right depicts the average latency for all packets types. These averages were derived from 10 test trials per packet size. In all cases the maximum port density (96 Fast Ethernet) was used .

Appendix 3:
Extreme Networks Fast to Gigabit Ethernet Test Results

Extreme Networks recently took part in an industry test concerning Switch Ethernet hubs, which provide both Fast and Gigabit Ethernet connectivity. The focus of the test was to examine the maturity of the industry and manufacturers ability to provide components which would support server farm environments. Based upon many years of tracking the Switch Ethernet industry, Strategic Network felt that Fast-to-Gigabit Ethernet switches would find their way into corporate IT infrastructures via the need for more bandwidth in the server farm. To this effect, RFC 1942 tests of Throughput, Latency and Packet Loss Rate were performed, measuring the effectiveness of trunking multiple streams of Fast Ethernet traffic between switches using Gigabit Ethernet technology.

Throughput

Throughput evaluations were made over a full range of datagram sizes (64Kb to 1518Kb) and while using 10, 9 and 6 streams of Fast Ethernet. As depicted in the throughput graph above, Extreme's components performed flawlessly. Full line rate was achieved for 10, 9 and 6 streams of data. The chart is a comparison of throughput for

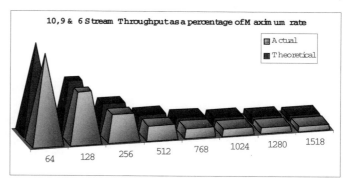

10, 9 and 6 streams of Fast Ethernet against the theoretical maximum throughput rate. All streams achieved full line rate. Clearly the components had switching power to spare.

Packet Loss Rate

Packet Loss Rate for a device can be one of the more introspective data points. Invariably packet loss points to some potential problem with buffer schemes, switch fabric design or queuing. In the case of Extreme, none of the above seem to apply. SNL found no packet loss during any of the tests conducted in the lab. All packet sizes and rates were handled without incident.

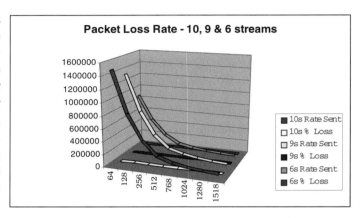

Latency

Latency represents the third factor SNL considered during test. Delay through a switch can lead to high rates of retransmission and imply deep queues within the switch. SNL looks for latencies that are considered "acceptable"

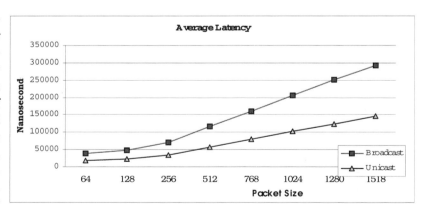

and for consistency over a variety of packet flows. As one can see from the chart, the latency for both broadcast and unicast are well within acceptable limits. Unicast latencies are very small, making end-to-end traffic very efficient. Buffering and queuing are obviously not in the critical path to getting packets through the switch.

Summary

SNL found Extreme's components to be very reliable and a good performer for the scope of this test. All of the data collected was well within acceptable ranges and exceptionally error free. Based upon these results Strategic Networks highly recommends including Extreme in IT evaluation projects since their presence is sure to create some competition, and maybe even win a few!

INDEX

A

Accelar switches
    routing switches in case study, 140-45
    tests on 1000 series, 67-72
Address Resolution Protocol (ARP) traffic, 57
Address tables, 63. *See also* Routing tables
AppleTalk, 76, 116
Applications
    in case study of Layer 3 switching, 110-11,
      134-35, 137, 146-47
    effect of broadcast storms on processing of,
      35-36
    effects of increasing numbers, 110-11, 117-
      18, 122
    impact on networks, 159-62
    increasing numbers of, 125, 140-41
    site backbone, 48
Application-specific integrated circuits (ASICs)
    and classical routers, 56
    in CoreBuilder 3500, 75, 128
    in IP9000 Gigabit Router, 83
    programmable, 73
    and routing switches, 58, 142
    in Summit switches, 78-79
    vs. RISC, 56-57
Architecture
    of Accelar 1000 series, 69-72
    in criteria for evaluating technology, 16-17, 19

of Layer 3 flow switching, 91-108
of Layer 2 switches, 41
Ascend, GRF 400 by, 86-88
ASICs. *See* Application-specific Integrated Circuits
ASIK algorithm, of Torrent, 66
ATM25, 1-2
ATM (Asynchronous Transfer Mode), 2. *See also* Multi-Protocol over ATM (MPOA)
    backbone, 115
    in case study of Layer 3 switching, 123
    cell format of, 41, 55
    classes of service, 12-13
    hardware, 120
    and high-speed ports, 43
    infrastructure, 105, 108, 118
    interfaces, 148
    networks, 100
    rate of deployment of, 154
    and Resource reSerVation (RSVP), 12-13
    shortcut paths, 121-22
    on standards for flow switching, 59
    supported by CoreBuilder 3500, 77
    switches, 124, 174
AutoClass (flow classification), 74-75
Availability dates
    for CoreBuilder 9000, 128
    for IP9000 Gigabit Router, 128